THE 500 GREATEST ALBUMS OF ALL TIME

INTRODUCTION BY
STEVEN VAN ZANDT

FOREWORD

L ET'S START WITH Number One – my Number One. *Meet the Beatles* – the first rock & roll album I ever bought; to me and most of my generation, the first great rock & roll album ever; and the essential reason why you're holding this book and reading these words – is Number 53 on this list. That can't be right. Everything on that record is the birth of nearly everything else here. • We know now that *Meet the Beatles* was the American version of the Beatles' second British album, *With the Beatles* – most of it, anyway. In those days, English albums had thirteen or fourteen tracks and usually did not include the hit singles. It wouldn't be cricket to expect fans to pay twice for the same song, would it? Well, guess what? We don't play cricket here, so American companies chopped up those U.K. LPs into ten-or-eleven-track platters, adding the singles and getting an extra album or three for every two English releases. • But the level of sophistication on *Meet the Beatles* is amazing. The Beatles did a lot of things, and they did them all well. But more than anything, they raised our standards, right

from the start. The songwriting was completely original, coming from American rhythm & blues, but combined with those Everly Brothers harmonies and unique chord changes. This was also a band with four singers. You could have a relationship with any or all of them. If you didn't like John Lennon, you liked Paul McCartney. If you were quiet, you went for George Harrison. If you were a real outcast, you loved Ringo! And if somebody can explain to me how George Martin went from making comedy records to being the most brilliant rock & roll producer in the world in exactly five minutes, please do so.

Suddenly, we went from this narrow relationship with music and the stars who made it, moving from single to single, to this extraordinary concentration of genius. Elvis Presley and Buddy Holly had made exciting, important albums before that: *Elvis Presley* [No. 56]; *The "Chirping" Crickets* [No. 415]. This was different. The Beatles made Albums.

I don't think the Beatles were trying to make great albums then. I'm sure they were focused on writing hit singles. But their not-quite-hit-single material was still high-quality stuff. Even their covers – which made up half of their first British album, *Please Please Me* [No. 39] – were terrific reinterpretations of our own rockabilly and R&B.

The Rolling Stones hit that same peak right away. My second favorite album of all time is their second American album, *12X5*, which also didn't exist in England. So it's difficult for me to get too upset at the A&R guys who created the U.S. versions of those early, great British LPs, because they accidentally had great taste!

And I will forever argue that "I've Just Seen a Face" belongs on the Beatles' *Rubber Soul* [No. 5] rather than *Help!* [No. 328] – where you found it in England – because as the all-important opening song on

our *Rubber Soul*, it heralded the Beatles' embrace of Bob Dylan and the Byrds' folk rock. *It feels better there, damnit!*

I hope you're happy now. You've got me all riled up.

But lists will do that to you. They are absolutely subjective, utterly frustrating, always incomplete – and they cause more arguments than religion and politics.

In other words, they're a lot of fun.

And we're not just taking on rock albums here. That would be too easy. We're throwing in folk, jazz, blues and gospel. But before we go any further, we should ask:

What is an album?

In the beginning, you got music two songs at a time, on these hard, ten-inch shellac discs that turned at 78 revolutions per minute. The word *album* comes from the photo-album-like books where you stored 78s. An album was literally a series of snapshots, musical pictures, bound in one place. The invention of the twelve-inch, long-playing record, spinning at 33-1/3, by the engineers at Columbia Records meant that you got a dozen of those images on a single disc. But the term stuck.

Albums were an adult thing too, in cost, content and attention span. Teenagers had their own technology: the seven-inch 45, the perfect fit for a two-and-a-half-minute rock & roll song. Even in 1964 and '65, I was still buying mostly singles. I wouldn't go into a store that way you do now, coming out with ten CDs at a time. An album was a serious investment ($3.79!).

The Beatles – and Dylan – changed that. Dylan's second album, 1963's *The Freewheelin' Bob Dylan* [No. 98], was the first example of an album being more important than a single, of a great album having no singles. By the mid-Sixties, I was buying *The Paul Butterfield Blues*

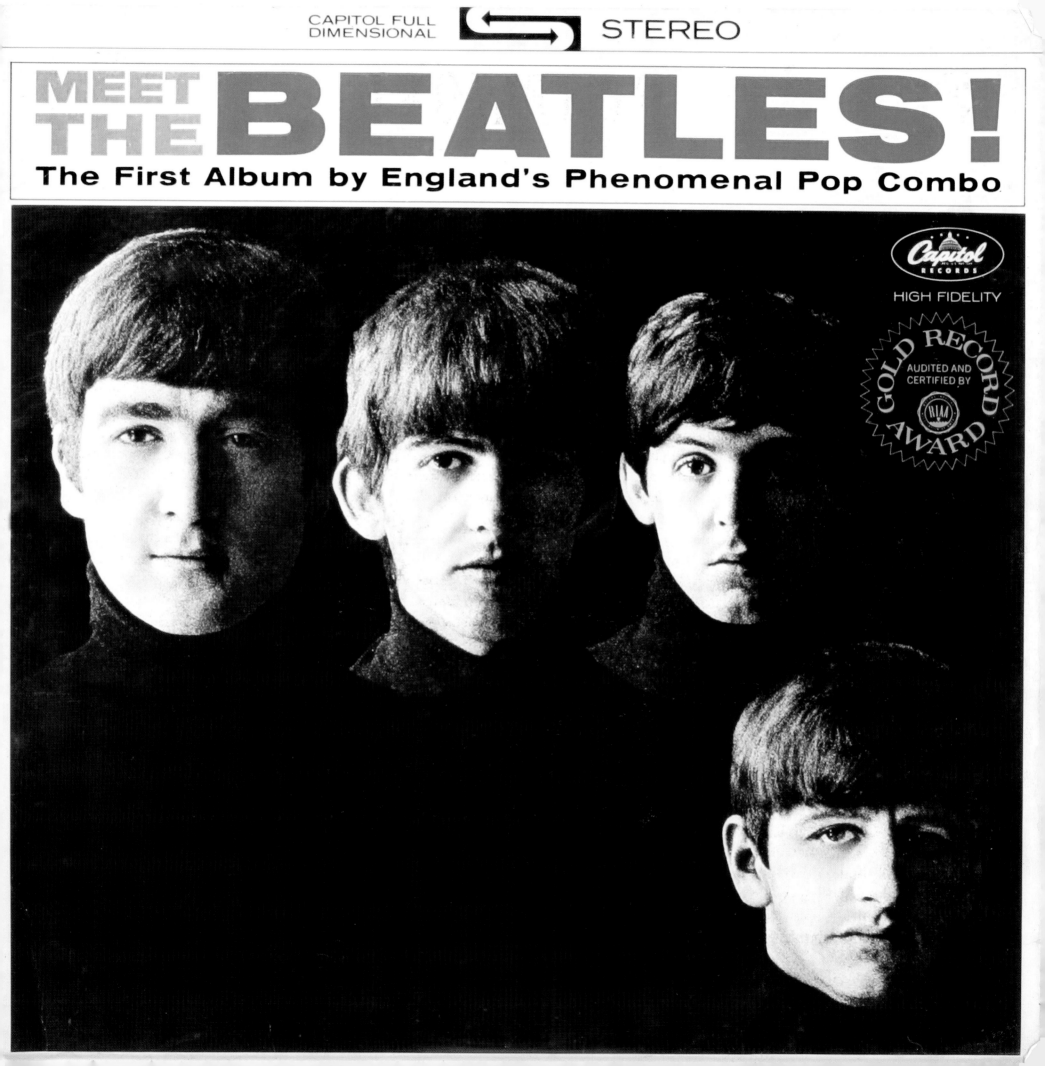

Band [No. 468], *Freak Out!* by the Mothers of Invention [No. 240], *Fresh Cream* [No. 102] and *Projections,* by the Blues Project – all important records for me that had no hit singles.

I must admit, I'm a sucker for a concept album. I love the art form used to its fullest potential, as Frank Sinatra first showed us in 1955, with *In the Wee Small Hours* [No. 101] – a coherent, theatrical experience in its performances and Sinatra's choice of songs. Miles Davis and Gil Evans explored the concept record instrumentally on 1960's *Sketches of Spain* [No. 352], with great success.

So I won't complain much about *Sgt. Pepper's Lonely Hearts Club Band* being Number One. It's not only a wonderful album but a perfect reflection of the world around it at the time. That is something a quality record will do. Some, like *Sgt. Pepper,* go on to influence the culture as well. All of a sudden, that album was a way that people defined themselves and lived their lives, the Beatles included.

Sometimes it's hard to evaluate those things until years later. I didn't know the Ramones were special in 1976, although I do remember defending them to my friends at the New York rock station WNEW. The DJs thought that first album, *Ramones* [No. 33], was a joke. But I heard the influences, and I knew the influences were cool. And by the way, where is 1980's *End of the Century* – a collision of two legends, the Ramones and Phil Spector, yielding one of the greatest singles of all time, "Do You Remember Rock 'n' Roll Radio?" – on this list? Nowhere, that's where!

I now have an entire radio format based on the Ramones. But at the time there was so much going on in music, and I was a little busy playing with Bruce Springsteen and Southside Johnny (*wheeeere's* Johnny?). Sometimes, you need a little distance to know how important something is. Then again, I've always been impressed by simplicity. That, to me, is the highest form of evolution. It's much harder to write "Louie Louie" or "Gloria" than "Stairway to Heaven." Nobody understands that until they try it.

I played on three of the Bruce Springsteen albums here – *Darkness on the Edge of Town* [No. 150], *The River* [No. 247] and *Born in the U.S.A.* [No. 85] – co-arranging all three and co-producing two of them. I can't actually tell you what it's like to record a classic album, though. You never know you're making one at the time. You're just fighting to get the thing done, to get something you're happy with and, if you're producing, that the artist is happy with. "Classic" and "greatest" don't come into it.

My challenge on *The River* was to make a record that sounded live, the way Bruce Springsteen and the E Street Band did in concert. We pretty much got there. The only problem was that Bruce then threw

out twenty of my favorite songs from the sessions – most of which ended up on the *Tracks* boxed set, still one of my favorite records.

For *Born in the U.S.A.,* the idea was to really get down to basics and avoid overdubbing altogether. So we didn't rehearse. That was the concept. Bruce showed us the songs in the studio, and we recorded – before we truly knew the songs. We did fifteen songs in three weeks – one a day. We stayed totally disciplined. If Bruce wanted to sing the song again, we played it with him again. Then I left – and he spent two more years working on the record, on three more songs, one of which was the album's first hit. Did we know we had seven Top Ten singles there? No. We were doing the best we could at the time.

Occasionally, you know you're on to something. You take into account the desire, the will, to do something extraordinary, or at least attempt it. I remember Bruce telling me about wanting to sum up all he knew about rock & roll in "Born to Run." But that's very different from "I know I'm making a classic." You only hope you're making one.

So what makes a classic? Greatness? Historical significance? Influence? All of those things. But our list also includes emotional favorites – no intellect required. And you will quibble about the order and what got left out. If rock & roll is religion to you, as much as it is to me, you will more than quibble.

For example: I believe the Who's first album, *The Who Sings My Generation,* is still their best. What's it doing at 232? There aren't twenty rock records better than that, let alone 235. And the Kinks' 1965 album, *The Kink Kontroversy,* remains their best non-best-of record, in spite of the critical acclaim heaped on *The Village Green Preservation Society* [No. 252]. Naturally, *Kontroversy* isn't here at all.

Also, no Youngbloods? *Tapestry* [No. 36] before *Beggars Banquet* [No. 58] and *Disraeli Gears* [No. 114]? And how about them Carpenters sneaking in at 174 ahead of New York Dolls [No. 211] and John Mayall's Blues Breakers with Eric Clapton [No. 193]?

That aside, these are all terrific records, many of them from a time when music mattered, when it was an integral part of our culture and an essential part of literally surviving the day.

I should know – I'm one of the survivors.

Now if we could only get all of these records in mono, so we could hear them the way God intended . . .

LITTLE STEVEN

EDITOR'S NOTE

THIS BOOK BEGAN in December of 2003, when ROLLING STONE published the RS 500, an issue devoted to the greatest records of all time. Our list of albums was selected by a blue-ribbon panel of experts and true fans: the singers, songwriters, musicians, producers, label executives, artist managers and critics, among others, who have shaped rock & roll in its first half-century. The 273 voters spanned every decade and genre of popular music, from the 1950s to the present, including Billie Joe Armstrong and Tré Cool of Green Day, the Edge of U2, Fats Domino, James Hetfield and Lars Ulrich of Metallica, Beck, Carole King, Jackson Browne, Ray Manzarek and John Densmore of the Doors, Dion DiMucci, Shirley Manson and Butch Vig of Garbage, Adam Yauch of the Beastie Boys, Missy Elliott and Little Steven. The voters were asked to select and rank their fifty top albums of all time. The ballot was open – any album was eligible – and we cast our net wide: Both folk patriarch Pete Seeger and pop princess Britney Spears voted (you can see a full list of voters on page 218). The ballots were tabulated according to a weighted point system developed by the accounting firm of Ernst & Young under the supervision of the editors of ROLLING STONE.

The 500 albums selected represent the most exciting and vital music ever recorded, from the shellac 78s made on November 23rd, 1936, by Robert Johnson in a San Antonio, Texas, hotel room – finally compiled on LP nearly thirty years after his death – to the twenty-first-century garage rock of the White Stripes. Our list was inclusive, but – our readers let us know – not perfect. Led Zeppelin fans were astounded that Zeppelin didn't crack the top 10; Deadheads were even more amazed that the Grateful Dead didn't crack the top 200. Other readers complained about the presence of compilation albums and greatest-hits packages, a fair criticism, but one that would have left out the pioneer artists who did their best work on singles in the days before the LP, including Chuck Berry, Little Richard, Jerry Lee Lewis, Howlin' Wolf, Hank Williams, John Lee Hooker and Muddy Waters. No list of the greatest rock & roll albums would be complete without these artists. Still, for this book ver-

sion of the RS 500 I have eliminated a few compilation albums that simply repeated material appearing elsewhere on albums that made the list. I've also combined the two volumes of Robert Johnson's *King of the Delta Blues Singers* – the LPs on which many of the voters first heard Johnson (Bob Dylan is pictured alongside a copy of the first volume on the cover of *Bringing It All Back Home*) – into the more readily available *Complete Recordings*. That left room for eight new albums to bubble up from the bottom of our tally. I'm sorry to tell you that still leaves *Workingman's Dead* at No. 259.

But I can tell you that these 500 albums – which are credited to the labels that currently have them in print – have shaped and defined the music we call rock & roll. Country, blues, gospel, pop, soul, R&B, funk, hip-hop, acid-rock, heavy metal, punk – every way there is to scream and shout, soothe and seduce, get up to get down, and keep on moving – it's all here. Each of these albums have been crucial to rock's history, its present or its future. And each one testifies to how much the music has shaped and defined us. My guess is you'll find a lot your own history here. I know I do: The first albums I ever bought were Bruce Springsteen's *Born to Run* [No. 18] and Elvis Costello's *Armed Forces* [No. 474]. I started making my own list that day in 1979, and I haven't stopped since.

JOE LEVY
DEPUTY MANAGING EDITOR
ROLLING STONE

1 Sgt. Pepper's Lonely Hearts Club Band

THE BEATLES *CAPITOL 1967*

Sgt. Pepper's Lonely Hearts Club Band is the most important rock & roll album ever made, an unsurpassed adventure in concept, sound, songwriting, cover art and studio technology by the greatest rock & roll group of all time. From the title song's regal blasts of brass and fuzz guitar to the orchestral seizure and long, dying piano chord at the end of "A Day in the Life," the thirteen tracks on *Sgt. Pepper's Lonely Hearts Club Band* are the pinnacle of the Beatles' eight years as recording artists. John Lennon, Paul McCartney, George Harrison and Ringo Starr were never more fearless and unified in their pursuit of magic and transcendence.

Issued in Britain on June 1st, 1967, and a day later in America, *Sgt. Pepper's Lonely Hearts Club Band* is also rock's ultimate declaration of change. For the Beatles, it was a decisive goodbye to matching suits, world tours and assembly-line record making. "We were fed up with being Beatles," McCartney said decades later, in *Many Years From Now,* Barry Miles' McCartney biography. "We were not boys, we were men . . . artists rather than performers."

At the same time, *Sgt. Pepper* formally ushered in an unforgettable season of hope, upheaval and achievement: the late 1960s and, in particular, 1967's Summer of Love. In its iridescent instrumentation, lyric fantasias and eye-popping packaging, *Sgt. Pepper* defined the opulent revolutionary optimism of psychedelia and instantly spread the gospel of love, acid, Eastern spirituality and electric guitars around the globe. No other pop record of that era, or since, has had such an immediate, titanic impact. This music documents the world's biggest rock band at the very height of its influence and ambition.

"It was a peak," Lennon confirmed in his 1970 ROLLING STONE interview, describing both the album and his collaborative relationship with McCartney. "Paul and I definitely were working together," Lennon said, and *Sgt. Pepper* is rich with proof: McCartney's burst of hot piano and school-days memoir ("Woke up, fell out of bed . . .") in Lennon's "A Day in the Life," a reverie on mortality and infinity; Lennon's impish rejoinder to McCartney's chorus in "Getting Better" ("It can't get no worse").

"*Sgt. Pepper* was our grandest endeavor," Starr said, looking back, in the 2000 autobiography *The Beatles Anthology.* "The greatest thing about the band was that whoever had the best idea – it didn't matter who – that was the one we'd use. No one was standing on their ego, saying, 'Well, it's mine,' and getting possessive." It was Neil Aspinall, the Beatles' longtime assistant, who suggested they reprise the title track, just before the grand finale of "A Day in the Life," to complete *Sgt. Pepper*'s theatrical conceit: an imaginary concert by a fictional band, played by the Beatles.

The first notes went to tape on December 6th, 1966: two takes of McCartney's music-hall confection "When I'm Sixty-Four." (Lennon's lysergic reflection on his Liverpool childhood, "Strawberry Fields Forever," was started two weeks earlier but issued in February 1967 as a stand-alone single.) But *Sgt. Pepper*'s real birthday is August 29th, 1966, when the Beatles played their last live concert, in San Francisco. Until then, they had made history in the studio – *Please Please Me* (1963), *Rubber Soul* (1965), *Revolver* (1966) – between punishing tours. Off the road for good, the Beatles were free to be a band away from the hysteria of Beatlemania.

McCartney went a step further. On a plane to London in November '66, as he returned from a vacation in Kenya, he came up with the idea of an album by the Beatles in disguise, an alter-ego group that he subsequently dubbed Sgt. Pepper's Lonely Hearts Club Band. "We'd pretend to be someone else," McCartney explained in *Anthology.* "It liberated you – you could do anything when you got to the mike or on your guitar, because it wasn't you."

Only two songs on the final LP, both McCartney's, had anything to do with the Pepper character: the title track and Starr's jaunty vocal showcase "With a Little Help From My Friends," introduced as a number by Sgt. Pepper's star crooner, Billy Shears. "Every other song could have been on any other album," Lennon insisted later. Yet it is hard to imagine a more perfect setting for the Victorian jollity of Lennon's "Being for the Benefit of Mr. Kite!" (inspired by an 1843 circus poster) or the sumptuous melancholy of McCartney's "Fixing a Hole," with its blend of antique shadows (a harpsichord played by the Beatles' producer George Martin) and modern sunshine (double-tracked lead guitar executed with ringing precision by Harrison). The Pepper premise was a license to thrill.

It also underscored the real-life cohesion of the music and the group that made it. Of the 700 hours the Beatles spent making *Sgt. Pepper* (engineer Geoff Emerick actually tallied them) from the end of 1966 until April 1967, the group needed only three days' worth to complete Lennon's lavish daydream "Lucy in the Sky With Diamonds." "A Day in the Life," the most complex song on the album, was done in just five days. (The oceanic piano chord was three pianos hit simultaneously by ten hands belonging to Lennon, McCartney, Starr, Martin and Beatles roadie Mal Evans.) No other Beatles appear with Harrison on his sitar-perfumed sermon on materialism and fidelity, "Within You Without You," but the band wisely placed the track at the halfway point of the original vinyl LP, at the beginning of Side Two: a vital meditation break in the middle of the jubilant indulgence.

The Beatles at the press conference for the release of "Sgt. Pepper's," May 19th, 1967. "It was a peak," John Lennon said. "Paul and I were definitely working together."

The Beatles' exploitation of multitracking on *Sgt. Pepper* transformed the very act of studio recording (the orchestral overdubs on "A Day in the Life" marked the debut of eight-track recording in Britain: two four-track machines used in sync). And *Sgt. Pepper*'s visual extravagance officially elevated the rock album cover to a work of art. Michael Cooper's photo of the Beatles in satin marching-band outfits, in front of a cardboard-cutout audience of historical figures, created by artist Peter Blake, is the most enduring image of the psychedelic era. *Sgt. Pepper* was also the first rock album to incorporate complete lyrics to the songs in its design.

Yet *Sgt. Pepper's Lonely Hearts Club Band* is the Number One album of the RS 500 not just because of its firsts — it is simply the best of everything the Beatles ever did as musicians, pioneers and pop stars, all in one place. A 1967 British print ad for the album declared, "Remember, Sgt. Pepper's Lonely Hearts Club Band Is the Beatles." As McCartney put it, the album was "just us doing a good show."

The show goes on forever.

N-16156 A Capitol Re-Issue
MONOPHONIC

The Beach Boys Pet Sounds

Sloop John B. / Caroline No
Wouldn't It Be Nice / You Still Believe In Me
That's Not Me / Don't Talk (Put Your Head on My Shoulder)
I'm Waiting For The Day / Let's Go Away For Awhile
God Only Knows / I Know There's An Answer / Here Today
I Just Wasn't Made For These Times / Pet Sounds

2 Pet Sounds

THE BEACH BOYS *CAPITOL 1966*

"Who's gonna hear this shit?" Beach Boys singer Mike Love asked the band's resident genius, Brian Wilson, in 1966, as Wilson played him the new songs he was working on. "The ears of a dog?" Confronted with his bandmate's contempt, Wilson made lemonade of lemons. "Ironically," he observed, "Mike's barb inspired the album's title." • Barking dogs — Wilson's dog Banana among them, in fact — are prominent among the found sounds on the album. The Beatles made a point of echoing them on *Sgt. Pepper's Lonely Hearts Club Band* — an acknowledgment that *Pet Sounds* was the inspiration for the Beatles' masterpiece. That gesture actually completed a circle of influence: Wilson initially conceived of *Pet Sounds* as an effort to top the Beatles' *Rubber Soul.*

Wilson essentially made *Sounds* without the rest of the band, using them only to flesh out the vocal arrangements. He even considered putting the album out as a solo project, and the first single, "Caroline, No," was released under his own name. The deeply personal nature of the songs, which Wilson co-wrote primarily with lyricist

The Beach Boys with a crucial collaborator

Tony Asher, further distinguished the album from the Beach Boys' typical fare. Its luxurious sound conveys a heartbreaking wistfulness, as songs such as "I Just Wasn't Made for These Times" and "I'm Waiting for the Day" bid farewell to the innocent world of the early Sixties and to the Beach Boys' fun-in-the-sun hits.

Unfortunately, Capitol Records proved no more enamored of *Pet Sounds* than had Love; the label actually considered not releasing the album at all. Not yet vindicated by history, Wilson withdrew further into his inner world. "At the last meeting I attended concerning *Pet Sounds*," Wilson wrote in his autobiography (which took the name of the album's opening track, "Wouldn't It Be Nice") about his dealings with Capitol's executive brain trust, "I showed up holding a tape player and eight prerecorded, looped responses, including 'No comment,' 'Can you repeat that?' 'No' and 'Yes.' Refusing to utter a word, I played the various tapes when appropriate."

3 Revolver

THE BEATLES *CAPITOL 1966*

"I don't see too much difference between *Revolver* and *Rubber Soul*," George Harrison once said. "To me, they could be Volume One and Volume Two." *Revolver* extends the more adventurous aspects of its predecessor – its introspection, its nascent psychedelia, its fascination with the possibilities of the studio – into a dramatic statement of generational purpose. The album, which was released in August 1966, made it thrillingly clear that what we now think of as "the Sixties" was fully – and irreversibly – under way.

Part of that revolutionary impulse was visual. Klaus Voormann, one of the Beatles' artist buddies from their days in Hamburg, Germany, designed a striking photo-collage cover for *Revolver*; it was a crucial step on the road to the even trippier, more colorful imagery of *Sgt. Pepper's Lonely Hearts Club Band*, which would come less than a year later.

And then there's the music. The most innovative track on the album is John Lennon's "Tomorrow Never Knows." Attempting to distill an LSD trip into a three-minute song, Lennon borrowed lyrics from Timothy Leary's version of *The Tibetan Book of the Dead* and recorded his vocal to sound like "the Dalai Lama singing from the highest mountaintop." Tape loops, a backward guitar part (Paul McCartney's blistering solo on "Taxman," in fact) and a droning tamboura completed the experimental effect, and the song proved hugely influential. For his part, on "Eleanor Rigby" and "For No One," McCartney mastered a strikingly mature form of art song, and Harrison, with "Taxman," "I Want to Tell You" and "Love You To," challenged Lennon-McCartney's songwriting dominance.

Revolver, finally, signaled that in popular music, anything – any theme, any musical idea – could now be realized. And, in the case of the Beatles, would be.

The Fabs in 1966: On "Revolver" they mastered the studio. Next stop: "Sgt. Pepper."

BOB DYLAN HIGHWAY 61 REVISITED

4 Highway 61 Revisited

BOB DYLAN *COLUMBIA 1965*

Bruce Springsteen has described the beginning of "Like a Rolling Stone," the opening song on Bob Dylan's Highway 61 Revisited, as the "snare shot that sounded like somebody'd kicked open the door to your mind." The response of folk singer Phil Ochs to the entire album was even more rhapsodic. "It's impossibly good. . . ." he said. "How can a human mind do this?" • Recorded in an astonishing six days and released in August 1965, Highway 61 Revisited – named after the road that runs from Dylan's home state of Minnesota down through the Mississippi Delta – is one of those albums that, quite simply, changed everything. In and of itself, "Like a Rolling Stone," which was rumored to be about Andy Warhol acolyte Edie Sedgwick, forever altered the landscape of popular music – its "vomitific" lyrics (in Dylan's memorable term), literary ambition and sheer length (6:13) shattered limitations of every kind. But that was literally only the beginning. "Ballad of a Thin Man" delivered the definitive Sixties comment on the splintering hip/straight fault line: "Something is happening here, but you don't know what it is/Do you, Mr. Jones?" If anyone questioned whether or not Dylan had truly "gone electric," the roaring rock & roll of "From a Buick 6" and "Tombstone Blues" – both powered by legendary guitarist Mike Bloomfield of the Paul Butterfield Blues Band – left no doubt.

The album ends with "Desolation Row," a swirling eleven-minute surrealist night journey of indescribable power. Confronted with the dilemma of providing an ending to an album so bursting with ideas, Dylan evokes a Hieronymus Bosch-like season in hell that, in retrospect, seems to foretell all the Sixties cataclysms to come. "The *Titanic* sails at dawn," he sings wearily near the song's end. "Everybody is shouting, 'Which side are you on?'" That "Desolation Row" is an all-acoustic track – a last-minute decision on Dylan's part – is one final stroke of genius: a spellbinding new vision of folk music to close the album that, for the time being at least, destroyed folk music. The gesture was simultaneously touching and a devastating "Fuck you!"

Not that Dylan wasn't having fun all the while as well. The toy siren that opens the album's title track was keyboardist's Al Kooper's playful way of policing the recording sessions for *Highway 61 Revisited*. "If anybody started using drugs anywhere," he explained, "I'd walk into the opposite corner of the room and just go *whooooooooo*."

5 | Rubber Soul

THE BEATLES *CAPITOL 1965*

Released in December 1965 – and capping a year defined by groundbreaking singles such as Bob Dylan's "Like a Rolling Stone" and the Rolling Stones' "(I Can't Get No) Satisfaction" – *Rubber Soul* finds the Beatles rising to meet the challenge their peers had set. Characteristically, they achieved new musical sophistication and thematic depth without sacrificing a whit of pop appeal. Producer George Martin described *Rubber Soul* as "the first album to present a new, growing Beatles to the world," and so it was.

The band's development expressed itself in a variety of overlapping ways. On the U.K. version (the only one available on CD), "Drive My Car" presents a comic character study of a sort not previously in the Beatles' repertoire. More profoundly, however, Dylan's influence suffuses the album, accounting for the tart emotional tone of "Norwegian Wood," "I'm Looking Through You," "You Won't See Me" and "If I Needed Someone." (Dylan would return the compliment the following year, when he offered his own version of "Norwegian Wood" – titled "4th Time Around" – on *Blonde on Blonde,* and consequently made Lennon "Paranoid.") Lennon's "Nowhere Man," which he later acknowledged as a depressed self-portrait, and the beautifully reminiscent "In My Life" both reflect the more serious and personal style of songwriting that Dylan had suddenly made possible.

George Harrison's sitar on "Norwegian Wood" – the first time the instrument was used in a pop song – and Paul McCartney's fuzz bass on "Think for Yourself" document the band's increasing awareness that the studio could be more than a pit stop between tours. Harrison called *Rubber Soul* "the best one we made," because "we were suddenly hearing sounds that we weren't able to hear before." And as for why the band's hearing had grown so acute, well, that was another aspect of the times. "There was a lot of experimentation on *Rubber Soul,*" said Ringo Starr, "influenced, I think, by the substances."

In Atlanta, 1965, under the influence of Bob Dylan and other substances

what's going on

MARVIN GAYE

TS310

ORCHESTRA CONDUCTED
AND ARRANGED BY
DAVID VAN DePITT

6 What's Going On

MARVIN GAYE *MOTOWN 1971*

"In 1969 or 1970, I began to re-evaluate my whole concept of what I wanted my music to say," Gaye once said about the creation of *What's Going On.* "I was very much affected by letters my brother was sending me from Vietnam, as well as the social situation here at home. I realized that I had to put my own fantasies behind me if I wanted to write songs that would reach the souls of people. I wanted them to take a look at what was happening in the world."

The last thing Motown wanted its fans to think about, however, was "what was happening in the world." So with Gaye determined to shatter the label's hugely successful pop formula and address issues such as the Vietnam War, civil rights and the environment, Motown founder Berry Gordy was not pleased, to say the least. He claimed that "What's Going On" was the worst song he had ever heard. As for "Mercy Mercy Me (The Ecology)," Gordy asserted that he didn't even know what the word *ecology* meant. For his part, Gaye said he would never record for Motown again unless "What's Going On" was put out as a single. After initially being rejected by Motown's quality-control committee, it was; when it became a Top Five hit, the album – and a burst of socially conscious music from Motown – followed soon after.

Producing the album amid a haze of marijuana smoke, Gaye made one intuitively brilliant decision after another – from letting the tapes roll as his friends mingled and chatted to recording the rehearsal exercises of saxophonist Eli Fountain.

Strange but true: Gaye's masterpiece was initially rejected by Motown.

When Fountain complained that he had just been goofing around, Gaye replied, "Well, you goof exquisitely. Thank you." And that's how the plaintive saxophone line that announces *What's Going On* came to be.

7 Exile on Main Street

THE ROLLING STONES *VIRGIN 1972*

A dirty whirl of blues and boogie, the Rolling Stones' 1972 double LP "was the first grunge record," guitarist Keith Richards crowed proudly last year. But inside the deliberately dense squall – Richards' and Mick Taylor's dogfight riffing, the lusty jump of the Bill Wyman/Charlie Watts rhythm engine, Mick Jagger's caged-animal bark and burned-soul croon – is the Stones' greatest album and Jagger and Richards' definitive songwriting statement of outlaw pride and dedication to grit. In the existential shuffle "Tumbling Dice," the exhausted country beauty "Torn and Frayed" and the whiskey-soaked church of "Shine a Light," you literally hear the Stones in exile: working at Richards' villa in the south of France, on the run from media censure, British drug police (Jagger and Richards already knew the view from behind bars) and the country's onerous tax code. The music rattles like battle but also swings with clear purpose – unconditional survival – in "Rocks Off" and "All Down the Line." As Richards explained, "The Stones don't have a home anymore – hence the Exile – but they can still keep it together. Whatever people throw at us, we can still duck, improvise, overcome." Great example: Richards recorded his jubilant romp "Happy" with just producer

The Stones cut their greatest album while tax exiles in France.

Jimmy Miller on drums and saxman Bobby Keys – while waiting for the other Stones to turn up for work. *Exile on Main Street* is the Stones at their fighting best, armed with the blues, playing to win.

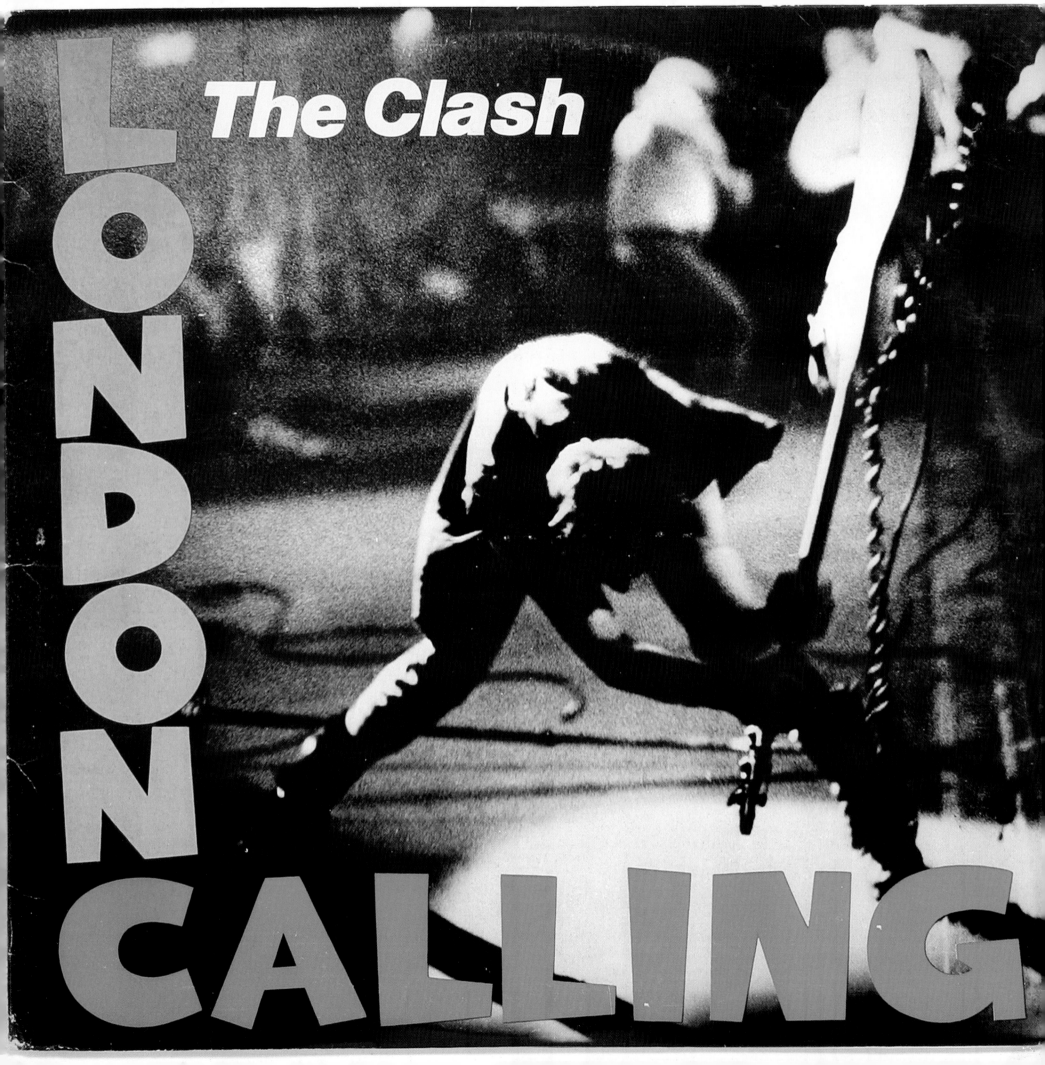

8 London Calling

THE CLASH *EPIC 1980*

Recorded in 1979 in London, which was then wrenched by surging unemployment and drug addiction, and released in America in January 1980, the dawn of an uncertain decade, *London Calling* is nineteen songs of apocalypse fueled by an unbending faith in rock & roll to beat back the darkness. Produced with no-surrender energy by legendary Sixties studio madman Guy Stevens, the Clash's third album sounds like a free-form radio broadcast from the end of the world,

skidding from bleak punk ("London Calling") to rampaging ska ("Wrong 'Em Boyo") and disco resignation ("Lost in the Supermarket"). The album was made in dire straits too. Although the Clash fired singles into the Britain's Top Forty with machine-gun regularity, the band was heavily in debt and openly at war with their record company.

Singer-guitarists Joe Strummer and Mick Jones, the Clash's Lennon and McCartney, wrote together in Jones' grandmother's flat, where he was living for lack of dough. "Joe, once he learned how to type, would bang the lyrics out at a high rate of good stuff," Jones noted. "Then I'd be able to bang out some music while he was hitting the typewriter." A news story about a terrorist bombing in the Mediterranean inspired "Spanish Bombs." "Lost in the Supermarket" was based on Jones' upside-down life as a rock star living in public

housing with his grandmother.

Strummer, Jones, bassist Paul Simonon and drummer Topper Headon spent three months rehearsing and demo-ing songs in a garage in the Pimlico section of London – "with one light and filthy carpet on the walls for soundproofing," recalled Strummer in 1989. "We felt that we were struggling," he said, "about to slide down a slope or something, grasping with our fingernails. And there was nobody to help us."

But Steven was on hand for inspiration. He threw chairs around the room "if he thought a track needed zapping up," according to Strummer. The album ends with "Train in Vain," a rousing song of fidelity (originally unlisted on the back cover) that became the sound of triumph: the Clash's first Top Thirty single in the U.S.

At left: The Fender bass smashed by Paul Simonon at a 1979 New York concert, captured on the cover of "London Calling"

9

Blonde on Blonde

BOB DYLAN *COLUMBIA 1966*

Released on May 16th, 1966, rock's first studio double LP by a major artist was, as Dylan declared in 1978, "the closest I ever got to the sound I hear in my head... that thin, that wild-mercury sound." There is no better description of the album's manic brilliance. After several false-start sessions in New York in the fall of 1965 and January 1966 with his killer road band the Hawks – "One of Us Must Know (Sooner or Later)" was the only keeper – Dylan blazed through the rest of *Blonde on Blonde*'s fourteen tracks in two three-day runs at Columbia's Nashville studios in February and March 1966.

The pace of recording echoed the amphetamine velocity of Dylan's songwriting and touring schedule at the time. But the combined presence of trusted hands like organist Al Kooper and Hawks guitarist Robbie Robertson with expert local sessionmen including drummer Kenneth Buttrey and pianist Hargus "Pig" Robbins created an almost contradictory magnificence: a tightly wound tension around Dylan's quicksilver language and incisive singing in barrelhouse surrealism such as "Rainy Day Women #12 and 35" and "Stuck Inside of Mobile With the Memphis Blues Again." Amid the frenzy, Dylan delivered some of his finest, clearest songs of comfort and desire: the sidelong beauty "Sad Eyed Lady of the Lowlands," recorded in just one take, and "I Want You," the title of which Dylan almost used for the album.

In 1966, on tour with the Hawks and on "Blonde on Blonde," Dylan let loose the wild sound in his head.

the BEATLES

A1436386

10 | The Beatles (The White Album)

THE BEATLES *CAPITOL 1968*

Beyond its stylish minimalism, the stark white cover of *The Beatles*, better known as the White Album, served a symbolic purpose. For the first time, the Beatles couldn't put a picture of themselves on the cover – because they were falling apart as a team. By 1968, John Lennon, Paul McCartney and George Harrison were all working separately as songwriters, each one singing his own songs solo while the rest of the band played backup. • Yet the creative tension that went into the White Album resulted in one of the most intense and adventurous rock albums ever made. Lennon pursued his hard-edged vision into the cynical wit of "Sexy Sadie" and "Happiness Is a Warm Gun," as well as the childlike yearning of "Julia" and "Dear Prudence." McCartney's playful pop energy came through in "Martha My Dear" and his inversion of Chuck Berry's American values, "Back in the U.S.S.R." Harrison's spiritual yearning led him to "Long, Long, Long" and "While My Guitar Gently Weeps," featuring a guest guitar solo from Eric Clapton. Even Ringo Starr contributes his first original, the country-tinged "Don't Pass Me By." The Beatles tried a little of everything, dabbling in folk ("Cry Baby Cry"), metal ("Helter Skelter"), avant-garde tape collage ("Revolution #9"), blues ("Yer Blues") and every other genre they could think of.

They wrote the songs while on retreat with the Maharishi Mahesh Yogi in India, taking a break from the celebrity whirl. As Lennon later said, "We sat in the mountains eating lousy vegetarian food and writing all these songs." They came back with more great tunes than they could release, and competed fiercely during the sessions. "I remember having three studios operating at the same time," Harrison recalled. "Paul was doing some overdubs in one, John was in another, and I was recording some horns or something in a third." The sessions became so tense that Ringo Starr quit the band in frustration for a few days. When he returned to the studio, his bandmates decorated his drum kit with flowers to celebrate. But even at each other's throats, they were spurring each other on to new musical heights. "I think it was a very good album," said McCartney. "It stood up, but it wasn't a pleasant one to make."

11 Sunrise

ELVIS PRESLEY *RCA 1976*

Many believe rock & roll was born on July 5th, 1954, at Sun Studios in Memphis. Elvis Presley, guitarist Scotty Moore and bassist Bill Black were horsing around with "That's All Right," a tune by bluesman Arthur Crudup, when producer Sam Phillips stopped them and asked, "What are you doing?" "We don't know," they said. Phillips told them to "back up and do it again." The A side of Presley's first single (backed with a version of Bill Monroe's "Blue Moon of Kentucky"), "That's All

Right" was issued by Sun, on July 19th. It may or may not be the first rock & roll record. But the man who would be King was officially on wax. Bridging black and white, country and blues, his sound was playful and revolutionary, charged by a spontaneity and freedom that changed the world. Presley released four more singles on Sun – including definitive reinventions of Wynonie Harris' "Good Rockin' Tonight" and Junior Parker's "Mystery Train" – before moving on to immortality at RCA. But this double CD collects everything he cut at the studio, including alternate takes and the 1953 acetate he recorded as a gift for his mother as a shy and awkward recent high school graduate.

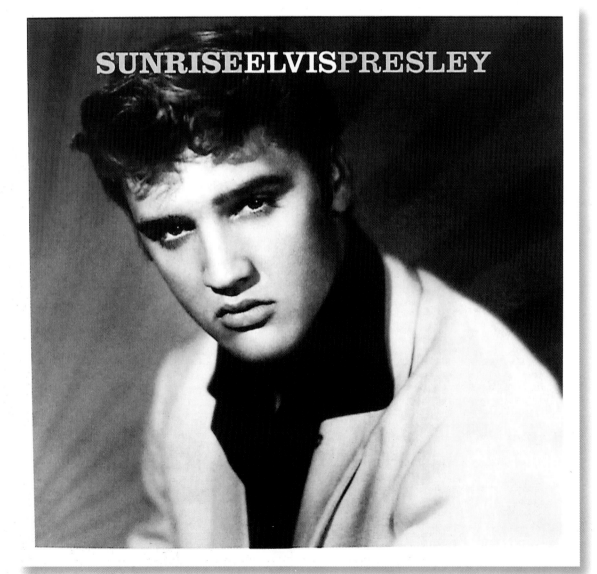

12 | Kind of Blue

MILES DAVIS *COLUMBIA/LEGACY 1959*

This painterly masterpiece is one of the most important, influential and popular albums in jazz. At the time it was made, *Kind of Blue* was also a revolution all its own. Turning his back on standard chord progressions, trumpeter Miles Davis used modal scales as a starting point for composition and improvisation – breaking new ground with warmth, subtlety and understatement in the thick of hard bop. Davis and his peerless band – bassist Paul Chambers, drummer Jimmy Cobb, pianist Bill Evans and the titanic sax team of John Coltrane and Cannonball Adderley – soloed in uncluttered settings, typified by "melodic rather than harmonic variation," as Davis put it. Two numbers, "All Blues" and "Freddie Freeloader" (the latter featured Wynton Kelly at the ivories in place of Evans), were in twelve-bar form, but Davis' approach allowed his players a cool, new, collected freedom. Evans wrote in his original liner notes, "Miles conceived these settings only hours before the recording dates and arrived with sketches which indicated to the group what was to be played. Therefore, you will hear something close to pure spontaneity in these performances." Or as the late critic Robert Palmer wrote, "*Kind of Blue* is, in a sense, all melody – and atmosphere." The bass line in "So What" is now among the most familiar obbligatos in jazz, and there is no finer evocation of the late-night wonder of jazz than the muted horns in "All Blues."

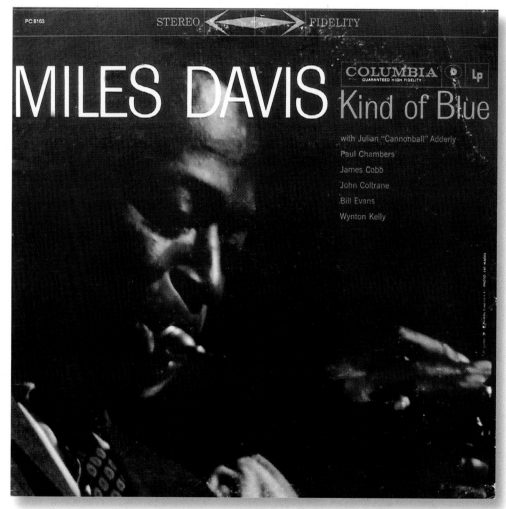

13 The Velvet Underground

THE VELVET UNDERGROUND AND NICO *MGM/VERVE 1967*

"We were trying to do a Phil Spector thing with as few instruments as possible," John Cale, the classically trained pianist and viola player of the Velvet Underground, once said of this record. It was no idle boast. Much of what we take for granted in rock would not exist without this New York band or its seminal debut, *The Velvet Underground and Nico*: the androgynous sexuality of glitter; punk's raw noir; the blackened-riff howl of grunge and noise rock.

It is a record of fearless breadth and lyric depth. Singer-songwriter Lou Reed documented carnal desire and drug addiction with a pop wisdom he learned as a song-factory composer for Pickwick Records. Cale introduced the power of pulse and drone (from his work in early minimalism); guitarist Sterling Morrison and drummer Maureen Tucker played with tribal force; Nico, a German vocalist briefly added to the band by manager Andy Warhol, brought an icy femininity to the heated ennui in Reed's songs. Rejected as nihilistic by the love crowd in '67, the Banana Album (so named for its Warhol-designed cover), is the most prophetic rock album ever made.

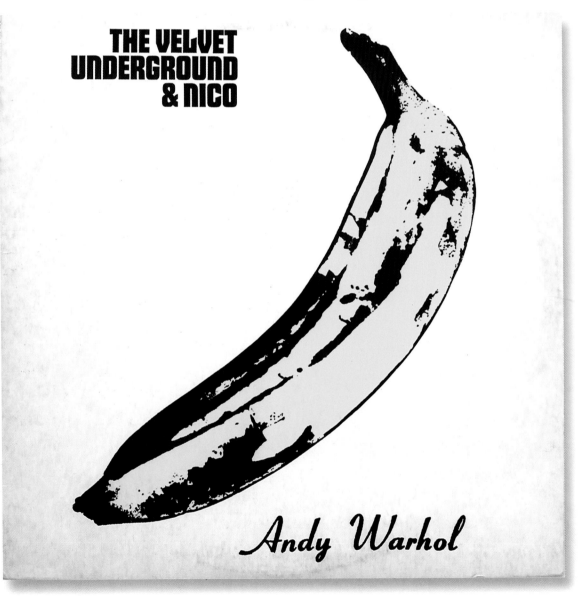

14 Abbey Road

THE BEATLES *CAPITOL 1969*

"It was a very happy record," said producer George Martin, describing this album in *The Beatles Anthology*. "I guess it was happy because everybody thought it was going to be the last." Indeed, *Abbey Road* – recorded in two months during the summer of 1969 – almost never got made at all. That January, the Beatles were on the verge of a breakup, exhausted and angry with one another after the disastrous sessions for the aborted *Get Back* LP, later salvaged as *Let It Be* [see

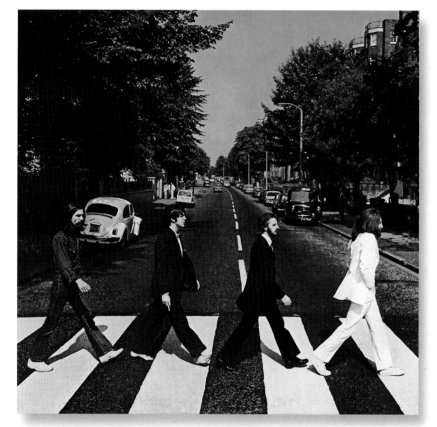

No. 86]. Yet determined to go out with the same glory with which they had first entranced the world at the start of the decade, the group reconvened at EMI's Abbey Road Studios to make their most polished album: a collection of superb songs cut with an attention to refined detail, then segued together (especially on Side Two) with conceptual force. There was no thematic link, other than the Beatles' unique genius. John Lennon veered from the stormy metal of "I Want You (She's So Heavy)" to the exquisite vocal sunrise of "Because." Paul McCartney was saucy ("Oh! Darling"), silly ("Maxwell's Silver Hammer") and deliciously bitter ("You Never Give Me Your Money"). George Harrison proved his long-secret worth as a composer with "Something" (later covered by Frank Sinatra) and the folk-pop diamond "Here Comes the Sun," written in his friend Eric Clapton's garden after a grim round of business meetings. And Lennon, McCartney and Harrison reputedly sang more three-part harmony here than on any other Beatles album. *Let It Be* was the group's final release, but this album was their real goodbye: The completion of "I Want You (She's So Heavy)" on August 20th marked the last time all four members were together in the studio they had made famous.

15 | Are You Experienced?

THE JIMI HENDRIX EXPERIENCE *MCA 1967*

This is what Britain sounded like in late 1966 and early 1967: ablaze with rainbow blues, orchestral guitar feedback and the personal cosmic vision of black American emigré Jimi Hendrix. Rescued from dead-end gigs in New York by ex-Animal Chas Chandler, Hendrix arrived in London in September 1966, quickly formed the Experience with bassist Noel Redding and drummer Mitch Mitchell and in a matter of weeks was recording the songs that comprised his epochal debut.

Hendrix's incendiary guitar was historic in itself, the luminescent sum of his chitlin-circuit labors with Little Richard and the Isley Brothers and his melodic exploitation of amp howl. But it was the pictorial heat of songs like "Manic Depression" and "The Wind Cries Mary" that established the transcendent promise of psychedelia. Hendrix made soul music for inner space. "It's a collection of free feeling and imagination," he said of the album. "Imagination is very important." Widely assumed to be about an acid trip, "Purple Haze" had "nothing to do with drugs," Hendrix insisted. " 'Purple Haze' was all about a dream I had that I was walking under the sea."

16 | Blood on the Tracks

BOB DYLAN *COLUMBIA 1975*

Bob Dylan once introduced this album's opening song, "Tangled Up in Blue," onstage as taking him ten years to live and two years to write. It was, for him, a pointed reference to the personal crisis – the collapse of his marriage to Sara Lowndes – that at least partly inspired this album, Dylan's best of the 1970s. In fact, he wrote all of these lyrically piercing, gingerly majestic folk-pop songs in two months, in mid-1974. He was so proud of them that he privately auditioned almost all of the album, from start to finish, for pals and peers including Mike Bloomfield, David Crosby and Graham Nash before cutting them in September – in just a week, with members of the bluegrass band Deliverance. But in December, Dylan played the record for his brother David in Minneapolis, who suggested recutting

some songs with local musicians. The final *Blood* was a mix of New York and Minneapolis tapes; the New York versions are slower, more pensive, while the Minneapolis versions are faster and wilder. Together, they frame the gritty anguish in Dylan's vocals, as he rages through some of his most passionate, confessional songs – from adult breakup ballads like "You're a Big Girl Now" and "If You See Her, Say Hello" to the sharp-tongued opprobrium of "Idiot Wind," his greatest put-down song since "Like a Rolling Stone." "A lot of people tell me they enjoyed that album," Dylan said soon after it became an instant commercial and critical success. "It's hard for me to relate to that – I mean people enjoying that type of pain." Yet Dylan had never turned so much pain into so much musical splendor.

17 | Nevermind

NIRVANA *GEFFEN 1991*

The overnight-success story of the 1990s, Nirvana's second album and its totemic first single, "Smells Like Teen Spirit," shot up from the Northwest underground – the nascent grunge scene in Seattle – to kick Michael Jackson off the top of the *Billboard* album chart and blow hair metal off the map. No album in recent history had such an overpowering impact on a generation – a nation of teens suddenly turned punk – and such a catastrophic effect on its main creator. The

weight of success led already troubled singer-guitarist Kurt Cobain to take his own life in 1994. But his slashing riffs, corrosive singing and deviously oblique writing, rammed home by the Pixies-via-Zeppelin might of bassist Krist Novoselic and drummer Dave Grohl, put the warrior purity back in rock & roll. Lyrically, Cobain raged in code – shorthand grenades of inner tumult and self-loathing. His genius, though, in songs like "Lithium," "Breed" and "Teen Spirit" was the soft-loud tension he created between verse and chorus, restraint and assault. Cobain was a pop lover at heart – and a Beatlemaniac: *Nevermind* co-producer Butch Vig remembers hearing Cobain play John Lennon's "Julia" at sessions. Cobain also fought to maintain his underground honor. Ultimately, it was a losing battle, but it is part of this album's enduring power. Vig recalls when Cobain was forced to overdub the guitar intro to "Teen Spirit" because he couldn't nail it live with the band: "That pissed him off. He wanted to play [the song] live all the way through."

18 | Born to Run

BRUCE SPRINGSTEEN *COLUMBIA 1975*

Bruce Springsteen spent everything he had – patience, energy, studio time, the physical endurance of his E Street Band – to ensure that his third album was a masterpiece. His reputation as a perfectionist begins here: There are a dozen guitar overdubs on the title track alone. He was also spending money he didn't have. Engineer Jimmy Iovine had to hide the mounting recording bills from the Columbia paymasters. "The album became a monster," Springsteen told his biographer, Dave Marsh. "It just ate up everyone's life." But in making *Born to Run*, Springsteen was living out the central drama in the album's tenement-love operas ("Backstreets," "Jungleland") and gun-the-engine rock & roll ("Thunder Road," "Born to Run"): the fight to reconcile big dreams with crushing reality. He found it so hard to get on tape the sound in his head – the Jersey-bar dynamite of his live gigs, Phil Spector's Wagnerian grandeur, the heartbreaking melodrama of Roy Orbison's hits – that Springsteen nearly scrapped *Born to Run* for a straight-up concert album. But his make-or-break attention to detail – including the iconic cover photo of Springsteen leaning onto saxman Clarence Clemons, a perfect metaphor for Springsteen's brotherly reliance on the E Street Band – assured the integrity of *Born to Run*'s success. In his determination to make a great album, Springsteen produced a timeless, inspiring record about the labors and glories of aspiring to greatness.

19 | Astral Weeks

VAN MORRISON *WARNER BROS. 1968*

This is music of such enigmatic beauty that, thirty-five years after its release, *Astral Weeks* still defies description. There was no precedent for it in Van Morrison's previous success: the bright, rolling pop of his 1967 Top Ten hit, "Brown Eyed Girl"; his earlier spell as the leader of Irish R&B punks Them and writer of the garage-rock standard "Gloria." And Morrison — a notoriously private man for whom singing and songwriting have long been a form of emotional armor as well

as release — never sounded as warm and ecstatic, more sensual and vulnerable, as he did on *Astral Weeks.* It was, in part, the sound of sweet relief. Morrison was newly signed to artist-friendly Warner Bros., after a rough ride with his previous U.S. label, Bang, when he made *Astral Weeks* in the summer of 1968. This was to be his first full-fledged solo album, and he used the opportunity to explore the physical and dramatic range of his voice in his extended poetic-scat singing in "Beside You" and "Ballerina." Morrison also turned his back on straight pop-song structure, setting these hallucinatory reveries on his native Belfast (the daydream memoir "Cypress Avenue," the hypnotic portrait of "Madame George") to wandering melodies connecting the earthy poetry in Celtic folk and American R&B. The crowning touch was the superior jazz quintet — including acoustic bassist Richard Davis and drummer Connie Kay of the Modern Jazz Quartet — created by producer Lewis Merenstein to color the mists and shadows. Years later, Davis claimed that the album's basic tracks were all done in one three-hour session and that Morrison never told the musicians what he wanted from them or what the lyrics meant. Maybe he didn't know how. *Astral Weeks* is Morrison going deep inside himself, to the far corners of his life and art, without a net or fear. He was never this open, and naked, again.

20 | Thriller

MICHAEL JACKSON *EPIC 1982*

Michael Jackson towered over the 1980s the way Elvis Presley dominated the 1950s, and *Thriller* is the reason why. Still in his early twenties when *Thriller* was released, the R&B child star of the 1970s had ripened into a Technicolor soulman: a singer, dancer and songwriter with incomparable crossover instincts. He and producer Quincy Jones established the something-for-everyone template of *Thriller* on 1979's *Off the Wall*, on which Jackson captures the rare mania of his

life – the applause and paranoia; the need for love and the fear of commitment – in a crisp fusion of pop hooks and dance beats. On *Thriller*, the pair heighten the sheen (the jaunty gloss of "The Girl Is Mine," with a guest vocal by Paul Mc-Cartney), pump up the theater (the horror-movie spectacular "Thriller") and deepen the funk. With its locomotive cadence and acrobatic-metal guitar solo by Eddie Van Halen, "Beat It" was arguably the first industrial-disco Number One. (Jackson had such an impeccable nose for the down-and-dirty that Jones called him Smelly.) But the most thrilling thing about *Thriller* was the autobiography busting through the gloss: the angry hiss of denial in Jackson's voice in the funk-rock noir of "Billie Jean"; the to-hell-with-haters cock strut of "Wanna Be Startin' Somethin'." Jackson was at the peak of his art and adulthood. It is hard now to separate the wonder of *Thriller* from its commercial stature (Number One for thirty-seven weeks, seven Top Ten singles, eight Grammys) and Jackson's current nightmare of tabloid celebrity and self-destructive egomania. But there was a time when he was truly the King of Pop. This is it.

Chuck Berry in '55:
Rock's first singer-
songwriter

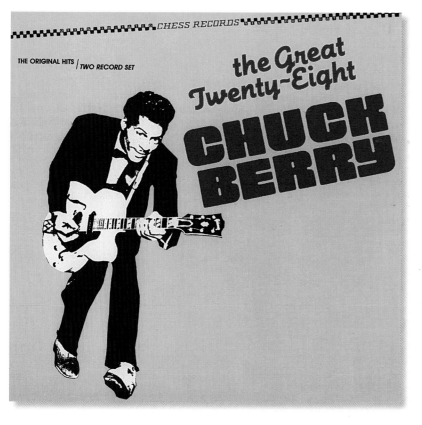

21 **The Great Twenty-Eight**

CHUCK BERRY
CHESS 1982

In the latter half of the Fifties, Berry released a string of singles that defined the sound and spirit of rock & roll. "Maybellene," a fast, countryish rocker about a race between a Ford and a Cadillac, kicked it all off in 1955, and one classic hit followed another, each powered by Berry's staccato, country-blues-guitar gunfire: "Roll Over Beethoven," "School Day," "Rock & Roll Music," "Sweet Little Sixteen," "Johnny B. Goode," "Back in the U.S.A." What was Berry's secret? In the maestro's own words, "The nature and backbone of my beat is boogie, and the muscle of my music is melodies that are simple." This collection culls the best of that magic from 1955 to 1965.

22 **The Complete Recordings**

ROBERT JOHNSON
COLUMBIA 1961

"You want to know how good the blues can get?" Keith Richards asked. "Well, this is it." The bluesman in question was Robert Johnson, who lived from 1911 to 1938 in the Mississippi Delta, and whose guitar prowess was so great, it inspired stories that, in exchange for his amazing gift, he had sold his soul to the devil. In his only two recording sessions, Johnson cut just twenty-nine songs, but their evanescent passion has resonated through the decades, crucial inspiration for everyone from Chicago blues originator Elmore James to British blues inheritors like the Stones and Eric Clapton. Every one of his songs (along with twelve alternate takes) is included here – a holy grail of the blues.

John and Yoko in Amsterdam at their 1969 bed-in for peace

Plastic Ono Band

JOHN LENNON

When John Lennon shocked the world by singing, "I don't believe in Beatles," on "God," the controversial centerpiece of his 1970 solo album *Plastic Ono Band*, he was drawing a line in the sand – between his old band and the future. "One has to completely humiliate oneself to be what the Beatles were ... you're doing exactly what you don't want to do with people you can't stand," Lennon told ROLLING STONE at the time of the album's release. "That's what I'm saying on this album: 'I remember what it's all about now, you fuckers – fuck you!'" Lennon's memories of that time were shaken up, and loose, by intense therapy sessions he and Yoko Ono underwent in California with "primal scream" expert Arthur Janov; in these sessions, Lennon explored complex feelings about his relationships, the tragedy of his mother's death and the recent dissolution of the Beatles – all themes that resonate on *Plastic Ono Band*. "John's songs came out of deep inside him," Ono says. "They were written about what we learned in primal therapy. It renewed our vitality – John was a different person after that. He started to open up."

According to Ono, this brutal new introspection caused a musical shift as well: "He was baring his soul here, so we made everything stark. 'Working Class Hero' is just the sound of John and his guitar, and he sang 'My Mummy's Dead' right into a cassette tape – it was so funky. That song is connected to John's childhood home in Liverpool. It's just a little boy in a room telling you his mummy's dead." Lennon limited his backing band to just Ringo Starr on percussion and longtime Beatles friend Klaus Voormann on bass, but Ono notes pianist Billy Preston's vital contribution to "God": "Without Billy's piano on 'God,' it would not have been that beautiful – it's the most naked, controversial song, but he gave a positive lift to it." The song, she adds, "was a new start for John, in terms of leaving the past as baggage. John announced his independence through these songs. When it came out, people were shocked. But it was appreciated in time."

23 Plastic Ono Band

JOHN LENNON
CAPITOL 1970

Also known as the "primal scream" album, referring to the painful therapy that gave rise to its songs, *Plastic Ono Band* was Lennon's first proper solo album and rock & roll's most self-revelatory recording. Lennon attacks and denies idols and icons, including his own former band ("I don't believe in Beatles," he sings in "God"), to hit a pure, raw core of confession that, in its echo-drenched, garage-rock crudity, is years ahead of punk. He deals with childhood loss in "Mother" and skirts blasphemy in "Working Class Hero": "You're still fucking peasants as far as I can see." But the unkindest cut came in his frank 1970 ROLLING STONE interview. "The Beatles was nothing," Lennon stated acerbically.

24 Innervisions

STEVIE WONDER
MOTOWN 1973

Wonder may be blind, but he reads the national landscape, particularly regarding black America, with penetrating insight on *Innervisions*. Fusing social realism with spiritual idealism, he brings expressive color and irresistible funk to his synth-based keyboards on "Too High" (a cautionary anti-drug song) and "Higher Ground" (which echoes Martin Luther King Jr.'s message of transcendence). The album's centerpiece is "Living for the City," a cinematic depiction of exploitation and injustice. Just three days after *Innervisions* was released, Wonder suffered serious head injuries and lay in a four-day coma after the car he was traveling in collided with a logging truck.

Ladies love Cool James: Brown outside the Apollo with fans

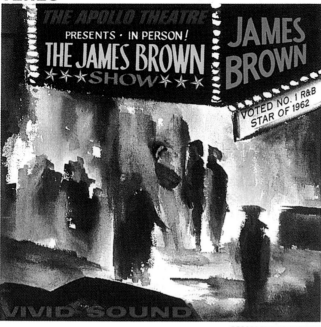

STEREO

THE APOLLO THEATRE PRESENTS · IN PERSON! THE JAMES BROWN SHOW — JAMES BROWN — VOTED NO. 1 R&B STAR OF 1962

VIVID SOUND

RECORDED LIVE AT THE FAMOUS APOLLO THEATRE, NEW YORK CITY

FLEETWOOD MAC RUMOURS

25 Live at the Apollo

JAMES BROWN
POLYGRAM 1963

This may be the greatest live album ever recorded. From the breathless buildup of the spoken intro through terse, sweat-soaked early hits such as "Try Me" and "Think" into eleven minutes of the raw ballad "Lost Someone," climaxing with a frenzied nine-song medley and ending with "Night Train," *Live at the Apollo* is pure, uncut soul. And it almost didn't happen. Brown defied King Records label boss Syd Nathan's opposition to a live album by arranging to record a show himself – on October 24th, 1962, the last date in a run at Harlem's Apollo Theater. His intuition proved correct; *Live at the Apollo* – the first of four albums Brown recorded there – charted for sixty-six weeks.

26 Rumours

FLEETWOOD MAC
REPRISE 1977

Here, Fleetwood Mac turned private turmoil into gleaming, melodic public art. The band's two couples – bassist John and singer-keyboard player Christine McVie, who were married; guitarist Lindsey Buckingham and vocalist Stevie Nicks, who were not – broke up during the protracted sessions for *Rumours*. This lent a highly charged, confessional aura to such songs as Buckingham's "Go Your Own Way," Nicks' "Dreams," Christine's "Don't Stop" and the group-composed anthem to betrayal, "The Chain." The Mac's catchy exposés, produced with California-sunshine polish, touched a nerve: *Rumours* became the sixth-best-selling album of all time.

*Bono onstage in
Holland during
the "Joshua Tree"
tour, 1987*

27 The Joshua Tree

U2
ISLAND 1987

"America's the promised land to a lot of Irish people," U2 singer Bono told ROLLING STONE. "I'm one in a long line of Irishmen who made the trip." On U2's fifth full album, the band immerses itself in the mythology of the United States, while guitarist the Edge exploits the poetic echo of digital delay, drowning his trademark arpeggios in rippling tremolo. While many of these songs are about spiritual quests – "Where the Streets Have No Name," "I Still Haven't Found What I'm Looking For" – U2 fortify the solemnity with the outright joys of rock & roll, although one of the most moving songs is "Running to Stand Still," a stripped-down slide-guitar ballad about heroin addiction.

28 Who's Next

THE WHO
MCA 1971

Pete Townshend suffered a nervous breakdown when his planned follow-up to the rock opera *Tommy,* the ambitious, theatrical *Lifehouse,* fell apart. But he was left with an extraordinary cache of songs that the Who honed for what became their best studio album, *Who's Next.* "Won't Get Fooled Again," "Bargain" and "Baba O'Riley" (named in tribute to avant-garde composer Terry Riley) all beam with epic majesty, often spiked with synthesizers. "I like synthesizers," Townshend said, "because they bring into my hands things that aren't in my hands: the sound of the orchestra, French horns, strings. . . . You press a switch and it plays it back at double speed."

29 Led Zeppelin

LED ZEPPELIN
ATLANTIC 1969

On their first album, Led Zeppelin were still in the process of inventing their own sound, moving on from the heavy rave-ups of guitarist Jimmy Page's previous band, the Yardbirds. But from the beginning, Zeppelin had the astonishing fusion of Page's lyrical guitar playing and Robert Plant's paint-peeling love-hound yowl. "We were learning what got us off most and what got people off most," said Plant. Yet the template for everything Zeppelin achieved in the 1970s is here: brutal rock ("Communication Breakdown"), thundering power balladry ("Your Time Is Gonna Come"), acid-flavored folk blues ("Babe I'm Gonna Leave You").

30 Blue

JONI MITCHELL
REPRISE 1971

"The *Blue* album, there's hardly a dishonest note in the vocals," Mitchell told ROLLING STONE in 1979. "At that period of my life, I had no personal defenses. I felt like a cellophane wrapper on a pack of cigarettes. I felt like I had absolutely no secrets from the world, and I couldn't pretend in my life to be strong. Or to be happy." With song after song of regrets and sorrow, this may be the ultimate breakup album. Its whispery minimalism is also Mitchell's greatest musical achievement. Stephen Stills and James Taylor lend an occasional hand, but in "California," "Carey" and "This Flight Tonight," Mitchell sounds utterly alone in her melancholy, turning the sadness into tender art.

Mitchell feeling better after her "Blue" period, 1975

Live bleeding (from left): Mick Jagger, Mick Taylor and Keith Richards

Let It Bleed

THE ROLLING STONES

Two of the greatest Rolling Stones albums, *Beggars Banquet* and *Let It Bleed*, were born during an intense period of tumult and creativity. From March 1968 through November 1969, the Stones recorded both albums while losing one guitarist (Brian Jones), hiring another (Mick Taylor), filming *The Rolling Stones Rock and Roll Circus*, touring the U.S., and staging milestone concerts in London (Hyde Park) and outside San Francisco (Altamont).

Moreover, the Stones got caught up in the unrest over Vietnam and other issues like everyone else. As a result, *Let It Bleed* was the most powerful and troubling of all Stones records. "Well, it's a very rough, very violent era," Mick Jagger reflected in a ROLLING STONE interview. "The Vietnam War. Violence on the screens, pillage and burning." *Let It Bleed* was released in the U.S. in 1969, just days before events at Altamont bore out the Stones'

recorded portents.

Three songs from *Let It Bleed* – "Midnight Rambler," "You Can't Always Get What You Want" and "You Got the Silver," featuring Keith Richards' first lead vocal – came from the prolific sessions for *Beggars Banquet* [see No. 58] in the spring of 1968. The other six – including the apocalyptic "Gimme Shelter" – were cut at sessions stretching from May through July 1969. *Beggars Banquet* and *Let It Bleed* were produced at Olympic Studios in London by Jimmy Miller, who would work with the Stones through 1973's *Goats Head Soup.*

Al Kooper, who played keyboards and French horn on "You Can't Always Get What You Want," says, "Mick was really the producer. He knew what he wanted, and he was doing just about everything."

"I don't know that Mick ever did anything other than from a producer's level, really," notes engineer Glyns Johns. "Certainly Jimmy Miller had an active role, but it was more of a co-production than not."

As for Brian Jones, Kooper recalls, "He was just sort of lying in the corner on his stomach, reading an article on botany." Kooper was particularly impressed with the Stones' epicurean tastes. "There was a great deal of cannabis and the like passed around," he says, chuckling. "At dinnertime, these two vans pulled up and put out a spread of food the likes of which I have never seen in a studio: lamb chops, curried dishes, class-A desserts. A pot smoker's dream!"

31 | Bringing It All Back Home

BOB DYLAN
COLUMBIA 1965

"It's very complicated to play with electricity," Dylan said in the summer of 1965. "You're dealing with other people. . . . Most people who don't like rock & roll can't relate to other people." But on Side One of this pioneering album, Dylan amplifies his cryptic, confrontational songwriting with guitar lightning and galloping drums. "Subterranean Homesick Blues" and "Maggie's Farm" are loud, caustic and funny as hell. Dylan returns to solo acoustic guitar on the four superb songs on Side Two, including the scabrous "It's Alright, Ma (I'm Only Bleeding)" and the closing ballad, "It's All Over Now, Baby Blue," arguably his finest, most affectionate song of dismissal.

32 | Let It Bleed

THE ROLLING STONES
ABKCO 1969

The record kicks off with the terrifying "Gimme Shelter," the song that came to symbolize not only the catastrophe of the Stones' free show at Altamont but the death of the utopian spirit of the 1960s. And the entire album burns with apocalyptic cohesion: the sex-mad desperation of "Live With Me"; the murderous blues of "Midnight Rambler"; Keith Richards' lethal, biting guitar on "Monkey Man"; the epic moralism, with honky-tonk piano and massed vocal chorus, of "You Can't Always Get What You Want," which Mick Jagger wrote on acoustic guitar in his bedroom. "Somebody said that we could get the London Bach Choir," Jagger recalled, "and we said, 'That will be a laugh.'"

Johnny and Joey deliver the message of punk to London, 1977

33 | Ramones

RAMONES
WARNER ARCHIVES/RHINO 1976

"Our early songs came out of our real feelings of alienation, isolation, frustration – the feelings everybody feels between seventeen and seventy-five," said singer Joey Ramone. Clocking in at just under twenty-nine minutes, *Ramones* is a complete rejection of the spangled artifice of 1970s rock. The songs were fast and anti-social, just like the band: "Beat on the Brat," "Blitzkrieg Bop," "Now I Wanna Sniff Some Glue." Guitarist Johnny Ramone refused to play solos – his jackhammer chords became the lingua franca of punk – and the whole record cost just over $600 to make. But Joey's leather-tender plea "I Wanna Be Your Boyfriend" showed that even punks need love.

34 | Music From Big Pink

THE BAND
CAPITOL 1968

"Big Pink" was a pink house in Woodstock, New York, where the Band – Dylan's '65-66 backup band on tour – moved to be near Dylan after his motorcycle accident. While he recuperated, the Band backed him on the demos later known as *The Basement Tapes* [see No. 288 and made its own debut. Dylan offered to play on the album; the Band said no thanks. "We didn't want to just ride his shirttail," drummer Levon Helm said. Dylan contributed "I Shall Be Released" and co-wrote two other tunes. But it was the rustic beauty of the Band's music and the incisive drama of its own reflections on family and obligations, such as "The Weight," that made *Big Pink* an instant homespun classic.

35 | The Rise and Fall of Ziggy Stardust and the Spiders From Mars

DAVID BOWIE
VIRGIN 1972

This album documents one of the most elaborate self-mythologizing schemes in rock, as Bowie created the glittery, messianic alter ego Ziggy Stardust ("well-hung and snow-white tan"). The glam rock Bowie made with guitarist Mick Ronson is an irresistible blend of sexy, campy pop and blues power, with enduring tracks like "Hang On to Yourself" and "Suffragette City." The anthem "Ziggy Stardust" was one of rock's earliest, and best, power ballads. "I consider myself responsible for a whole new school of pretensions," Bowie said. "They know who they are. Don't you, Elton? Just kidding. No, I'm not."

36 | Tapestry

CAROLE KING
SONY 1971

For a decade, King wrote pop songs with her then-husband, Gerry Goffin: hits such as Little Eva's "The Loco-Motion" (Eva Boyd was the couple's baby sitter) and the Monkees' "Pleasant Valley Sunday." Then King's friend James Taylor encouraged her to sing her own tunes. She slowed down "Will You Love Me Tomorrow?" (originally a hit for the Shirelles in 1961), heightening the melancholy inside, while her warm, earnest singing brought out the sadness in "It's Too Late" and the earthy joy on "I Feel the Earth Move." On *Tapestry*, King remade herself as an artist and created the reigning model for the 1970s female singer-songwriter.

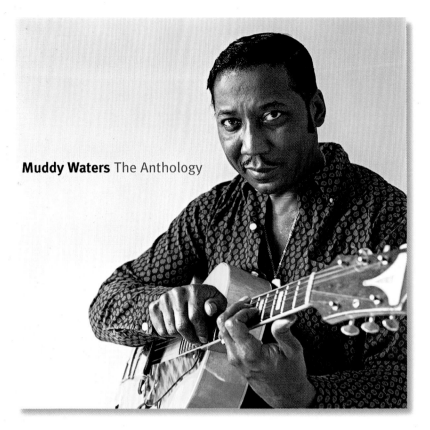

Muddy Waters The Anthology

37 | Hotel California

THE EAGLES
ELEKTRA/ASYLUM 1976

In pursuit of note-perfect Hollywood-cowboy ennui, the Eagles spent eight months in the studio polishing take after take after take. As Don Henley recalled, "We just locked ourselves in. We had a refrigerator, a pingpong table, roller skates and a couple of cots. We would go in and stay for two or three days at a time." With guitarist Joe Walsh replacing Bernie Leadon, the band backed off from straight country-rock in favor of the harder sound of "Life in the Fast Lane." The highlight is the title track, a monument to the rock-aristocrat decadence of the day and a feast of triple-guitar interplay. "Every band has their peak," Henley said. "That was ours."

38 | The Anthology

MUDDY WATERS
CHESS/MCA 2001

Waters started out playing acoustic Delta blues in Mississippi, but when he moved to Chicago in 1943, he needed an electric guitar to be heard over the tumult of South Side clubs. The sound he developed was the foundation of Chicago blues – and rock & roll; the thick, bleeding tones of his slide work anticipated rock-guitar distortion by nearly two decades. Hendrix adapted Waters' "Rollin' Stone" for "Voodoo Chile," Dylan found inspiration in it for "Like a Rolling Stone," and Jagger and Richards took their band's name from it. The fifty cuts on these two CDs run from guitar-and-stand-up-bass duets to full-band romps – and they still just scratch the surface of Waters' legacy.

Papa was a rolling stone: Muddy Waters lays it down.

They'll go far: The Beatles with George Martin, 1962.

39 Please Please Me

THE BEATLES
CAPITOL 1963

The Beatles recorded ten of the fourteen songs on their British debut album at EMI's Abbey Road studio in just over twelve hours on February 11th, 1963. In efficiency terms alone, it's one of the greatest first albums in rock. The Beatles had already invented a bracing new sound for a rock band – an assault of thrumming energy and impeccable vocal harmonies – and they nailed it using the covers and originals in their live repertoire: the Shirelles' "Boys" and Arthur Alexander's "Anna"; the Lennon-McCartney burners "There's a Place" and "I Saw Her Standing There." John Lennon finished up by shredding what was left of his vocal cords on two takes of "Twist and Shout."

40 Forever Changes

LOVE
RHINO 1967

"When I did that album," singer Arthur Lee said, "I thought I was going to die at that particular time, so those were my last words." Lee is still touring – and still playing this album live. It's about time: Love's third record is his crowning achievement. A biracial cult band from L.A. that rarely gigged out of town in its 1960s heyday, Love were Lee's vehicle for a pioneering folk-rock turned into elegant armageddon with the symphonic sweep and mariachi-brass drama of "Alone Again Or," "Andmoreagain" and "You Set the Scene." And Lee – recently released from prison – now brings extra pathos to "The Red Telephone" when he sings "Served my time, served it well."

It's lager time! The Sex Pistols toast their notoriety. 1976.

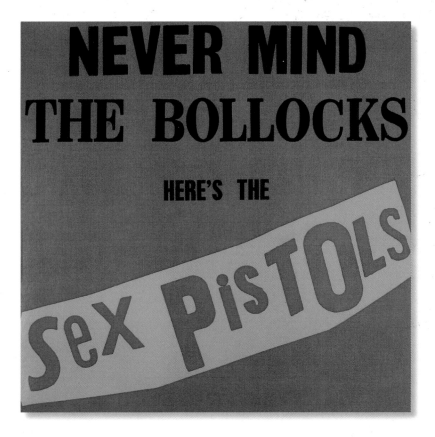

41 ## Never Mind the Bollocks, Here's the Sex Pistols

THE SEX PISTOLS
WARNER BROS. 1977

"If the sessions had gone the way I wanted, it would have been unlistenable for most people," Johnny Rotten said. "I guess it's the very nature of music: If you want people to listen, you're going to have to compromise." But few heard it that way at the time. The Pistols' only studio album sounds like a rejection of everything rock & roll – and the world itself – had to offer. True, the music was less shocking than Rotten himself, who sang about abortions, anarchy and hatred on "Bodies" and "Anarchy in the U.K." But *Never Mind . . .* is the Sermon on the Mount of U.K. punk – and its echoes are everywhere.

42 ## The Doors

THE DOORS
ELEKTRA 1967

After blowing minds as the house band at the Whisky-a-Go-Go, where they were fired for playing the Oedipal drama "The End," the Doors were ready to unleash their organ-driven rock on the world. "On each song we had tried every possible arrangement," drummer John Densmore said, "so we felt the whole album was tight." "Break On Through (to the Other Side)," "Twentieth-Century Fox" and "Crystal Ship" are pop-art lighting for Top Forty attention spans. But the Doors hit pay dirt by editing one of their jam songs for airplay: "Light My Fire," written by guitarist Robbie Krieger when Jim Morrison told everybody in the band to write a song with universal imagery.

Patti Smith Horses

43 The Dark Side of the Moon

PINK FLOYD
EMI 1973

"I think every album was a step towards *Dark Side of the Moon*," keyboardist Rick Wright said. "We were learning all the time; the techniques of the recording and our writing was getting better." As a culmination of their inner-space explorations of the early 1970s, the Floyd toured the bulk of *Dark Side* in Britain for months prior to recording. But in the studio, the band articulated bassist Roger Waters' reveries on the madness of everyday life with melodic precision ("Breathe," "Us and Them") and cinematic luster (Clare Torry's guest vocal aria "The Great Gig in the Sky"). *Dark Side* is one of the best-produced rock albums ever, and "Money" may be rock's only Top Twenty hit in 7/8 time.

44 Horses

PATTI SMITH
ARISTA 1975

From its first defiant line, "Jesus died for somebody's sins, but not mine," the opening shot in a bold reinvention of Van Morrison's garage-rock classic "Gloria," Smith's debut album was a declaration of committed mutiny, a statement of faith in the transfigurative powers of rock & roll. *Horses* made her the queen of punk, but Smith cared more for the poetry in rock. She sought the visions and passions that connected Keith Richards and Rimbaud—and found them, with the intuitive assistance of a killing band (pianist Richard Sohl, guitarist Lenny Kaye, bassist Ivan Kral and drummer Jay Dee Daugherty) and her friend Robert Mapplethorpe, who shot the cover portrait.

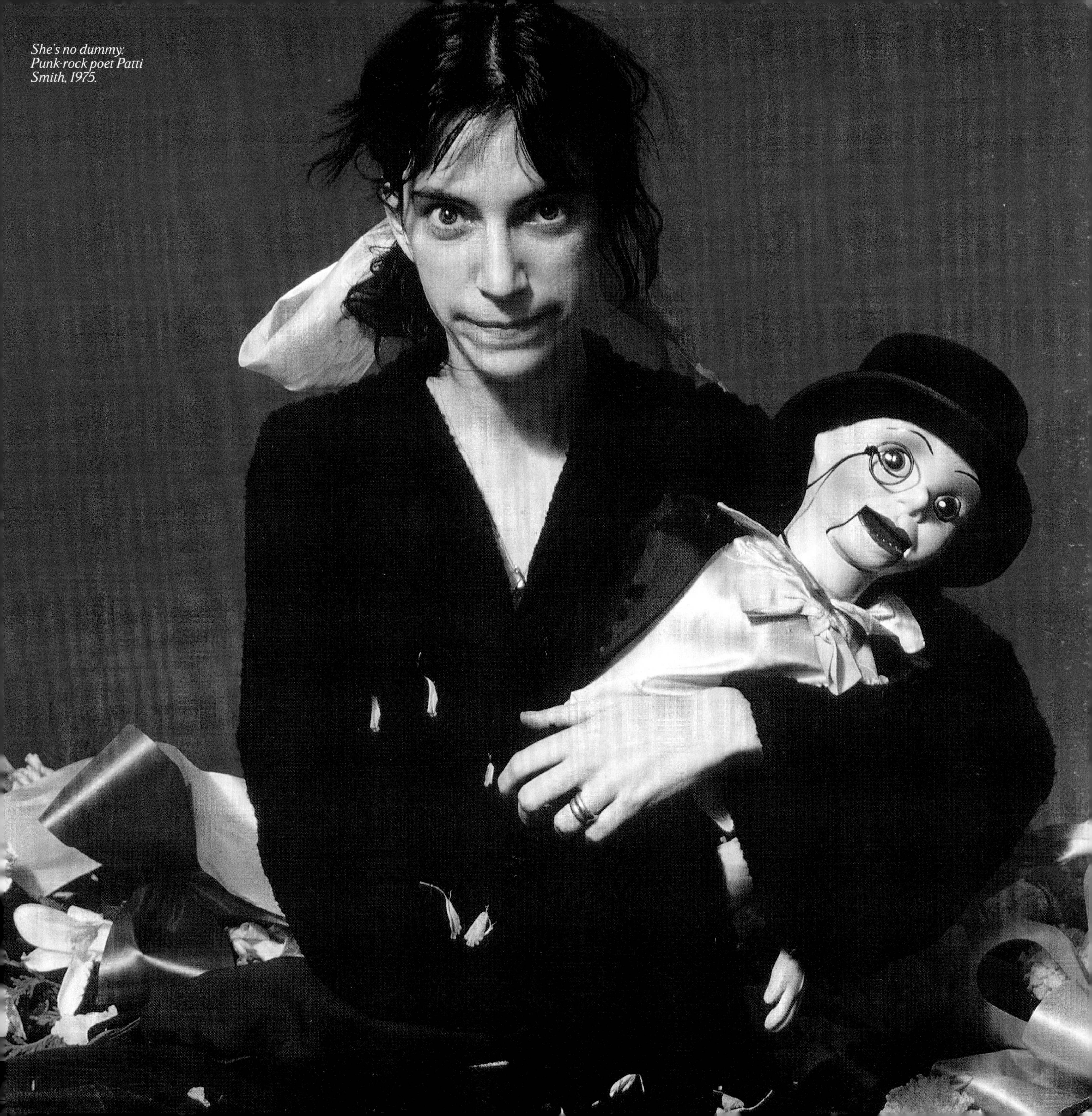

She's no dummy: Punk-rock poet Patti Smith, 1975.

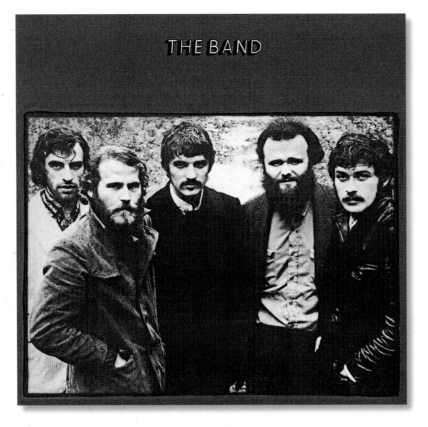

45 | The Band

THE BAND
CAPITOL 1969

The band was four-fifths Canadian – drummer Levon Helm was from Arkansas – but its second album was all American. Guitarist Robbie Robertson's songs vividly evoke the country's pioneer age – "Across the Great Divide," "The Night They Drove Old Dixie Down" – while reflecting the state of the nation in the 1960s. The Band's long life on the road resonates in the brawn of Garth Hudson's keyboards and Helm's juke-joint attack. But Robertson's stories truly live in Helm's growl, Rick Danko's high tenor and Richard Manuel's spectral croon. "Somebody once said he had a tear in his voice," Helm said of Manuel. "Richard had one of the richest textured voices I'd ever heard."

46 | Legend

BOB MARLEY AND THE WAILERS
POLYGRAM 1984

Marley said, "Reggae music too simple for [American musicians]. You must be inside of it, know what's happening, and why you want to play this music. You don't just run go play this music because you think you can make a million off it." Ironically, this set of the late reggae idol's greatest hits has sold in the millions. In a single disc, it captures everything that made him an international icon: his nuanced songcraft, his political message (and savvy), and – of course – the universal soul he brought to Jamaican rhythm and Rastafarian spirituality in the gunfighter ballad "I Shot the Sheriff," the comforting swing of "No Woman, No Cry" and the holy promise of "Redemption Song."

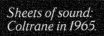
Sheets of sound:
Coltrane in 1965.

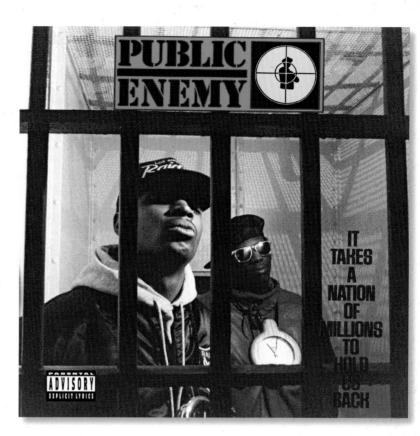

47 | A Love Supreme

JOHN COLTRANE
IMPULSE 1964

Two important things happened to Coltrane in 1957: The saxophonist left Miles Davis' employ to join Thelonious Monk's band and hit new heights in extended, ecstatic soloing. Coltrane also kicked heroin addiction, a vital step in a religious awakening that climaxed with this legendary album-long hymn of praise. The indelible four-note theme of the first movement, "Acknowledgment," is the humble foundation of the suite. But Coltrane's majestic, often violent blowing (famously described as "sheets of sound") is never self-aggrandizing. Coltrane soars with nothing but gratitude and joy. You can't help but go with him.

48 | It Takes a Nation of Millions to Hold Us Back

PUBLIC ENEMY
DEF JAM 1988

Loud, obnoxious, funky, avant-garde, political, uncompromising, hilarious – Public Enemy's brilliant second album is all of these things and, on nearly every track, all at once. Chuck D booms intricate rhymes with a delivery inspired by sportscaster Marv Albert; sidekick Flavor Flav raps comic relief; and production team the Bomb Squad build mesmerizing, multilayered jams, pierced with shrieking sirens. The title and roiling force of "Bring the Noise" is truth in advertising. "If they're calling my music 'noise,'" said Chuck D, "if they're saying that I'm really getting out of character being a black person in America, then fine – I'm bringing more noise."

49 | At Fillmore East

THE ALLMAN BROTHERS BAND
MERCURY 1971

Although this double album is unbeatable testimony to the Allman Brothers' improvisational skills, it is also evidence of how they connected with the crowds at New York's Fillmore East to give birth to rock's greatest live double LP. "The audience would kind of play along with us," singer-organist Gregg Allman said of those March 1971 shows. "They were right on top of every single vibration coming from the stage." The guitar team of Duane Allman and Dickey Betts was at its peak, seamlessly fusing blues and jazz in "Whipping Post" and "In Memory of Elizabeth Reed." But their telepathy was cut short: Just three months after the album's release, Duane died in a motorcycle accident.

50 | Here's Little Richard

LITTLE RICHARD
SPECIALTY 1957

"I came from a family where my people didn't like rhythm and blues," Little Richard told ROLLING STONE in 1970. "Bing Crosby, 'Pennies From Heaven,' Ella Fitzgerald was all I heard. And I knew there was something that could be louder than that, but didn't know where to find it. And I found it was *me*." Richard's raucous debut collected singles such as "Good Golly, Miss Molly," in which his rollicking boogie-woogie piano and falsetto scream ignited the unfettered possibilities of rock & roll. "Tutti Frutti" still contains what has to be considered the most inspired rock lyric on record: "A wop bop alu bop, a wop bam boom!"

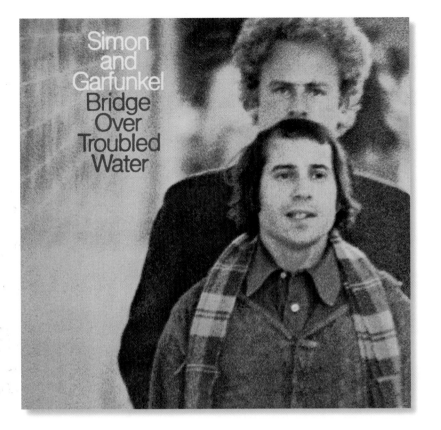

51 Bridge Over Troubled Water

SIMON AND GARFUNKEL
COLUMBIA/LEGACY 1970

On their fifth and final studio album, Paul Simon and Art Garfunkel were pulling away from each other: Simon assembled some of it while Garfunkel was in Mexico starting his acting career with a part in the film version of *Catch-22*. Garfunkel vetoed Simon's song "Cuba Sí, Nixon No," and Simon nixed Garfunkel's idea for a Bach chorale. What remains is the partnership at its best: wry, wounded songs with healing harmonies such as "The Boxer," though the gorgeous title track was sung by Garfunkel alone, despite his resistance. "He felt I should have done it," Simon told ROLLING STONE in 1972. "And many times I'm sorry I didn't do it."

"By the time the single and the album were out, we were in the throes of a breakup. We were having a hard time during the recording of that album, yet we made it work."

ART GARFUNKEL
(RS 534, SEPTEMBER 8TH, 1988)

52 Greatest Hits

AL GREEN
CAPITOL 1975

Green made some of the most visionary soul music of the Seventies in Memphis with producer Willie Mitchell. "In Memphis, you just do as you feel," he told ROLLING STONE in 1972. "It's not a modern, up-to-par, very glamorous, big-red-chairs-and-carpet-that-thick studio. It's one of those places you can go into and stomp out a good soul jam." In collaboration with Mitchell, Green was a natural album artist, making love-and-pain classics such as *Call Me.* But this collection makes a unified album in itself, compiling hits like "Let's Stay Together" and "Tired of Being Alone" into a flawless twelve-song suite: strong as death, sweet as love.

53 Meet the Beatles

THE BEATLES
CAPITOL 1964

For Americans in the full grip of Beatlemania, this was the first album they could buy. *Meet* took the Fabs' second British record, *With the Beatles,* dropped five covers and added three tracks, including the singles "I Want to Hold Your Hand" and "I Saw Her Standing There." (This arguably made a hash of the Beatles' artistic intentions, yet made for a much better record.) The Lennon-McCartney were on a roll that would be unmatched in rock history, and at this point they were a real team. They wrote "I Want to Hold Your Hand" together on a piano in the basement of Jane Asher, Paul McCartney's actress girlfriend – as John Lennon put it, "eyeball to eyeball."

Hendrix at the newly opened Electric Lady, 1970. A month later, he was dead.

Electric Lady

52 WEST EIGHTH STREET, NEW YORK

Located in New York's Greenwich Village, the building was once a supper club owned by Rudy Vallée. When Jimi Hendrix bought it in 1968, he wanted to turn it into a nightclub until Eddie Kramer, Hendrix's engineer, forced him to look at the numbers. "He was spending thousands of dollars to block out time at other studios just to jam," Kramer says. "I told him that a studio was the way to go." Hendrix poured more than $1 million into Electric Lady and in May 1970 began to use the facility to practice (he often recorded at the Record Plant in New York, though there are hours of unreleased material at Electric Lady). Being owned and operated by a musician, the studio included creature comforts like plush lounges and psychedelically painted walls. Electric Lady officially opened for business on August 27th, 1970. But Hendrix died less than a month later, on September 18th, in London.

"I was so happy at the start of the day – I had just gotten my green card," says Kramer, a native of South Africa. "Then I got to the studio, and everyone was crying. I just went blank."

Not surprisingly, the complex is something of a shrine. Studio A remains exactly as it was during Hendrix's time, and Studio B (nicknamed Purple Haze) has the world's only purple mixing console. Not to mention the ghosts in residence. "The Clash swore that Jimi put an extra guitar track on *Sandinista!*," says Mary Campbell, the studio's manager from 1983 to 2003. "Doors slam, floors creak. The place has a magic."

RS 500 ALBUMS RECORDED AT ELECTRIC LADY

Patti Smith – *Horses*

The Clash – *Sandinista!*

Weezer – *Weezer*

D'Angelo – *Voodoo*

54 | The Birth of Soul: The Complete Atlantic R&B

RAY CHARLES
ATLANTIC 1991

Soul music, you may have heard, is a blend of the holy and the filthy: gospel and blues rubbing up against each other. What you may not have heard is that Charles was just about the first person to perfect that mix. Charles was knocking around Seattle when Atlantic bought out his contract in 1952. For the next eight years, he turned out brilliant singles such as "What'd I Say" and "I Got a Woman." He was inventing the sound of ecstasy, three minutes at a time. This box collects every R&B side he cut for Atlantic, though his swinging take on "My Bonnie" will have you thinking it covers his Atlantic jazz output as well.

55 | Electric Ladyland

THE JIMI HENDRIX EXPERIENCE
MCA 1968

Hendrix's third album was the first he produced himself, a fever dream of underwater electric soul cut in round-the-clock sessions at the Record Plant in New York. Hendrix would leave the Record Plant to jam at a club around the corner, the Scene, and "Voodoo Chile" – fifteen minutes of live-in-the-studio blues exploration with Steve Winwood on organ and the Jefferson Airplane's Jack Cassidy on bass – reflects those excursions. In addition to psychedelic Delta blues, there was the precision snap of "Crosstown Traffic" and a cover of "All Along the Watchtower" that took Bob Dylan into outer space before touching down with a final burst of spectral fury.

56 Elvis Presley

ELVIS PRESLEY
RCA 1956

In November 1955, RCA Records bought Presley's contract, singles and unreleased master tapes from Sun Records for $35,000. His first full-length album came out six months later, with tracks drawn from both the Sun sessions and from further recording at RCA's studios in New York and Nashville. "There wasn't any pressure," guitarist Scotty Moore said of the first RCA sessions. "They were just bigger studios with different equipment. We basically just went in and did the same thing we always did." On tracks such as "Blue Suede Shoes," that meant revved-up country music with the sexiest voice anyone had ever heard.

57 Songs in the Key of Life

STEVIE WONDER
MOTOWN/UNIVERSAL 1976

Making this record, Wonder would often stay in the studio forty-eight hours straight, not eating or sleeping, while everyone around him struggled to keep up. "If my flow is goin', I keep on until I peak," he said. The flow went so well, Wonder released twenty-one songs, packaged as a double album and a bonus EP. The highlights are the joyful "Isn't She Lovely" and "Sir Duke," but Wonder also displays his mastery of funk, jazz, Afrobeat and even a string-quartet minuet. Nineteen years later, Coolio turned the haunting groove of the quiet "Pastime Paradise" into the Number One single "Gangsta's Paradise."

Songs in the Key of Life

Stevie Wonder

Months before the recording sessions for *Songs in the Key of Life* ended, the musicians in Stevie Wonder's band had T-shirts made up that proclaimed, WE'RE ALMOST FINISHED. It was the stock answer to casual fans and Motown executives and everybody who'd fallen in love with Wonder's early-Seventies gems – 1972's *Talking Book*, 1973's *Innervisions* and 1974's *Fulfillingness' First Finale* – and who had been waiting two years for the next chapter. Wonder was one of the hottest stars in pop at the time: He toured with the Rolling Stones and dashed off a string of inescapable singles including "Superstition" and "You Haven't Done Nothin'." "We felt like the whole world was waiting for this," recalls keyboardist Greg Phillinganes.

Wonder said the title came to him in a dream; many in the industry advised him against making a double album, but, as he told the BBC, "I believed there was a lot that needed to be said."

More, in fact, than he could fit on a double album – also included was a bonus EP, seven-inch single with four more songs from the sessions.

Songs, released in 1976, encompasses an incredible range of life experiences – from the giddy joy of a baby in the bathtub ("Isn't She Lovely," featuring the cries and giggles of Wonder's infant daughter, Aisha Morris) through tributes to his musical heroes ("Sir Duke") to dismay about the indifference of the wealthy ("Village Ghetto Land"). Wonder would begin recording alone, laying down a foundation on the electric piano or drums. Then he'd mumble through an outline of the vocals. He would summon musicians as needed. Sometimes that meant phone calls at odd hours. "The band was on retainer, and if he was onto something, he'd call, and you had to come," says Phillinganes. "It'd be three in the morning, you'd have to drive [to the studio], but it was always a hang when you got there."

Though the blind singer would memorize many of the lyrics, some songs had four or five intricate verses, so somebody had to prompt him. Often it was engineer John Fischbach, reading lines into the headphone mix just seconds before Wonder sang them. "He never got thrown off hearing the words," marvels Fischbach. "Most people couldn't sing at all like that. But his vocals had so much power and presence to them."

Keys of life: Wonder plays for dance students in Harlem. 1976.

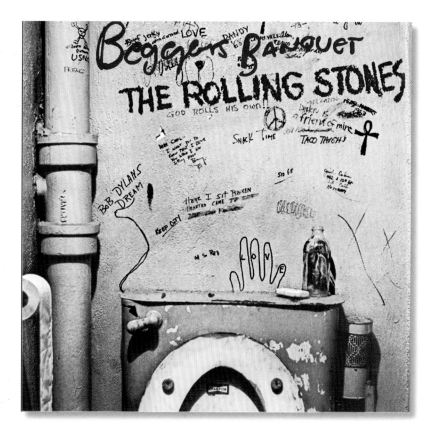

58 | Beggars Banquet

THE ROLLING STONES
ABKCO 1968

"When we had been in the States between 1964 and '66, I had gathered together this enormous collection of records, but I never had any time to listen to them," Keith Richards recalled. "In late 1966 and '67, I unwrapped them and actually played them." After the wayward psychedelia of *Their Satanic Majesties Request,* and with guitarist Brian Jones largely AWOL, Richards' record collection led the Rolling Stones back to their version of America: country music on "Dear Doctor," the blues on "Prodigal Son" and urban riots on "Street Fighting Man." And "Sympathy for the Devil," of course, is an anthem for the darkness in every human heart.

59 | Trout Mask Replica

CAPTAIN BEEFHEART AND HIS MAGIC BAND
REPRISE 1969

On first listen, *Trout Mask Replica* sounds like a wild, incomprehensible rampage through the blues. Don Van Vliet (a.k.a. Captain Beefheart) growls, rants and recites poetry over chaotic guitar licks. But every note was precisely planned in advance – to construct the songs, the Magic Band rehearsed twelve hours a day for months on end in a house with the windows blacked out. (Producer and longtime friend Frank Zappa was then able to record most of the album in less than five hours.) The avant-garde howl of tracks such as "Ella Guru" and "My Human Gets Me Blues" have inspired modern musical primitives like Tom Waits and PJ Harvey.

60 | Greatest Hits

SLY AND THE FAMILY STONE
EPIC 1970

Sly and the Family Stone created a musical utopia: an interracial group of men and women who blended funk, rock and positive vibes. Sly Stone, the Family mastermind, was one of the 1960s' most ambitious artists, mixing up the hardest funk beats with hippie psychedelia in hits such as "Thank You Falettin Me Be Mice Elf Agin." *Greatest Hits* ranges from gospel-style ballads ("Everybody Is a Star") to rump shakers ("Everyday People"). Stone discovered his utopia had a ghetto, and he brilliantly tore the whole thing down on *There's a Riot Goin' On* [see No. 100]. But nothing can negate the joy of this music.

61 | Appetite for Destruction

GUNS N' ROSES
GEFFEN 1987

The biggest-selling debut album of the Eighties, *Appetite* features a lot more than the yowl of Indiana-bred W. Axl Rose, the only thing still remaining of the original G n' R. Guitarist Slash gave the band blues emotion and punk energy, while the rhythm section brought the funk on hits such as "Welcome to the Jungle." When all the elements came together, as in the final two minutes of "Paradise City," G n' R left all other Eighties metal bands in the dust, and they knew it too. "A lot of rock bands are too fucking wimpy to have any sentiment or any emotion," Rose said. "Unless they're in pain."

62 | Achtung Baby

U2
ISLAND 1991

After fostering a solemn public image for years, U2 loosened up on *Achtung Baby,* recorded in Berlin with Brian Eno and Daniel Lanois. They no longer sounded like young men sure of the answers; now they were full of doubt and longing. "It's a con, in a way," Bono told ROLLING STONE about the album in 1992. "We call it *Achtung Baby,* grinning up our sleeves in all the photography. But it's probably the heaviest record we've ever made." "One" may be their most gorgeous song, but it's a dark ballad about a relationship in peril and the struggle to keep it together. Yet the emotional turmoil made U2 sound more human than ever.

*Lady Soul at work, January 1969:
Duane Allman, Aretha Franklin,
Cissy Houston, Sylvia Shemwell,
Jerry Wexler and Arif Mardin
(from left) at Muscle Shoals*

Muscle Shoals

1000 ALABAMA AVENUE, SHEFFIELD, ALABAMA

Founded in 1969 by white session men Jimmy Johnson, David Hood, Barry Beckett and Roger Hawkins, Muscle Shoals was an anomaly in racially charged Alabama. "There were all these cars outside, blacks and whites mingling," Hood says. "I don't think people in town understood what it was." Funded with seed money from Atlantic Records, the original building at 3614 Jackson Highway was an old casket warehouse turned into a one-room studio. After Aretha Franklin and Wilson Pickett cut hits there, others came for some Muscle Shoals magic. The Rolling Stones recorded part of *Sticky Fingers* there; Paul Simon worked on his solo LP *There Goes Rhymin' Simon* after falling in love with the Staple Singers' smash "I'll Take You There." "He called Al Bell of Stax and said, 'I love the Jamaican musicians you used. Can I have their number?'" says Hood. "Al said, 'Sure, but they're not Jamaican. They're four white boys.'"

RS 500 ALBUMS RECORDED AT MUSCLE SHOALS

Aretha Franklin – *I Never Loved a Man the Way I Love You*

Paul Simon – *There Goes Rhymin' Simon*

Boz Scaggs – *Boz Scaggs*

63 | Sticky Fingers
THE ROLLING STONES
VIRGIN 1971

Drummer Charlie Watts remembered the origin of *Sticky Fingers* as the songs Mick Jagger wrote while filming the movie *Ned Kelly* in Australia. "Mick started playing the guitar a lot," Watts said. "He plays very strange rhythm guitar . . . very much how Brazilian guitarists play, on the upbeat. It is very much like the guitar on a James Brown track – for a drummer it's great to play with." New guitarist Mick Taylor, replacing Brian Jones, stretches out the Stones sound in "Sway," "Can't You Hear Me Knocking" and "Moonlight Mile." But "Brown Sugar" is a classic Stones stomp, and two of the best cuts are country songs: one forlorn ("Wild Horses") and one funny ("Dead Flowers").

64 | Back to Mono (1958-1969)
PHIL SPECTOR
ABKCO 1991

When the Righteous Brothers' Bobby Hatfield first heard "You've Lost That Lovin' Feelin'," with partner Bill Medley's extended solo, he asked, "But what do I do while he's singing the whole first verse?" Producer Phil Spector replied, "You can go directly to the bank!" Spector built his Wall of Sound out of hand claps, massive overdubs and orchestras of percussion, making some of the most frenzied teenage-lust pop ever heard. This box has hits such as the Ronettes' "Be My Baby," Darlene Love's "A Fine Fine Boy" and the Crystals' "Da Doo Ron Ron," which Spector called "a little symphony for the kids."

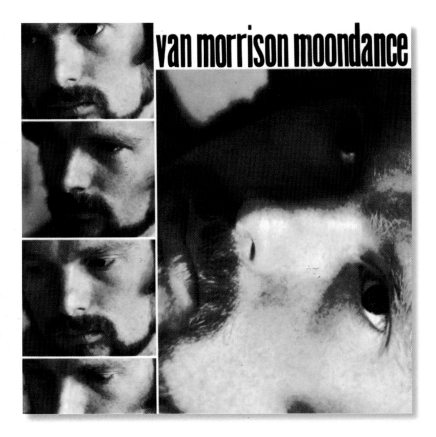

65 ## Moondance

VAN MORRISON
WARNER BROS. 1970

"That was the type of band I dig," Morrison said of the *Moondance* sessions. "Two horns and a rhythm section – they're the type of bands that I like best." Morrison took that soul-band lineup and blended it with jazz, blues, poetry and vivid memories of his Irish childhood, until songs such as "And It Stoned Me" and "Caravan" felt like lucid dreams. In the title hit, Morrison turns the words over and over in his mouth, not scatting so much as searching for the sound of magic. "Into the Mystic" serves as an apt summary: To listen to the album is to get your passport stamped for Morrison's world of ecstatic visions.

66 ## Led Zeppelin IV

LED ZEPPELIN
ATLANTIC 1971

"I put a lot of work into my lyrics," Robert Plant told ROLLING STONE in 1975. "Not all my stuff is meant to be scrutinized, though. Things like 'Black Dog' are blatant let's-do-it-in-the-bath-type things, but they make their point just the same." On their towering fourth, rune-titled album, Led Zeppelin match the raunch of "Black Dog" with Plant's most poetic lyrics for the inescapable epic ballad "Stairway to Heaven," while guitarist Jimmy Page veers from the blues apocalypse of "When the Levee Breaks" to the mandolin-driven "Battle of Evermore." ("It sounded like a dance-around-the-maypole number," Page later confessed.)

67 | The Stranger

BILLY JOEL
COLUMBIA 1977

On this record, Billy Joel found the recipe for success: a bottle of red, a bottle of white and a sharp eye for the local color of New York street life. The piano man sharpens his story-telling gifts with a Scorsese-style sense of humor and compassion, whether he's singing about a down-and-out Little Italy hustler in "Movin' Out (Anthony's Song)," the *femme fatale* in "She's Always a Woman to Me" or the doomed Long Island greaser couple Brenda and Eddie in "Scenes From an Italian Restaurant." Meanwhile, he hit the pop charts with the Grammy-winning "Just the Way You Are" (written for his first wife and manager, Elizabeth) which became a wedding-band standard.

68 | Off the Wall

MICHAEL JACKSON
EPIC 1979

"The ballads were what made *Off the Wall* a Michael Jackson album," Jackson remembered of his big solo splash, which spun off four Top Ten hits and eclipsed the sucess of the Jackson 5. "I'd done ballads with [my] brothers, but they had never been too enthusiastic about them and did them more as a concession to me than anything else." At the end of "She's Out of My Life," you can hear Jackson actually break down and cry in the studio. But the unstoppable dance tracks on *Off the Wall* remain more or less perfect examples of why disco didn't suck. "Don't Stop Till You Get Enough," "Rock With You" and "Burn This Disco Out" still get the party started today.

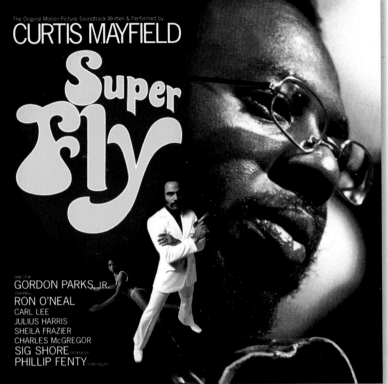

69 | Superfly

CURTIS MAYFIELD

RHINO 1972

Isaac Hayes' *Shaft* came first – but that record had one great single and a lot of instrumental filler. It was Mayfield who made a blaxploitation-soundtrack album that packed more drama than the movie it accompanied. Musically, *Superfly* is astonishing, marrying lush string parts to deep bass grooves, with lots of wah-wah guitar. On top, Mayfield sings in his worldly-wise falsetto, narrating the bleak ghetto tales of "Pusherman" and "Freddie's Dead," telling hard truths about the drug trade and black life in the 1970s. "I don't take credit for everything I write," Mayfield said. "I only look upon my writings as interpretations of how the majority of people around me feel."

70 | Physical Graffiti

LED ZEPPELIN

ATLANTIC 1975

While visiting India, Robert Plant and Jimmy Page got onstage at a Bombay club to jam for an audience who had no idea who they were. The owner gave them a bottle of Indian whiskey and asked them to return the next night. *Physical Graffiti* is the ultimate in Zeppelin's attempts to fuse East and West, exploring the Arabic and Indian sonorities of "Kashmir" and "In the Light." It's Zeppelin's most eclectic album, featuring down-and-dirty blues ("Black Country Woman," "Boogie With Stu"), pop balladry ("Down by the Seaside"), metal riffs ("The Wanton Song") and the eleven-minute "In My Time of Dying." An excessive album from the group that all but invented excess.

Keith Richards lays down a guitar part during a Stones session at Olympic in 1967.

Olympic Studios

117 CHURCH ROAD, BARNES, LONDON

During the day, Olympic's two recording suites housed session musicians and fifty-piece orchestras working on film scores. At night, the rockers came and, because the orchestras never put their instruments away, things got interesting. "People were always fooling around with violins, horns, everything," says Eddie Kramer, who engineered all of Jimi Hendrix's albums. "When we recorded 'Little Wing' [for *Axis: Bold As Love*], Jimi picked up a glockenspiel and said, 'Hey, man, start the tape.' There was no conscious effort to be experimental. It was such a fertile playground, and shit just happened to be there."

Olympic fostered a family atmosphere, with recording sessions often spilling over to the Red Lion Pub across the street. "On any given night, the Stones were mingling with the Who or Eric Clapton," recalls producer Andy Johns, who got his start assisting Kramer on the Hendrix albums and went on to engineer records for the Stones and Led Zeppelin. "Jaguars were double-parked outside."

While the friendly environment was attractive, Olympic's technical prowess was the real draw. "Dick Swettenham built the most amazing mixers, with very innovative features for back then," says Johns. "They looked like something out of *Star Trek*. It was right when stereo sound was becoming the way to work, and Dick was the mad scientist. He'd appear at 5 A.M. to make tea for everyone and then disappear back into his hole. Amazing."

The Jimi Hendrix Experience – *Are You Experienced?*

The Rolling Stones – *Let It Bleed*

The Who – *Who's Next*

71 After the Gold Rush

NEIL YOUNG
WARNER BROS. 1970

For his third album, Young fired Crazy Horse (the first of many times he would do so), picked up an acoustic guitar and headed to his basement. He installed recording equipment in the cellar of his Topanga Canyon home near Los Angeles, leaving room for only three or four people. There, Young made an album of heartbreaking ballads such as "Tell Me Why" and "Don't Let It Bring You Down." The music is gentle, but never smooth. Nils Lofgren, then a seventeen-year-old hotshot guitarist, squeezed into the sessions – but Young assigned him to the piano, an instrument he had never played in his life.

72 Star Time

JAMES BROWN
POLYDOR 1991

So great is Brown's impact that even with seventy-one songs on four CDs, *Star Time* isn't quite comprehensive – between 1956 and 1984, Brown placed an astounding 103 singles on the R&B charts. But every phase of his career is well represented here: the pleading, straight-up R&B of "Please, Please, Please"; his instantaneous reinvention of R&B with "Papa's Got a Brand New Bag," where the rhythm takes over and the melody is subsumed within the groove; his spokesmanship for the civil-rights movement in "Say It Loud – I'm Black and I'm Proud (Pt. 1)"; his founding document of Seventies funk, "Sex Machine"; and his blueprint for hip-hop in "Funky Drummer."

73 Purple Rain

PRINCE AND THE REVOLUTION
WARNER BROS. 1984

The blockbuster soundtrack to Prince's semi-autobiographical movie was raunchy enough to inspire Tipper Gore to form the Parents Music Resource Center. It also showcases Prince's abilities as a guitarist, especially on "Let's Go Crazy." The breakthrough hit, "When Doves Cry," has no bass track: Looking for a different sound, Prince removed it, making one more unforgettable single. The title track was inspired by Bob Seger, of all people – when Prince was touring behind 1999 [see No. 162], Seger was playing many of the same markets. Prince didn't understand his appeal but decided to try writing a crossover hit, a ballad in the Seger mode.

74 Back in Black

AC/DC
ATLANTIC 1980

In the middle of album rehearsals, singer Bon Scott went on a drinking spree; he choked on his own vomit and was found dead in the back seat of a car. After two days of mourning, guitarist Malcolm Young thought, "Well, fuck this, I'm not gonna sit around mopin' all fuckin' year." He called his brother, guitarist Angus Young, and they went back to work with replacement vocalist Brian Johnson. The resulting album has the relentless logic of a sledgehammer. *Back in Black* might be the purest distillation of hard rock ever: The title track, "Hells Bells" and "You Shook Me All Night Long" have all become enduring anthems of strutting blues-based guitar.

75 Otis Blue

OTIS REDDING
ATCO 1965

Redding's third album includes covers of three songs by Sam Cooke, Redding's idol, who had died the previous December. Their styles were different: Cooke, smooth and sure; Redding, raw and pleading. But Redding's versions of "Shake" and "A Change Is Gonna Come" show how Cooke's sound and message helped shape Redding's Southern soul, heard here in his originals "Respect" and "I've Been Loving You Too Long" and in a cover of the Rolling Stones' "(I Can't Get No) Satisfaction," which was itself inspired by the Stax/Volt sound. "I use a lot of words different than the Stones' version," Redding noted. "That's because I made them up."

76 Led Zeppelin II

LED ZEPPELIN
ATLANTIC 1969

This album – recorded on the fly while the band was touring – opens with one of the most exhilarating guitar riffs in rock & roll: Jimmy Page's searing stutter in "Whole Lotta Love." As Page told ROLLING STONE, "On the second LP, you can hear the real group identity coming together," by which he meant the unified might of his own white-blues sorcery, John Bonham's hands-of-God drumming, Robert Plant's love-god howl and surprisingly tender lyrics (the gorgeous "Thank You"), and John Paul Jones' firm bass and keyboard colors. Other great reasons to bang your head: "The Lemon Song," "Heartbreaker" and "Ramble On."

77 | Imagine

JOHN LENNON
CAPITOL 1971

After the primal-scream therapy of *Plastic Ono Band* [see No. 23], Lennon softened up on his second solo album. There is still the stinging "Gimme Some Truth" and Lennon's evisceration of Paul McCartney, "How Do You Sleep?" – both featuring George Harrison on guitar. But there is also the aching soul of "Jealous Guy" and the irresistible "Oh Yoko!" *Imagine* is self-consciously luminescent, pointedly embraceable. Lennon said of the title track: "Anti-religious, anti-nationalistic, anti-conventional, anti-capitalistic, but because it is sugarcoated it is accepted. . . . Now I understand what you have to do. Put your political message across with a little honey."

"We knew what we were going to do. We knew this was going to be a Beatle-orientated album. It was going to be John making a political statement, but a very commercial one as well. He played me the piano lick for 'Imagine,' which was very good. And I said, 'Just write it.' I always thought that song was like the national anthem. It is now – and it should be."

PHIL SPECTOR
(RS 837, MARCH 30TH, 2000)

John Lennon's handwritten lyrics to "Imagine"

78 | The Clash

THE CLASH
EPIC 1977

"I haven't got any illusions about anything," Joe Strummer said. "Having said that, I still want to try to change things." That youthful ambition bursts through the Clash's debut, a machine-gun blast of songs about unemployment ("Career Opportunities"), race ("White Riot") and the Clash themselves ("Clash City Rockers"). Most of the guitar was played by Mick Jones, because Strummer considered studio technique insufficiently punk. The American release was delayed two years and replaced some of the U.K. tracks with recent singles, including "Complete Control" – a complaint about exactly that sort of record-company shenanigans.

79 | Harvest

NEIL YOUNG
REPRISE 1972

Harvest yielded Neil Young's only Number One hit, "Heart of Gold," and helped set the stage for the Seventies soft-rock explosion – both James Taylor and Linda Ronstadt sing on the album. Along with Young, they were in Nashville to appear on Johnny Cash's CBS-TV variety show the week that *Harvest* was cut with an odd group of accomplished session musicians that included bassist Tim Drummond, who had played with James Brown. The sound was Americana – steel guitar, slide guitar, banjo – stripped down and rebuilt with every jagged edge exposed. The standout tracks include "Old Man" and "The Needle and the Damage Done."

PAUL·SIMON
GRACELAND

80 | Odessey and Oracle

THE ZOMBIES
BIG BEAT 1969

The Zombies broke up two weeks after they completed *Odessey and Oracle,* in December 1967, and the album wasn't released in the U.S. until 1969, after Al Kooper had heard a British pressing and lobbied his label, CBS, to release it here. But its baroque psychedelic-pop arrangements continue to exert a powerful influence – Beck and Fountains of Wayne have each covered its songs live. Recorded in London at both Abbey Road and a Stones haunt, Olympic Studios, *Odessey* combined the adventure of *Sgt. Pepper* with the concision of British Invasion pop. And "Time of the Season" went on to become a Number Three hit.

81 | Graceland

PAUL SIMON
WARNER BROS. 1986

Frustrated by the experience of writing good songs that didn't come to life in the studio, Simon set out "to make really good tracks," as he later put it. "I thought, 'I have enough songwriting technique that I can reverse this process and write this song after the tracks are made.' " Simon risked severe criticism by going to South Africa (then under apartheid) and working with the best musicians from the black townships. With the fluid energy and expertise of guitarist Ray Phiri and the vocal troupe Ladysmith Black Mambazo, Simon created an album about isolation and redemption that transcended "world music" to become the whole world's soundtrack.

82 | Axis: Bold As Love

THE JIMI HENDRIX EXPERIENCE
REPRISE 1968

Hendrix's first album remade rock & roll with guitar magic that no one had ever even dreamed of before; his second album was just plain magic. It started with some musings on extraterrestrial life, then got really far out: jazzy drumming, funky balladry, liquid guitar solos, dragonfly heavy metal and the immortal stoner's maxim from "If 6 Was 9": "I'm the one who's got to die when it's time for me to die, so let me live my life the way I want to." All over the album, Hendrix was inventing new ways to make the electric guitar roar, sing, talk, shriek, flutter and fly. And with the delicate "Little Wing," he delivered one of rock's most cryptic and bewitching love songs.

83 | I Never Loved a Man the Way I Love You

ARETHA FRANKLIN
RHINO 1967

Franklin's Atlantic debut is the place where gospel music collided with R&B and rock & roll and became soul. The Detroit-born preacher's daughter was about $80,000 in debt to her previous label, Columbia, when Atlantic producer Jerry Wexler signed her in 1966. "I took her to church," Wexler said, "sat her down at the piano and let her be herself." She immediately cut the album's title hit, a slow fire of ferocious sexuality, while her storefront-church cover of Otis Redding's "Respect" – Franklin's first Number One pop single – became the marching song for the women's and civil-rights movements.

84 | Lady Soul

ARETHA FRANKLIN
RHINO 1968

Franklin's third Atlantic album in less than two years is another classic, with "You Make Me Feel (Like a Natural Woman)," "Ain't No Way" and a slinky version of the Rascals' "Groovin'." It was a year of triumph and turbulence for Franklin: Although she made the cover of *Time*, the magazine reported details of her rocky marriage to Ted White, then her manager. But Franklin channeled that frenzy into performances of funky pride and magisterial hurt. Among the best: the grand-prayer treatment of Curtis Mayfield's "People Get Ready" and her explosive anguish on the hit cover of Don Covay's "Chain of Fools."

85 | Born in the U.S.A.

BRUCE SPRINGSTEEN
COLUMBIA 1984

Springsteen wrote most of these songs in a fit of inspiration that also gave birth to the harrowing *Nebraska* [see No. 221]. "Particularly on the first side, it's actually written very much like *Nebraska*," he said. "The characters and the stories, the style of writing – except it's just in the rock-band setting." It was a crucial difference: The E Street Band put so much punch into the title song that millions misheard its questioning allegiance as mere flag-waving instead. The immortal force of the album is in Springsteen's frank mix of soaring optimism and the feeling of, as he put it, being "handcuffed to the bumper of a state trooper's Ford."

The Beatles at work in Studio 2 at Abbey Road, March 1963

Abbey Road

3 ABBEY ROAD, LONDON

Tucked away on a residential street in the upscale London neighborhood of St. John's Wood, Abbey Road easily blends into the landscape. But behind its doors lies the most famous studio complex in the world. The Beatles recorded nearly all of their albums there in the years between 1962 and 1969, working in Studio 2, a large, open room of 2,000 square feet. "It's a 'dead' room," says producer John Leckie, who was an engineer at Abbey Road from 1970 to '78. "'Dead' means the sound doesn't reverberate like you would think. Everyone can set up and see each other, with voices and music filling the entire space."

Pink Floyd were the other early giants who inhabited Studio 2, where they recorded, among other albums, their bizarro debut, *Piper at the Gates of Dawn*, and the operatic *Dark Side of the Moon*. They had the most technologically advanced equipment available, but, says Townsend, "The first time I walked into the studio, they were chopping wood for a sound effect." Pink Floyd also recruited one of the studio's security guards to record the "I've always been mad" line on *Dark Side of the Moon*'s "Speak to Me."

Owned by the record label EMI since it opened in 1931, Abbey Road had a stuffy reputation, with stories of employees scurrying around in uniforms of black pants, black ties and white lab coats. "That was only in the daytime," says Townsend. "And not everyone wore white coats. The guys who moved all the equipment from studio to studio wore brown ones."

RS 500 ALBUMS

The Beatles –
With the Beatles,
A Hard Day's Night,
Rubber Soul,
Revolver,
The White Album,
Sgt. Pepper's Lonely
Hearts Club Band,
Abbey Road,
Let It Be

Pink Floyd –
The Piper at the
Gates of Dawn,
The Dark Side of the Moon

Radiohead – *The Bends*

86 | Let It Be

THE BEATLES
CAPITOL 1970

Let It Be is the sound of the world's biggest pop group at war with itself. John Lennon is at his most acidic; George Harrison's "I Me Mine" is about the sin of pride, sung with plaintive exhaustion. Only Paul McCartney sounds focused, as if the title song were his personal survival mantra. The original concept was a live-in-the-studio album and film, begun in January 1969, that left the Beatles so weary they abandoned the project to make *Abbey Road*. Phil Spector went back to the tapes later, sweetening (or oversweetening, depending on who you ask) ballads like "Across the Universe" and "The Long and Winding Road" with strings and backup singers.

87 | The Wall

PINK FLOYD
HARVEST/CAPITOL 1979

Pink Floyd's most elaborately theatrical album was inspired by their own success: the alienating enormity of their tours after *The Dark Side of the Moon* [see No. 43], which was when bassist-lyricist Roger Waters first hit upon the wall as a metaphor for isolation and rebellion. He finished a demo of the work by July 1978; the double album then took the band a year to make. Rock's ultimate self-pity opera, *The Wall* is also hypnotic in its indulgence: the totalitarian thunder of "In the Flesh?," the suicidal languor of "Comfortably Numb," the Brechtian drama of "The Trial." Rock-star hubris has never been more electrifying.

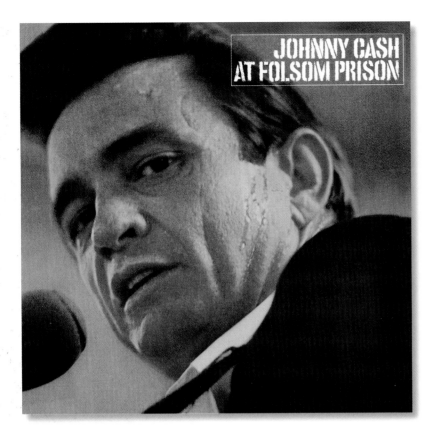

88 | At Folsom Prison

JOHNNY CASH
COLUMBIA/LEGACY 1968

By the late Sixties, Cash was ignored by country radio and struggling for a comeback. *At Folsom Prison* was a million-seller that reignited his career. A year later, he was writing liner notes for Bob Dylan's *Nashville Skyline* and logging four weeks at Number One with his second prison album, *At San Quentin.* But *At Folsom Prison* is essential Cash. Backed by a tough touring band, including fellow Sun Records alum Carl Perkins on guitar, Cash guffaws his way through "Cocaine Blues," "25 Minutes to Go" (a countdown to an execution) and "Folsom Prison Blues," with its line about shooting a man just to watch him die. The 2,000 inmates in attendance roar their approval.

89 | Dusty in Memphis

DUSTY SPRINGFIELD
RHINO 1969

Born in London, Springfield was a great soul singer hidden inside a white British pop queen – racking up Motown-style hits such as "I Only Want to Be With You" – when Atlantic producer Jerry Wexler brought her way down South, to Memphis, to make this album. She was so intimidated by the idea of recording with session guys from her favorite Aretha Franklin and Otis Redding hits that she never actually managed to sing a note there. Her vocals were overdubbed later, when the sessions moved to New York. But the result was blazing soul and sexual honesty ("Breakfast in Bed," "Son of a Preacher Man") that transcended both race and geography.

Dusty in Memphis

Dusty Springfield

Dusty went to Memphis, but "she refused to sing!" reports legendary soul producer Jerry Wexler. The London-born Springfield, who died in 1999, was known for pop gems such as "I Only Want to Be With You," "Wishin' and Hopin'" and, as she put it, "big, ballady things." But she loved Southern soul, and she chose Wexler to produce her fifth album based on his work with Wilson Pickett and Aretha Franklin.

Wexler booked session time at Muscle Shoals, in Alabama, and handpicked eighty songs for Springfield – everything from gospel soul like "Son of a Preacher Man" (which Aretha Franklin would later record) to big, ballady things including "The Windmills of Your Mind." Initially, Springfield nixed them all. A few months later, she approved fifteen, but Muscle Shoals was booked. So Wexler brought her to Chips Moman's American Studios in Memphis.

Located in a business district of town, American was steeped more in legend than atmosphere; the studio was "bare-bones, functional, not too pretty," Wexler says. The house band, working with Wexler and co-producers Arif Mardin and Tom Dowd, cut basic tracks. They'd learned not to wait for Springfield, who arrived late every day – she would come only in full makeup, which took hours. And she never actually put down a vocal. "I couldn't even get pilot vocals out of her," says Wexler. "She was used to recording with a full orchestra, but we were going against the naked track. People who are used to singing with support feel lost." Mardin theorized that Springfield "felt intimidated to sing in the same vocal booth that Wilson Pickett had sung in." Wexler puts it more bluntly: "It was self-consciousness and neurotic self-involvement."

The sessions moved back to Manhattan, where Mardin and Dowd added strings, horns and a Hungarian zither. And Springfield finally sang. "She absorbed what was going on [at American]," says Wexler. And indeed, her vocals mixed heartbreak with sultry frankness and the soulful sound Springfield had been hoping for – but only after the backing tracks were turned up to an excruciating level. "I put an ear to her headphones and I almost lost it!" says Wexler. "How she delivered those supernal vocals without hearing herself, I'll never be able to figure out."

Springfield arrived late, in full makeup, to the Memphis sessions.

90 | Talking Book

STEVIE WONDER
MOTOWN/UNIVERSAL 1972

"I don't think you know where I'm coming from," Wonder warned Motown executives in 1971. "I don't think you can understand it." Indeed, the two albums Wonder released in 1972 – *Music of My Mind* and *Talking Book* – rewrote the rules of the Motown hit factory. *Talking Book* was full of introspection and social commentary, with Wonder producing, writing and playing most of the instruments himself. "Superstition" and "You Are the Sunshine of My Life" were Number One singles; "Big Brother" is political consciousness draped in a light melody: "You've killed all our leaders/I don't even have to do nothin' to you/You'll cause your own country to fall."

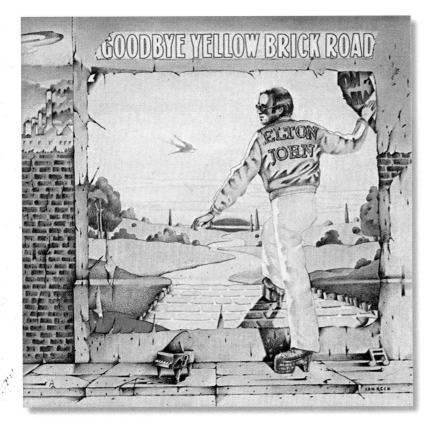

91 | Goodbye Yellow Brick Road

ELTON JOHN
UNIVERSAL 1973

Elton compared this double album to the Beatles' White Album, and why not? He was by this point the most consistent hitmaker since the Fab Four, and soon enough he would be recording with John Lennon. Everything about *Goodbye Yellow Brick Road* was supersonically huge, from the Wagnerian-opera-like combo of "Funeral for a Friend" and "Love Lies Bleeding" to the electric boots and mohair suit of "Bennie and the Jets." "Saturday Night's Alright for Fighting" was strutting rock & roll, "Candle in the Wind" paid tribute to Marilyn Monroe (and later, Princess Diana), and the title track harnessed the fantastical imagery of glam to a Gershwin-sweet melody.

92 | 20 Golden Greats

BUDDY HOLLY
MCA 1978

Holly spent his teenage years kicking around Texas playing straight country music – until, at nineteen, when he got a gig opening for Elvis Presley. With that, Holly later claimed, he became a rock & roller. For the next two years, he put his trademark vocal hiccup on springy rockabilly, orchestral ballads and Chuck Berry covers – an eclecticism that had a huge impact on the future Beatles. "Rave On," "Peggy Sue" and "Not Fade Away" made Holly one of rock's first great singer-songwriters. He was also its first major casualty: dead at twenty-two, in a plane crash after a show in Iowa in 1959. He was just getting started.

93 | Sign 'o' the Times

PRINCE
WARNER BROS. 1987

He'd fired his band, and his latest movie, *Under the Cherry Moon,* had flopped; just three years after *Purple Rain,* Prince was in the market for a comeback. So he recorded one of the great albums of the Eighties. *Times* is best known for the apocalyptic title track, the brontosaurus funk of "House-quake" and the gorgeous "If I Was Your Girlfriend." Yet the simplest moments are unforgettable: the "Sweet Jane"-style guitar plea of "The Cross," the Stax revamp on "Slow Love," a jilted girl's sadness in "I Could Never Take the Place of Your Man." "I hate the word *experiment,*" Prince said. "It sounds like something you didn't finish." Here, he finished.

94 | 40 Greatest Hits

HANK WILLIAMS
POLYDOR 1978

"Like a rolling stone, all alone and lost," Williams sang in "Lost Highway," "for a life of sin I have paid the cost." When he died on New Year's Day 1953 at age twenty-nine in the back seat of a Cadillac while en route to a gig in Canton, Ohio, Williams was the biggest star in country music, a charismatic songwriter and performer equally at home with lovesick ballads like "I'm So Lonesome I Could Cry" and long-gone-daddy romps such as "You're Gonna Change (Or I'm Gonna Leave)." Williams left his stamp on the decades of rock & roll that followed him, from the rockabilly of Elvis Presley to Bob Dylan's "Like a Rolling Stone" to the lovesick ballads of Beck's *Sea Change.*

95 Bitches Brew

MILES DAVIS

COLUMBIA/LEGACY 1970

In February 1969, Davis recorded *In a Silent Way*, a bold step into ambient funk and electric futurism. Then just six months later, he was back in the studio, driven by his desire to assemble "the best damn rock & roll band in the world." The idea was to connect his music to the audience of Jimi Hendrix and Sly Stone. The result was this double album of jazz-rock fusion, cut in three days of on-the-spot improvisations with an electric orchestra that included three keyboardists, three drummers, two bassists, saxophonist Wayne Shorter and guitarist John McLaughlin. The music was full of visceral thrills and the brooding darkness Davis brought to everything he touched.

96 Green River

CREEDENCE CLEARWATER REVIVAL

FANTASY 1969

The third Creedence Clearwater Revival album was their first classic LP, a tightly wrapped package of blistering guitar, roadhouse-rhythm snap and John Fogerty's backwoods howl. The lengthy jamming on CCR's previous LPs is gone, and Fogerty has found his lyrical voice — radio-ready essays in frontier living ("Green River," "Lodi") and working-stiff politics ("Bad Moon Rising," "Wrote a Song for Everyone"). As producer, he makes it all sound so gritty and easy, too — like CCR had cut it all in a toolshed. "All this overproduction is funny to me," Fogerty has said. "It doesn't make it mo' betta when you add more junk."

"It was approached in the way anti-intellectual rock people would hate. We went into it in depth before we worked out the plot; we worked out the sociological implications, the religious implications, the rock implications. We made sure every bit was solid. We went into the studio, got smashed out of our brains and made it. Then we listened, pruned and edited very carefully, then got smashed and did it all again."

PETE TOWNSHEND
(RS 37, JULY 12TH, 1969)

97 | Tommy

THE WHO
MCA 1969

"Rock opera" is one way to describe the pioneering ambition in Pete Townshend's musical exploration of childhood trauma, sexual abuse, repression and spiritual release (after all, it does have an overture). Here's another way: the slash and thunder of "My Generation" blown wide open. Driven by the hellbent drumming of Keith Moon, the Who surge and shine, igniting the drama in Townshend's melodies ("Pinball Wizard," "We're Not Gonna Take It"). "We worked out the sociological implications, the religious implications, the rock implications," he said. "When we'd done that, we went into the studio, got smashed out of our brains and made it."

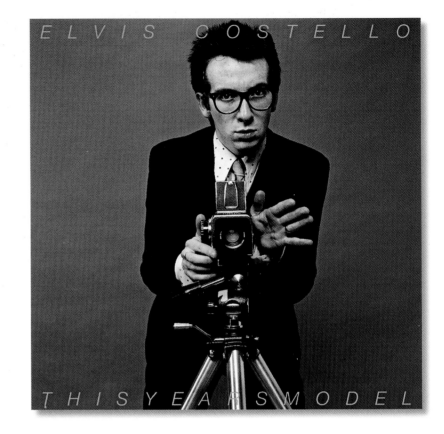

98 The Freewheelin' Bob Dylan

BOB DYLAN
COLUMBIA 1963

Dylan's second LP was released on May 27th, 1963 – three days after his twenty-second birthday. It was a tender age for such a historic triumph. On *Freewheelin'*, the poetry and articulate fury of Dylan's lyrics and his simple, compelling melodies transformed American popular songwriting. He later made light of the protest anthem "Blowing in the Wind" ("I wrote that in ten minutes," he said in 1966). But Dylan's wholly original grip on grit, truth and beauty in "A Hard Rain's A-Gonna Fall" and "Masters of War" still changes everyone who hears this album, four decades later.

99 This Year's Model

ELVIS COSTELLO
RHINO 1978

His second album and first with his crack backing band the Attractions, *This Year's Model* is the most "punk" of Costello's records – not in any I-hate-the-cops sense but in his emotionally explosive writing ("No Action," "Lipstick Vogue," "Pump It Up") and the Attractions' vicious gallop (particularly the psycho-circus organ playing of Steve Nieve). Many of the songs rattle with sexual paranoia, but the broadside against vanilla-pop broadcasting, "Radio, Radio" (a U.K. single added to the original U.S. vinyl LP), better reflects the general, righteous indignation of the album: Costello vs. the world. And Costello wins.

100 | There's a Riot Goin' On

SLY AND THE FAMILY STONE
EPIC 1971

This highly anticipated studio follow-up to Sly and the Family Stone's 1969 blast of hope, *Stand!*, was the grim, exact opposite: implosive, numbing, darkly self-referential. Sly Stone's voice is an exhausted grumble; the funk in "Family Affair," "Runnin' Away" and especially the closing downward spiral, "Thank You for Talkin' to Me Africa," is spare and bleak, fiercely compelling in its anguish over the unfulfilled promises of civil rights and hippie counterculture. "It is Muzak with its finger on the trigger," wrote critic Greil Marcus in *Mystery Train*. Take that as a recommendation.

101 | In the Wee Small Hours

FRANK SINATRA
CAPITOL 1955

In the Wee Small Hours, the first collection of songs Sinatra recorded specifically for an LP, sustains a midnight mood of loneliness and lost love – it's a prototypical concept album. From the title track, brought in on the bell tones of a celesta, through a trenchant recast of "This Love of Mine," a hit from his Tommy Dorsey days, Sinatra – reeling from his breakup with Ava Gardner – is never less than superb. His voice rarely hits the same downbeat as his languorous rhythm section, yet they're locked in a fluid step. Put your ear close to the speaker and you can hear the soft intake of his breath.

102 | Fresh Cream

CREAM
POLYGRAM 1967

Bassist Jack Bruce and drummer Ginger Baker had racked up credits with Graham Bond and Manfred Mann; guitarist Eric Clapton had inspired "Clapton Is God" graffiti all over London with the Yardbirds. Cream chose their name as a joke on their own supergroup credentials. Together, they gave a psychedelic pop spin on the blues, retooling Skip James' "I'm So Glad" and Muddy Waters' "Rollin' and Tumblin'," as well as originals such as "N.S.U." and "I Feel Free." *Fresh Cream* is tight and concise, a blueprint for the band's onstage jams. When Cream hit the U.S. acid-ballroom circuit, they stretched these tunes into quarter-hour improvisations.

103 | Giant Steps

JOHN COLTRANE
ATLANTIC 1960

With characteristic humility, Coltrane said the title of this album referred to the loping instrumental gait of his bassist, Paul Chambers. In fact, the LP was one of two giant steps Coltrane himself made in 1959: his playing on Miles Davis' epochal *Kind of Blue* and the recording of this, Coltrane's Atlantic debut. On seven originals, he played with a heated melodic enthusiasm – flying clusters of notes – that declared new possibilities for jazz improvisation and predicted the ferocious, harmonically open lyricism that would come with his mid-Sixties records on Impulse. "Mr. P.C.," "Cousin Mary," and "Spiral" became Coltrane's first classics.

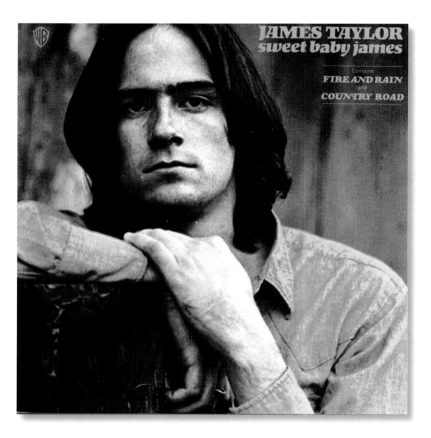

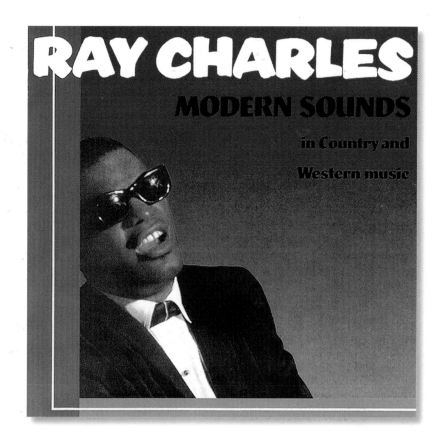

104 | Sweet Baby James

JAMES TAYLOR
WARNER BROS. 1970

Taylor's second album landed him on the cover of *Time* magazine, and its gentle melodies drew the blueprint for many of the Seventies singer-songwriters that followed. But he went through a private hell on his way to success; the hit "Fire and Rain" was inspired by Taylor's stay in a psychiatric institution in the mid-1960s (he had committed himself) and the suicide of a fellow patient. In the months before making this album, Taylor committed himself again, this time to kick heroin. His confessional lyrics set a new standard, as did the spare melodicism of his songs. But it was the quiet strength in his voice that makes this album a model of folk-pop healing.

105 | Modern Sounds in Country and Western Music

RAY CHARLES
RHINO 1962

Country and soul were deeply entangled Southern traditions and had been cross-pollinating for years. But *Modern Sounds* was still the audacious boundary-smasher its title promised, with Charles applying his gospel grit and luscious soul-pop strings to standards by Hank Williams ("Half as Much," "You Win Again," "Hey, Good Lookin'") and Eddy Arnold, whose lover's lament "You Don't Know Me" he recast as a parable about race relations in the light of the civil-rights struggle. *Modern Sounds* became the most popular album of Charles' career and includes the hits "I Can't Stop Loving You" and "Born to Lose."

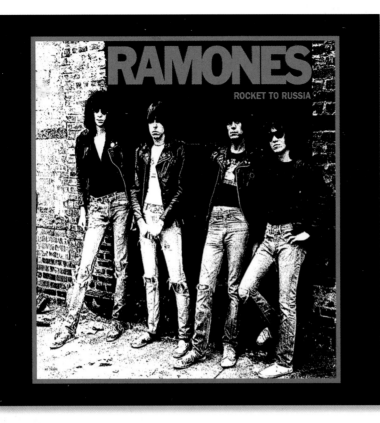

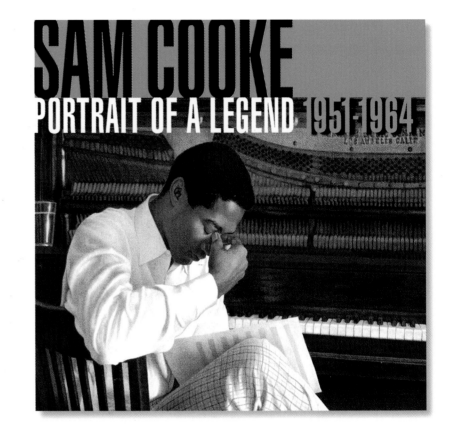

106 | Rocket to Russia

RAMONES
RHINO 1977

The Ramones wrote their third album on tour, as they took the gospel of three chords and ripped denim beyond New York's five boroughs. *Rocket to Russia* was also their first true studio triumph: an exuberant, polished bottling of the CBGB-stage napalm of *Ramones* and *Leave Home*. The razor-slashing hooks bring out the Top Forty classicism in "Rockaway Beach" and "Sheena Is a Punk Rocker," plus the lonely-boy poignancy of Joey Ramone's vocals in "I Don't Care" and "I Wanna Be Well." *Rocket to Russia* was also the last album made by the Ramones' founding four: Drummer Tommy Ramone left to be a full-time producer.

107 | Portrait of a Legend 1951-1964

SAM COOKE
ABKCO 2003

"Sam Cooke was the best singer who ever lived, no contest," asserted Atlantic Records' Jerry Wexler. Cooke was a gospel star who crossed over to rock & roll, helping to invent the music that would become known as soul. He kept the floridly emotional vocal style of gospel in his pop work, writing his own best hits ("Wonderful World," "You Send Me"). This collection spans his whole career, from his early work with gospel kings the Soul Stirrers to the civil-rights anthem "A Change Is Gonna Come," which became a posthumous hit after Cooke was shot to death at an L.A. motel in 1964.

Blaine: From Hebrew school to the Hall of Fame

The Beach Boys –
Pet Sounds

Hal Blaine

SESSION MAN

The smithsonian wants his drum kit. Hal Blaine, 74, has played drums with Basie, Elvis, Sinatra, the Beach Boys, Sonny and Cher – and just about everyone else. Blaine has lent his versatile sweet touch to more than 150 Number One singles, from "Be My Baby," by the Ronettes, to "Mr. Tambourine Man," by the Byrds. He was inducted into the Rock & Roll Hall of Fame in 2000.

What inspired you to start playing drums?

I was at Hebrew school, and across the street was a church. I used to watch the kids over there in a drum corps. The priest gave me a pair of sticks and a snare drum. Then my sister bought me my first kit. I'd sit on the front porch and do my own shows, showing off.

You've taken over the drum throne from band members. Was that ever weird?

Like, was Dennis Wilson upset that I played the drums [on Beach Boys sessions]? Gosh, no! He loved it. I was making thirty-five bucks a day in the studio, and Dennis was making $35,000 a night onstage. I took over from the regular drummer on about 175 records.

On the "Pet Sounds" sessions, Brian Wilson yells, "Take forty-six!" Was it that crazy?

That was a joke. It might have been take fourteen, but Brian would yell, "Take 120!" and everyone would laugh. It was always with a smile. He heard it in his head, and until he heard it on tape, he wanted to go for more. All those Hollywood sessions were fun, a party.

Even working with Phil Spector?

Oh, yeah. Brian used to stick his head in the door, even though there was a big sign that said "closed session." Phil would drag 'em in and say, "Give him a tambourine!"

What's your favorite drummer joke?

What do you call a drummer with no girlfriend? Homeless.

Simon and Garfunkel –
Bridge Over Troubled Water

Phil Spector –
Back to Mono (1958-1969)

The Mamas and the Papas –
If You Can Believe Your Eyes and Ears

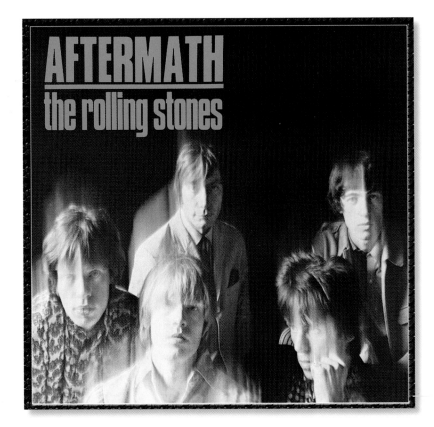

108 | Hunky Dory

DAVID BOWIE
VIRGIN 1970

Bowie, then twenty-four, arrived at the *Hunky Dory* cover shoot with a book of photographs of Marlene Dietrich: a perfect metaphor for this album's visionary blend of gay camp, flashy rock guitar and saloon-piano balladry. Bowie marked the polar ends of his artistic ambitions with tribute songs to Bob Dylan and Andy Warhol. In "Oh! You Pretty Things," "Quicksand" and "Changes," he invented and perfected a new style of rock & roll glamour. On "Life on Mars?," he sings to all the weirdos like himself who feel like aliens on Earth. Soon an entire army of kids would attempt to remake themselves in his spangled image, proving his point.

109 | Aftermath

THE ROLLING STONES
ABKCO 1966

Aftermath of what? Of the whirlwind fame that had resulted from releasing five albums in two years, for one thing. The Stones sound mean and jaded on *Aftermath*, writing bad-boy songs about Swinging London's overnight stars, groupies, hustlers and parasites. This is the first Stones album completely written by Jagger-Richards, a collection of tough riffs ("It's Not Easy") and tougher acoustic blues ("High and Dry"); of girls seeking kicks ("Under My Thumb") or just escape ("Think"); of zooming psychedelia ("Paint It, Black"), baroque-folk gallantry ("I Am Waiting") and epic groove (the eleven-minute "Going Home").

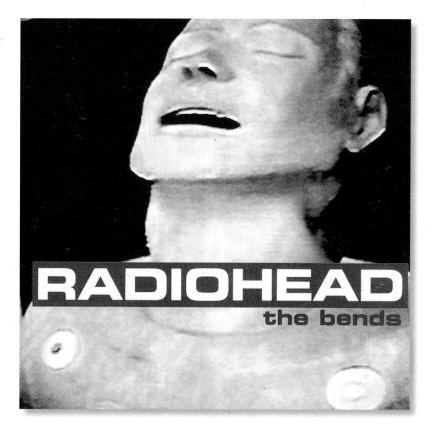

110 | Loaded

THE VELVET UNDERGROUND
WARNER BROS. 1970

The Velvet Underground made their most accessible album in 1970, during a summer comprised alternately of triumph and stress. They were playing their first New York shows in three years (at Max's Kansas City) and slowly falling apart. Drummer Maureen Tucker was on maternity leave; singer-guitarist-songwriter Lou Reed quit in August before the record was even finished. But Reed left behind a pair of hits ("Sweet Jane," "Rock 'n' Roll"), two of his finest ballads ("New Age," "Oh! Sweet Nuthin' ") and a record that highlights the R&B/doo-wop roots and Sun Records crackle buried deep inside the Velvets' noir-guitar maelstrom.

111 | The Bends

RADIOHEAD
CAPITOL 1995

If the first half of the Nineties was shaped by Nirvana, the template for the second half was set by Radiohead. Though the 1993 smash "Creep," from their debut, is itself indebted to Kurt Cobain, *The Bends*, their second album, is more grand, more operatic, marrying a majestic and somber guitar sound to Thom Yorke's anguished-choirboy vocals. "Fake Plastic Trees" was something of a radio hit, an introspective acoustic ballad of alienation. And not yet shying away from guitar anthems, Radiohead draw on the epic grandeur of U2 and the melancholy of the Smiths in "Nice Dream," "Just" and the haunting finale, "Street Spirit (Fade Out)."

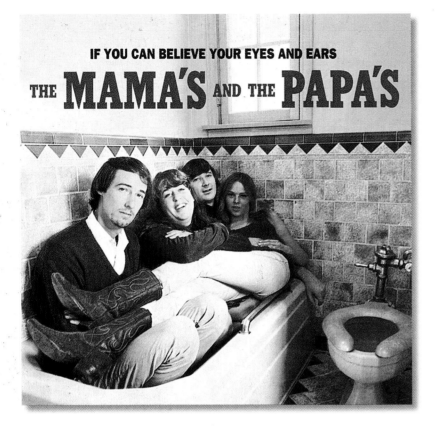

112 | If You Can Believe Your Eyes and Ears

THE MAMAS AND THE PAPAS
MCA 1966

"California Dreamin' " was this album's first hit, a warm breeze that inspired countless hippie migrants to hit the road for the West Coast in time for the Summer of Love. But Papa John Phillips came from New York, and under his group's sunny surface, the songs were full of darkness and wit. His fetching young bride, Michelle Phillips, Mama Cass Elliott and Denny Doherty joined him in gorgeous four-part harmonies over folk-rock guitars, but the songs were made of tough stuff, especially "Got a Feelin'," "Go Where You Wanna Go" and the junkie-seduction tale of "Straight Shooter."

113 | Court and Spark

JONI MITCHELL
ELEKTRA/ASYLUM 1974

Mitchell followed up *Blue* with the under-rated *For the Roses,* a set of harmonically and lyrically complex songs. *Court and Spark* is, in comparison, smoother and more straight-ahead; it became the biggest record of her career, hitting Number Two. Working with saxophonist Tom Scott's fusion group, L.A. Express, Mitchell settles into a folk-pop-jazz groove that remains a landmark of breezy sophistication, particularly on the Top Ten single "Help Me." Strange but true: A cover of "Twisted" by the scat-jazz vocal group Lambert, Hendricks and Ross closes the album — with stoner comics Cheech and Chong singing backup.

"*Court and Spark* was a turning point. In the state that I was at in my inquiry about life and direction and relationships, I perceived a lot of hate in my heart. I perceived my inability to love at that point, and it horrified me some."

(RS 296, JULY 26TH, 1979)

114 | Disraeli Gears

CREAM
UNIVERSAL 1967

Of all Cream's studio albums, *Disraeli Gears* is the sharpest and most linear. The power trio focused its instrumental explorations into colorful pop songs: "Strange Brew" (slinky funk), "Dance the Night Away" (trippy jangle), "Tales of Brave Ulysses" (a wah-wah freakout that Eric Clapton wrote with Martin Sharp, who created the kaleidoscopic cover art). The hit "Sunshine of Your Love" nearly didn't make it onto the record; the band had trouble nailing it until famed Atlantic Records engineer Tom Dowd suggested that Ginger Baker try a Native American tribal beat, a simple adjustment that locked the song into place.

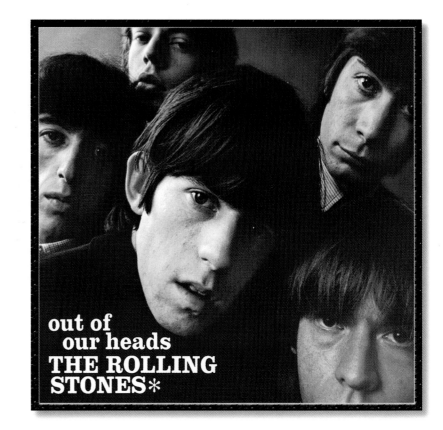

115 | The Who Sell Out

THE WHO
MCA 1967

The Who's third record was their first concept album, a tribute to the U.K.'s offshore pirate-radio stations. The band strung the songs together with mock commercials ("Heinz Baked Beans") and genuine radio jingles. It's the Who's funniest record – the sad love ballad "Odorono" turns out to be an ad for deodorant. The mini rock opera, "Rael," gave a hint of things to come (*Tommy* was two years away). The Who expanded their maximum R&B with "Armenia City in the Sky," "Tattoo" and "I Can See for Miles," which rode Pete Townshend's thrashiest power chords into the Top Ten.

116 | Out of Our Heads

THE ROLLING STONES
ABKCO 1965

Here's where the Stones started to leave the R&B and blues covers behind. Their fourth album in America – where the Stones' label disemboweled their U.K. releases to eke out more product – featured three defining Jagger-Richards originals, each a masterpiece of libidinal menace: "The Last Time," the gently vicious "Play With Fire" and "(I Can't Get No) Satisfaction," a song that is the very definition of riff. They also did great covers of Marvin Gaye, Otis Redding and Don Covay numbers, but for the first time on an album, the Stones were building an original songbook easily as hard and dark as they were themselves.

117 | Layla and Other Assorted Love Songs

DEREK AND THE DOMINOS
POLYGRAM 1970

Eric Clapton was tired of stardom, so he formed a new band where he could be just another one of the lads. But there was no mistaking the blues guitar on "Layla," as Clapton sang about falling in love with the wife of his best friend, George Harrison. The tortured love songs on *Layla* get a kick from guest Duane Allman, one of the few guitarists who could challenge Clapton – it's like a blues-guitar battle tape. Clapton and Allman had never met before the sessions, but their interplay in "Key to the Highway" and "Have You Ever Loved a Woman" is both harmonious and fiercely competitive: electric, brotherly love.

118 | At Last!

ETTA JAMES
MCA 1961

James was a self-described "juvenile delinquent" when R&B band boss Johnny Otis took her under his wing and made her a precociously sexual teenage star with 1954's "Roll With Me, Henry." Seven years later, James bloomed into a mature, fiery interpreter on this spellbinding LP. Against Riley Hampton's meaty orchestrations, James wraps her husky voice around strange bedfellows such as "Stormy Weather" and Willie Dixon's "I Just Want to Make Love to You," injecting them with rock & roll heart. She hit the pop and R&B charts with three of the songs here and, in the process, created a new vocal model: the crossover diva.

119 | Sweetheart of the Rodeo

THE BYRDS
COLUMBIA/LEGACY 1968

On release, this bold experiment in Nashville classicism was shunned by rock fans and country purists alike. But rural American song had been central to the Byrds' folk-rock sound; here, driven by junior Byrd Gram Parsons, the band highlighted that connection, dressing Bob Dylan and Merle Haggard songs in steel guitar and rock & roll drive, setting the stage for country rock. Legal hassles forced the removal of most of Parsons' lead vocals from the '68 LP (they're restored on CD), and he quit before it came out. But he left signs of his short, glorious future in his originals "Hickory Wind" and "One Hundred Years From Now."

120 | Stand!

SLY AND THE FAMILY STONE
EPIC 1969

Stand! is party politics at its most inclusive and exciting – Sly Stone at the top of his funk-rock-soul game. A DJ and producer in San Francisco during the Dawn of Hippie, Stone rides the bonfire momentum of the civil-rights movement in motivational-soul sermons such as "Stand!" and "You Can Make It If You Try" without denying the intrinsic divisions that threatened civil war ("Don't Call Me Nigger, Whitey"). There was also the uplifting pure-pop beauty of "Everyday People" as well as the R&B ecstasy of "I Want to Take You Higher" and swirling black psychedelia of "Sex Machine." It makes *Stand! a* greatest-hits album in all but name.

121 The Harder They Come

ORIGINAL SOUNDTRACK
HIP-O 1973

This was the album that took reggae worldwide. The movie was a Jamaican stew of *Robin Hood, High Sierra* and *Easy Rider* – reggae singer turns outlaw hero, goes on the run with guns blazing – with patois dialogue so thick that U.S. audiences needed subtitles. But the soundtrack needed no translation, introducing Babylon to the new beat. The film's star, Jimmy Cliff, sings four songs, including the hymn "Many Rivers to Cross." There are glorious one-shots (especially Scotty's demented "Draw Your Brakes") as well as artists such as Desmond Dekker ("007 [Shanty Town]") the Melodians ("Rivers of Babylon) and Toots and the Maytals ("Pressure Drop").

122 Raising Hell

RUN-DMC
ARISTA 1986

Man, did this record start something. Working for the first time with producer Rick Rubin, the Hollis crew of Run, D.M.C. and Jam Master Jay made an album so undeniable, it forced the mainstream to cross over to hip-hop. "Peter Piper" kicked the rhymes over avant-garde mixology, with a jingling cowbell sampled from an old jazz-fusion record. On "My Adidas," "It's Tricky" and "You Be Illin'," Run and D.M.C talked trash while the DJ made their day. They even hit MTV with a vandalistic cover of Aerosmith's "Walk This Way," featuring Steven Tyler and Joe Perry. After *Raising Hell,* nobody ever tried to call hip-hop a fad again.

123 | Moby Grape

MOBY GRAPE
SAN FRANCISCO SOUND 1967

What a beautiful mess Moby Grape were, and what an amazing noise they made on their debut album, a stunning artifact of San Francisco rock at its '67 peak. Jerry Miller, Peter Lewis, Don Stevenson, Bob Mosley and Skip Spence all sang like demons and wrote crisp pop songs packed with lysergic country-blues excitement. And the band's three guitarists – Miller, Spence and Lewis – created a network of lightning that made songs like "Omaha," "Changes" and "Hey Grandma" shine and sizzle. Columbia Records hyped this album to near death (issuing five singles at once), but the music is just as thrilling now as it was in '67. This is genuine hippie power pop.

124 | Pearl

JANIS JOPLIN
COLUMBIA/LEGACY 1971

On *Pearl*, Joplin finally made a solo album worthy of her mighty blues-mama voice. She had her first Number One album, *Cheap Thrills*, as lead singer of Big Brother and the Holding Company, and made an uneven solo debut with the 1969 *I Got Dem Ol' Kozmic Blues Again Mama!* But *Pearl* was more intimate, more assured, unleashing her Texas-bred wail on the country-style soul tune "Get It While You Can" and the hippie gospel goof "Mercedes Benz." "Me and Bobby McGee" gave her a Number One single, but Joplin did not live to enjoy her triumph. She died of a drug overdose in 1970, before the album was completed. She was twenty-seven.

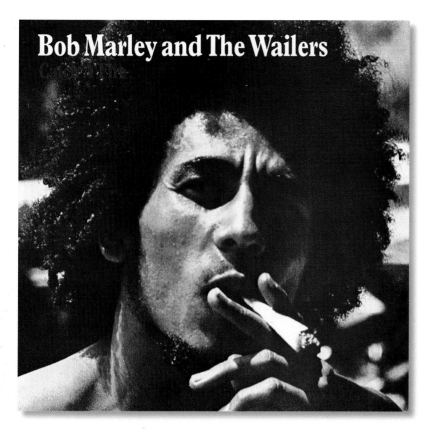

125 | Catch a Fire

BOB MARLEY AND THE WAILERS
ISLAND 1973

This was the album that introduced the whole world to Bob Marley, expanding his audience beyond Jamaica without diluting his bedrock reggae power. At the time, the Wailers were truly a unified band, fronted by three extraordinary singers in Marley, Peter Tosh and Bunny Livingston. The rhythm section of drummer Carlton Barrett and his brother, bassist Aston "Family Man" Barrett, defined the reggae beat. Producer and label boss Chris Blackwell subtly overdubbed and remixed the original Jamaican sessions for international ears, but the Wailers' ghetto rage comes across uncut in "Concrete Jungle" and "Slave Driver."

126 | Younger Than Yesterday

THE BYRDS
COLUMBIA 1967

Two years after being hailed as America's answer to the Beatles, these folk-rock pioneers were unraveling, commercially and internally – a situation Roger McGuinn and Chris Hillman addressed with this album's rousing, ironic opener, "So You Want to Be a Rock 'n' Roll Star." David Crosby, whom McGuinn would later fire, contributed a ravishing noir ballad, "Everybody's Been Burned," and Hillman bloomed as a writer, simultaneously reviving the Byrds' early magic and foreshadowing their adventures in country rock with "Time Between." "My Back Pages," the obligatory Dylan cover, is the album's elegiac centerpiece.

127 Raw Power

THE STOOGES
COLUMBIA 1973

Iggy Pop had dyed silver hair and a hard-drug habit when David Bowie took the rudderless Stooges under his wing and helped get them a deal with Columbia. "With Bowie," Pop wrote in his 1982 book, *I Need More*, "I didn't feel compelled to go to sleep every time something unpleasant happened." Quite the opposite: Pop turned every knob up and recruited new guitarist James Williamson, who played with hellbent ferocity in punk eruptions like "Search and Destroy," "Gimme Danger," and "Your Pretty Face Is Going to Hell." The original version became a classic despite the infamously bad sonics; Pop's 1998 remix added even more raw power.

128 Remain in Light

TALKING HEADS
WARNER BROS. 1980

David Byrne said *Remain in Light* "was done in bits and pieces, one instrument at a time." The result was a New Wave masterpiece powered by Byrne's revelation, as he put it on "The Great Curve," that "the world moves on a woman's hips." It combined thrust of a P-Funk dance party, the ancient-to-the-future rhythm hypnosis of Nigerian funkmaster Fela Kuti, and the studied adventurousness of the album's producer and Heads co-conspirator, Brian Eno. *Remain in Light* marked Talking Heads' transformation from avatars of the punk avant-garde to polyrhythmic magicians with hit-single appeal. Just try not dancing to "Once in a Lifetime."

129 Marquee Moon

TELEVISION
ELEKTRA 1977

When the members of Television materialized in New York, at the dawn of punk, they played an incongruous, soaring amalgam of genres: the noirish howl of the Velvet Underground, brainy art rock, the double-helix guitar sculpture of Quicksilver Messenger Service. As exhilarating in its lyrical ambitions as the Ramones' debut was in its brutal simplicity, *Marquee Moon* still amazes. "Friction," "Venus" and the mighty title track are jagged, desperate and beautiful all at once. As for punk credentials, don't forget the cryptic electricity and strangled existentialism of guitarist Tom Verlaine's voice and songwriting.

130 Paranoid

BLACK SABBATH
WARNER BROS. 1971

You think the massive idiot-box success of *The Osbournes* was a fluke? Try taking a time machine back to the early 1970s and telling rock critics they'll still be writing about *Paranoid* in 2005. But Sabbath ruled for bummed-out kids in the Seventies, and nearly every heavy-metal and extreme rock band of the last three decades – from Metallica and Nirvana to Marilyn Manson, Slipknot and every one of those acts lining up year after year to play Ozzfest – owes a debt of worship to Tony Iommi's crushing, granite-fuzz guitar chords, the Visigoth rhythm machine of Bill Ward and Geezer Butler, and Ozzy Osbourne's agonized bray in "Paranoid," "Iron Man" and "War Pigs."

131 | Saturday Night Fever

ORIGINAL SOUNDTRACK
POLYGRAM 1977

In the mid-Seventies, the Bee Gees swept away the arch pop of their Sixties hits and applied their silvery-helium harmonies to the creamy syncopation of disco. They made great albums in their new incarnation (such as 1975's *Main Course*) but none bigger or more influential than this soundtrack. In the past quarter-century, *Saturday Night Fever* has sold 30 million copies worldwide, and its musical worth justifies the numbers. The Bee Gees dominate ("Stayin' Alive" is the pulse of the picture as well as the album), but the Trammps' hotfunk assault "Disco Inferno" and Tavares' yearning "More Than a Woman" affirm disco's black-R&B roots.

132 | The Wild, the Innocent and the E Street Shuffle

BRUCE SPRINGSTEEN
COLUMBIA 1973

"Someday we'll look back on this/And it will all seem funny," Springsteen sings on "Rosalita (Come Out Tonight)." Reeling from the commercial fizzle of his debut LP, Springsteen threw off the "new Dylan" baggage and applied his Jersey-bar-band skills to some of the funniest tunes he'd ever write: "Rosalita," "Kitty's Back" and the boardwalk love song "4th of July, Asbury Park (Sandy)." The music is loose, jazzy and full of ambition – a studio take on the live muscle that Springsteen was already famous for – and "New York City Serenade" is the first of Springsteen's epic street operas.

the notorious B I G

r e a d y t o d i e

133 | Ready to Die

THE NOTORIOUS B.I.G.

BAD BOY 1994

"At the time I was making the album," B.I.G. told ROLLING STONE in 1995, "I was just waking up every morning, hustling, cutting school, looking out for my moms, the police, stickup kids; just risking my life every day on the street selling drugs, you know what I'm saying?" B.I.G. (a.k.a. Biggie Smalls) took all that gritty life experience and crammed it into *Ready to Die.* Almost single-handedly, Biggie shifted the focus back to East Coast rap. "Big Poppa" is the hit sex jam; on "Things Done Changed" and "Everyday Struggle," he relates gangsta tales in a voice as thick as his waistline. "I'm definitely a writer," Biggie said. "I don't even know how to freestyle."

Ready to Die

The Notorious B.I.G.

You're never sure you're creating a classic," P. Diddy says of producing the Notorious B.I.G.'s debut, 1994's landmark *Ready to Die*, "but I knew that if I had any chance in my lifetime to be associated with one, this was it."

Biggie Smalls was already a ghetto superstar in the Northeast before he went into the studio with Puffy; his raucous single "Party and Bullshit" was an underground hit, and he had stolen the show as the guest MC on singles by Mary J. Blige and Super Cat, among others. But recording an entire album of songs was a different matter, as B.I.G. would find out. "At first, B.I.G. would write these long rhymes, like ten minutes long, with no structure, no chorus – just him destroying the microphone and leaving it smoking," Diddy says. "It took a couple of months to teach him how to turn them into a song. As soon as he got it, though, he made songs like nobody else I've seen."

The first song recorded for *Ready to Die* was "Gimme the Loot," which cemented Biggie's trademark vivid confessional style. "'Gimme the Loot' captured how he felt when he was broke," Diddy says. "He really had strategies about how to rob people – this was his life." According to DJ Premier, who produced "Unbelievable," Biggie knew exactly what he wanted. "'Unbelievable' was the last song recorded for the album," Premier recalls. "Biggie called and said, 'The record is done – I just need that bangin' ghetto joint.' He gave me $5,000 to do it – bullshit money, but I had so much love for B.I.G., I said OK.

"I had to go on tour in a couple days," continues Premier, "which is why it's so simple. When B.I.G. first heard it, all I had was the 'Biggie Smalls is the illest' sample. He was like, 'Keep that, but not through the whole song. Then flip it around a little on the chorus and scratch in R. Kelly singing 'unbelievable' from "Your Body's Callin'." ' That sample was bananas – it melodically fit the music by coincidence. It was his idea, and it worked."

B.I.G. wasn't all business during recording, however. "One time, Biggie was butt-ass naked on the couch with a couple women in his hotel room," Premier remembers. "The girls were giving him a 'microphone check.' He asked me if I wanted one, and I said, 'Naw, I'm good.' Still, I thank him for that. One thing about B.I.G. – he would share!"

B.I.G.: With help from P. Diddy, he recalibrated the hip-hop world.

134 Slanted and Enchanted

PAVEMENT
MATADOR 1992

Pavement were the quintessential American underground rock band, and this is the quintessential indie-rock album. The playing is loose-limbed, the production laid-back and primitive, the lyrics quirky and playful, the melodies sweet and seductive. But the sound is as intense as the white noise of the Velvet Underground. *Slanted and Enchanted* is one of the most influential rock albums of the 1990s; its fuzzy recording style can be heard in the music of Guided By Voices, Liz Phair, Beck, the Strokes and the White Stripes. To double your pleasure, get the recent two-CD reissue, which features essential odds-and-ends and live tracks.

135 Greatest Hits

ELTON JOHN
POLYGRAM 1974

John has put out numerous greatest-hits packages over the years, but none as important as this single-disc collection released by MCA during the piano man's creative and commercial peak. It includes every one of his Top Ten singles of the period, from "Your Song" (1970) to "Don't Let the Sun Go Down on Me" (1974). A second, equally strong volume came out in 1977, filling in some blanks – "Levon," "Tiny Dancer," "Philadelphia Freedom" – just as John prematurely announced his retirement. But for one easy-to-digest disc, this set documents why Elton John was one of the biggest-selling pop stars of the Seventies.

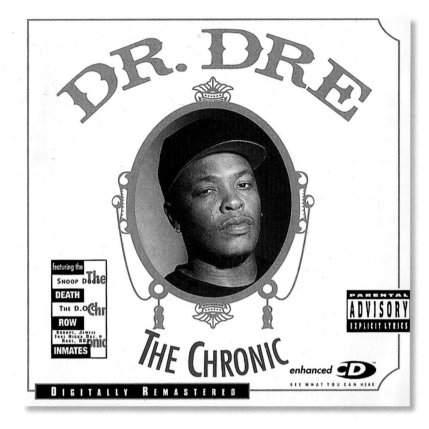

136 | Tim

THE REPLACEMENTS
WARNER BROS. 1985

Singer-guitarist Paul Westerberg once cited *Tim*'s stylistic bookends to describe both the longevity of the Replacements' influence and their lack of mainstream success. "My style is ultimately both kinds of things," he said. "Sometimes you just love the little acoustic songs, and other times you want to crank the goddamn amp up, and those two parts of me are forever entwined." Those extremes – the glammy power-chord swagger of "Bastards of Young," the quiet, strummy contemplation of "Here Comes a Regular" – became a crucial template for grunge, alternative country and, recently, the noisy introspection of emo.

137 | The Chronic

DR. DRE
DEATH ROW 1992

When George Clinton first heard hip-hop artists blending old records with new beats, he thought, "Damn, that's pretty tacky." Then Dr. Dre turned samples of Clinton's P-Funk sides into G-Funk, and Dr. Funkenstein approved, calling funk "the DNA of hip-hop and rap." Dre had already taken gangsta rap to the mainstream with his earlier group, N.W.A, but on *The Chronic*, he funked up the rhymes with a smooth bass-heavy production style and the laid-back delivery of then-unknown rapper Snoop Doggy Dogg. When Dre and Snoop dropped "Nuthin' But a 'G' Thang," there was no getting out of the way.

138 | Rejuvenation

THE METERS
SUNDAZED 1974

In 1974, when long, grueling guitar work-outs ruled the day, New Orleans producer Allen Toussaint was building hit records with a taut Morse-code style of rhythm guitar rooted in the marching-band and party beats of the Crescent City. That funky discipline defines this LP. The Meters were already respected Big Easy session players when they achieved a perfect balance of funk, rock and Dixie R&B on *Rejuvenation* gems such as "People Say" and "Hey Pocky A-Way." Listen closely and you'll hear Lowell George of Little Feat putting his slide guitar to work on "Just Kissed My Baby" – just enough to pan-sear this juicy cut.

139 | All That You Can't Leave Behind

U2
INTERSCOPE 2000

"Our best work has been in our thirties," Bono told ROLLING STONE in 2000. "We did some good work in our twenties, but it's getting better." U2's tenth album proved him right. Their previous effort, 1997's *Pop,* was under-realized; *All That You Can't Leave Behind* brought things back to essentials. The songs grapple with mortality – particularly the gospel-soul ballad "Stuck in a Moment You Can't Get Out Of" – and take on new resonance after September 11th. U2 bravely embraced those resonances the following October with a U.S. tour full of ecstasy, mourning and release.

"Our music in the early Eighties, it might have been ecstatic, but it wasn't really sexy, was it? Now we're sexy, and ecstatic. Now, literally, we're bringing up the rear."

BONO
(RS 860, JANUARY 18TH, 2001)

140 | Parallel Lines

BLONDIE
CAPITOL 1978

Here's where punk and New Wave broke through to a mass U.S. audience, thanks to the Number One hit "Heart of Glass," also known to Blondie fans as "The Disco Song." "I was trying to get that groove that the drummer for the Bee Gees had," said drummer Clem Burke, who credited Kraftwerk and the *Saturday Night Fever* soundtrack as influences on "Heart of Glass." *Parallel Lines* is a perfect synthesis of raw punk edge, Sixties-pop smarts and the cool New Wave glamour Blondie invented. Deborah Harry, of course, invented a new kind of rock & roll sex appeal that brought New York demimonde style to the mainstream. Madonna was surely watching.

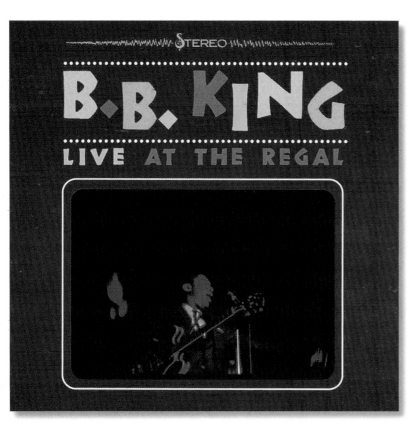

141 | Live at the Regal

B.B. KING
BEAT GOES ON 1965

By the mid-Sixties, King's career appeared to be winding down, as black audiences began to turn their backs on the blues. But the British blues revival – which saw the Rolling Stones making a pilgrimage to Chicago's Chess Studios – introduced the blues to young, white American rock fans. *Live at the Regal,* recorded in Chicago in 1964, paved the way for King's appearances on the rock-concert circuit and FM radio. It remains his definitive live set. His guitar sound was precise and powerful, driving emotional versions of some of his most influential songs, including "Everyday (I Have the Blues)" and "How Blue Can You Get?"

142 | A Christmas Gift for You

PHIL SPECTOR
ABKCO 1972

Hands down, the best holiday album in the history of pop music. Originally issued in 1963 under the title *A Christmas Gift for You From Philles Records,* it wasn't until the Beatles' Apple label reissued it almost a decade later that these gritty girl-group versions of Yuletide classics were really appreciated. Ronnie Spector of the Ronettes melts "Frosty the Snowman" and takes the innocence out of "I Saw Mommy Kissing Santa Claus." U2 later covered "Christmas (Baby Please Come Home)," but not even Bono could out-belt Ronnie's original. It all comes in a vortex of crashing drums and Phil Spector's exhilarating Wall of Sound production.

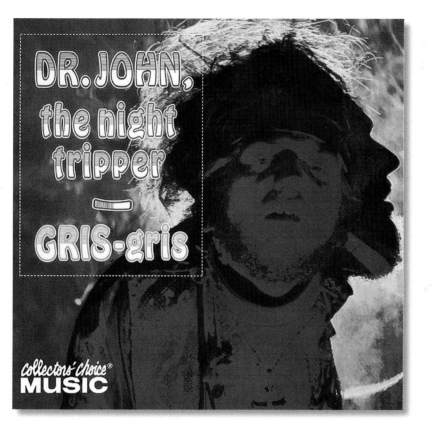

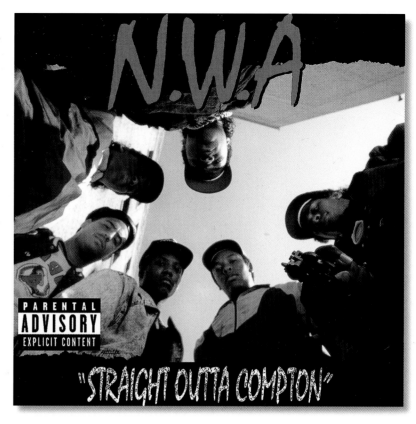

143 | Gris-Gris

DR. JOHN
COLLECTOR'S CHOICE 1968

Mac Rebennack was a New Orleans piano player on songs for Professor Longhair and Frankie Ford who moved to L.A. in the Sixties, where he played on Phil Spector sessions and encountered California psychedelia. Rechristening himself Dr. John Creaux the Night Tripper, he made this swamp-funk classic. *Gris-Gris* blends New Orleans R&B, voodoo chants and chemical inspiration. The groovy Afro-Caribbean percussion and creaky sound effects aren't just otherworldly – they seem to come from several other worlds all at once. John's secret: Even at his most Dr. Demento moments, he never lost sight of his hometown's earthy funk.

144 | Straight Outta Compton

N.W.A
PRIORITY 1988

This was the start of gangsta rap as well as the launching pad for the careers of Ice Cube, Eazy-E and Dr. Dre. While Public Enemy were hip-hop's political revolutionaries, N.W.A celebrated the thug life. "Do I look like a motherfucking role model?" Ice Cube asks on "Gangsta Gangsta": "To a kid looking up to me, life ain't nothing but bitches and money." Ice Cube's rage, combined with Dr. Dre's police-siren street beats, combined for a truly fearsome sound on "Express Yourself," "A Bitch Iz a Bitch" and "Straight Outta Compton." But it was the protest "Fuck Tha Police" that earned the crew its biggest honor: a threatening letter from the FBI.

145 | Aja

STEELY DAN
MCA 1977

If you were an audiophile in the late Seventies, you owned *Aja*. Steely Dan's sixth album is easy on the ears, thanks to both its meticulous production and its songs – this was Walter Becker and Donald Fagen's no-holds-barred stab at becoming a huge, mainstream jazz-pop success. And sure enough, thanks to sweet, slippery tracks like "Deacon Blues" and "Peg," this collegiate band with a name plucked from a William Burroughs novel and a songbook full of smart, cynical lyrics became bona fide superstars, shooting to the Top Five and selling platinum. And, yes, *Aja* even won a Grammy for Best Engineered album.

146 | Surrealistic Pillow

JEFFERSON AIRPLANE
RCA 1967

Psychedelic scholars have long tried to pin down just what the Grateful Dead's Jerry Garcia did on this album (besides contribute some guitar playing) to earn a credit as "musical and spiritual adviser." But the real trip is the Airplane's musical sorcery: a hallucinatory distillation of folk-blues vocals, garage-rock guitar and crisp pop songwriting. The effects were felt nationwide. Grace Slick's vocal showcases, "White Rabbit" and "Somebody to Love," made *Surrealistic Pillow* a commercial smash during San Francisco's Summer of Love, and Marty Balin's spectral "Today" is still the greatest ballad of that city's glory days.

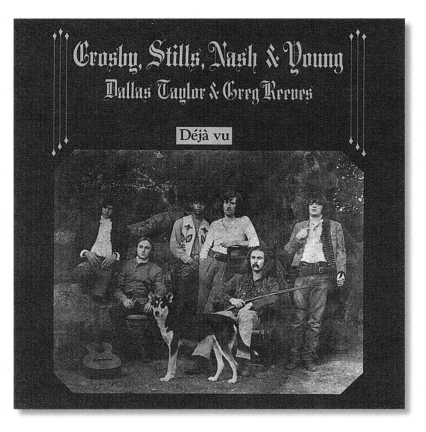

147 | Déjà Vu

CROSBY, STILLS, NASH AND YOUNG
ATLANTIC 1970

Neil Young was just getting his solo career under way when he joined his old Buffalo Springfield bandmate Stephen Stills, ex-Byrd David Crosby and former Hollie Graham Nash in the first of the West Coast supergroups. Young's vision and guitar transformed the earlier folk-rock CSN into a rock & roll powerhouse. The CSNY combination was too volatile to last, but on their best album, they offered pop idealism (Nash's "Teach Your Children"), militant blues (Crosby's "Almost Cut My Hair") and vocal-choir gallop (Stills' "Carry On"). The achingly plaintive "Helpless" and the explosive mini-opera "Country Girl" are prime early Young.

148 | Houses of the Holy

LED ZEPPELIN
ATLANTIC 1973

Led Zeppelin stuck close to their core sound on earlier albums – supercharged blues, celestial folk – but here they got into a groove. "D'yer Mak'er" (rhymes with "Jamaica") is their version of reggae, and "The Crunge" is a tribute to James Brown. "We thought of putting steps on the cover to help you do the dance," said Jimmy Page. The band also indulged its cosmic side with "The Rain Song" (featuring one of Plant's most amazing vocals), "The Song Remains the Same" and the Viking death chant "No Quarter." Confirming they were the biggest band on the planet, that summer Zeppelin's American tour broke box-office records established by the Beatles.

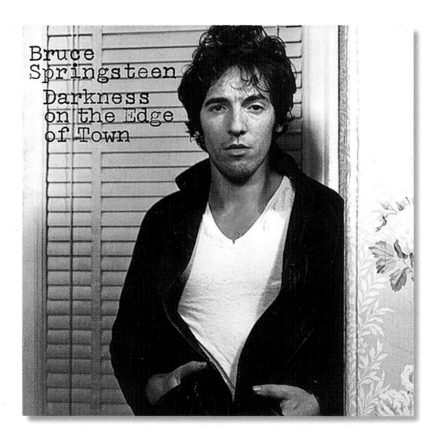

149 | Santana

SANTANA
COLUMBIA 1969

The first two times Santana tried to record their debut, they scrapped the tapes. But the third time, they came up with *Santana,* which combined Latin rhythms with jazz-inspired improvisation, hard-rock guitar and lyrical, B.B. King-style blues – and even had a hit single, "Evil Ways." The combination of rock guitar and funk percussion was undeniable. Back then, a lot of Carlos Santana's guitar playing was fueled by psychedelic drugs. "I don't recommend it to anybody and everybody," Santana told ROLLING STONE in 2000. "Yet for me, I feel it did wonders. It made me aware of splendor and rapture." For millions of people, Santana did the same thing.

150 | Darkness on the Edge of Town

BRUCE SPRINGSTEEN
COLUMBIA 1978

"When I was making this particular album, I just had a specific thing in mind," Springsteen told ROLLING STONE. "It had to be just a relentless . . . just a barrage of that particular thing." His obsession on this album is a common one: how you go on living in a mean world when your youthful dreams have fallen apart. Springsteen sang with John Lennon-style fury, as he chronicled the working-class dreams and despair of "Prove It All Night" and "The Promised Land," as well as his definitive car song, "Racing in the Streets." After the youthful exuberance of *Born to Run, Darkness* was the first sound of Springsteen's hard-won adult realism.

The future of rock & roll: Landau and Springsteen after a show in '74

Jon Landau

A ROLLING STONE writer before he graduated from college, Jon Landau parlayed music criticism into a career as a producer, working with the MC5 [No. 445], Bruce Springsteen (whom he now manages) and Jackson Browne [No. 387]. He has produced fewer than fifteen studio albums, but seven of them are in this book, including five by Springsteen [No. 18, 85, 150, 247 and 467].

What made you want to be a producer?
I played guitar in college, and I was offered a record contract. I didn't have the nerve to take that on. But I had the musical ideas and the chutzpah to tell other people what to do.

In 1974 you wrote, "I saw rock & roll's future, and its name is Bruce Springsteen." In 1975 you were producing "Born to Run."
He was my hero the day I met him; he's my hero today. I wrote a critique of his second album that said how great the songs were and how the production was underserving him. You could say I was auditioning in print for the job.

Did you two butt heads in the studio?
We were both very stubborn. When we drifted into disagreements, we were both like kids. I can communicate extremely well about lyrics. When you're dealing with a great songwriter, you want the power of their words to be very palpable, and I believe that's what we got on *Born to Run*.

You produced MC5's "Back in the USA" and Springsteen's "Born in the U.S.A." Do they have anything in common?
One thing they shared, in different ways, was a perspective about life in America. All the albums I've produced embody a critique of America and a celebration of Americans.

151 | The B-52's
THE B-52'S
WARNER BROS. 1979

The debut by the B-52's sounds like a bunch of high school friends cramming all their running jokes, goofy sounds and private nicknames into a New Wave record. "We never thought it would get past our circle of friends in Athens [Georgia]," vocalist Fred Schneider told ROLLING STONE. It turned out that nobody could resist the band's campy, arty funk, or the eccentric squeals and bouffant hairdos of Kate Pierson and Cindy Wilson. (Playing organ, Pierson also defined the band's sound.) They played toy instruments, and their thrift-store image was as inventive and colorful as their music – which, with "Rock Lobster," was pretty inventive and colorful.

152 | The Low End Theory
A TRIBE CALLED QUEST
JIVE 1991

Other people connected the dots between hip-hop and jazz – both were revolutionary forms of black music based in improvisation and flow – but A Tribe Called Quest' second album drew the entire picture. The sound is dominated by the low end of the title – they even recruited legendary jazz bassist Ron Carter (who'd worked with Thelonious Monk and Miles Davis). As Carter gets dope on the double bass, the Tribe discourse on matters ranging from the music industry ("Show Business") to sexual politics ("The Infamous Date Rape"). Each time Q-Tip rhymes over Carter's bass lines, the groove just gets deeper.

153 Moanin' in the Moonlight

HOWLIN' WOLF
CHESS 1959

Wolf was a big man – six feet three and 300 pounds of heavenly joy, as he put it in one song. His huge, eerie sound centered around his commanding growl and the explosive playing of two blues-guitar geniuses: Willie Johnson and Hubert Sumlin. This enormously influential collection of singles for Chess instructed the Rolling Stones, Eric Clapton, Jeff Beck and the rest of England in the ways of the blues. It includes Wolf compositions that became standards, such as "Smokestack Lightnin'" and "I Asked for Water (She Gave Me Gasoline)," and it starts with "Moanin' at Midnight," from his first recording session ever – at age forty-one.

154 Pretenders

THE PRETENDERS
WARNER BROS. 1980

After years of knocking around Ohio and England, writing record reviews and hanging with the Sex Pistols, Chrissie Hynde put together a band as tough as her attitude. The Pretenders' debut is filled with no-nonsense New Wave rock such as "Mystery Achievement" – plus a cover of "Stop Your Sobbing," by the Kinks' Ray Davies (three years later, the father of Hynde's child). The biggest hit was "Brass in Pocket," a song of ambition and seduction. Hynde, however, wasn't so sure about the song's success. "I was embarrassed by it," she said. "I hated it so much that if I was in Woolworth's and they started playing it, I'd have to run out of the store."

155 | Paul's Boutique

BEASTIE BOYS

CAPITOL 1989

"I went to this party in Los Angeles," recalled Adam Horovitz, "and they were playing this music, like . . . four break-beat records playing at the same time." The party soundtrack consisted of tracks by the Dust Brothers, who ended up co-producing this entire second record from the Beasties, providing the rap trio with some of the best samples ever put on wax, including the Ramones, Mountain and the Funky 4+1. *Paul's Boutique* is also an extended goof on *Abbey Road* [see No. 14], which was Paul McCartney's boutique — and like that record, it ambitiously stitches together song fragments in a way rarely seen before or since.

Paul's Boutique

The Beastie Boys

The Beastie Boys didn't exactly struggle under the burden of high expectations for their second album. "We were supposed to come out with 'Fight for Your Right to Party, Part Two' and fall on our faces," said Mike D. "Now we get people coming up and saying, 'I just have to thank you. . . . I got into *Paul's Boutique* in college.' "

Paul's Boutique has been called the *Sgt. Pepper* of hip-hop. "That's not totally inaccurate," says longtime Beastie studio whiz Mario Caldato Jr., who got his start with the Boys as engineer, "especially as we sampled a couple of Beatles joints." Indeed, the kaleidoscopic 1989 masterwork of found funk may go down as the most sampladelic album of all time. "Ninety-five percent of the record was sampled," Caldato says. "They spent over $250,000 for sample clearances.

The list of samples on the album is so long – they're still getting sued over it."

The Beasties had moved from New York to Los Angeles. They were in the midst of a painful divorce from their original label, Def Jam, and ready to start a new phase in their music. Matt Dike, head of the Delicious Vinyl label and a trendsetting L.A. DJ, heard about this and asked a mutual acquaintance to give the Beasties a pair of funky instrumental demos that he'd been working on with a production trio called the Dust Brothers (those two tracks would eventually become *Boutique* centerpieces "Shake Your Rump" and "Car Thief"). Production began in earnest. "The songs were really about the life we were living," Caldato says. "Staying at fancy hotels, eating at fancy restaurants, renting Beemers, chucking eggs at people," he says. "A lot of them are true stories. On 'Egg Man,' the words go 'Chuckin' eggs from the Mondrian Hotel at the cars goin' by,' and they did that. 'Chillin' like Bob Dylan'? Yeah, we were. We went to a Christmas party Dolly Parton had at her house. There were all these celebs, and there was Bob Dylan! We were like, 'Fuck, let's spark a joint. So we sparked a joint with Bob!' "

The Beasties, feeling sampladelic in their new L.A. digs.

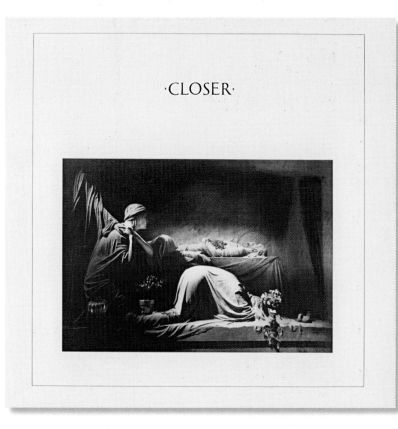

156 | Closer

JOY DIVISION
WARNER BROS. 1980

One of the most depressing albums ever made, with droning guitars and synthesizers, chilly bass lines, stentorian vocals and drums that sound as if they're steadily beating out the rhythm of doom. And that's not even considering the lyrics, which are about singer Ian Curtis' failing marriage and how he suffered from epilepsy. (Curtis hanged himself on May 18th, 1980, at the age of twenty-three — the rest of the band regrouped as New Order; see No. 357.) Though Joy Division fully earned their reputation as England's most harrowing punk band, they weren't always gloomy; on trips from Manchester to London, they'd pass the time by mooning other cars.

157 | Captain Fantastic and the Brown Dirt Cowboy

ELTON JOHN
MCA 1975

Bernie Taupin, John's lyricist, wanted to make a self-mythologizing album about his and John's rise to fame. The ballad "Someone Saved My Life Tonight," for example, was about a night when Taupin stopped John from committing suicide with a gas oven. While Taupin sweated over every line, his songwriting partner dashed off the music on a luxury ocean liner. "I'd tried to book the ship's music room, but an opera singer had it for the whole five days," John said. "The only time she wasn't there was when she scoffed her lunch for two hours. So every lunchtime I'd nip in there and grab the piano."

158 Alive

KISS
UNIVERSAL 1975

"We wanted to put out a souvenir, almost like when you go to the circus," said Kiss lead singer Paul Stanley. "I really enjoy myself onstage: prancing around, shaking my ass, shaking my head, playing the guitar between my legs. I enjoy it as much as the audience. Basically, I am entertaining myself up there." This double live album, recorded largely in Detroit (with some bonus material from Iowa, New Jersey and Ohio, plus a whole bunch of studio overdubs), was the breakthrough record for Kiss, with exuberant versions of "Strutter" and "Rock & Roll All Nite," plus a classic litany of alcohol choices in the intro to "Cold Gin."

159 Electric Warrior

T. REX
REPRISE 1971

"A successful, hit rock & roll record is a spell," T. Rex leader Marc Bolan told ROLLING STONE. And so, muttering "eye of Bowie, toe of Slade," Bolan cast a spell over all of England. He took his Tolkienesque hippie music and gave it a glammed-out Chuck Berry update on sexy singles like "Bang a Gong (Get It On)"; this was rock that thrusted, quivered and recklessly employed metaphors equating cars with sex ("You got a hubcap diamond star halo"). He outdid himself with "Jeepster," an entire song on the topic, vibrating with lust, a shuffling beat, lots of guitar and the sound of Bolan stomping on the studio floor.

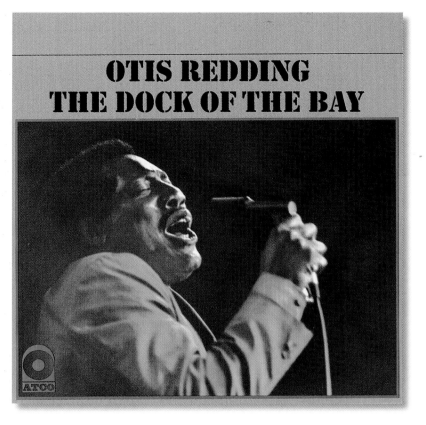

160 | The Dock of the Bay

OTIS REDDING
ATLANTIC 1968

On December 6th, 1967, Redding recorded "(Sittin' on) The Dock of the Bay," an experiment in "soul folk" influenced by the enthusiastic reception he'd gotten from the rock audience at the Monterey Pop Festival the previous June. Four days later, he was dead, when a plane he'd chartered went down over a Wisconsin lake. "Dock of the Bay" went on to become his biggest hit, a pop and R&B Number One. Guitarist Steve Cropper assembled this collection using unreleased sessions. So strong was Redding's output that both *Dock of the Bay* and the latter posthumous set, *The Immortal Otis Redding,* rank as essential soul albums.

161 | OK Computer

RADIOHEAD
CAPITOL 1997

Radiohead recorded their third album in the mansion of actress Jane Seymour while she was filming *Dr. Quinn, Medicine Woman. OK* is where the band began pulling at its sound like taffy, seeing what happened, not worrying if it was still "rock." What resulted is a slow, haunting album with unforgettable tracks such as "Karma Police." Guitarist Jonny Greenwood said, "I got very excited at the prospect of doing string parts that didn't sound like 'Eleanor Rigby,' which is what all string parts have sounded like for the past thirty years. . . . We used violins to make frightening white-noise stuff, like the last chord of 'Climbing Up the Walls.'"

162 | 1999
PRINCE
WARNER BROS. 1982

"I didn't want to do a double album," Prince said, "but I just kept on writing. Of course, I'm not one for editing." The second half of 1999 is just exceptional sex-obsessed dance music; the first half is the best fusion of rock and funk achieved to that date, and it lays out the blueprint for Prince's next decade. Except for a few background hand claps and vocals, Prince plays most every instrument himself and creates a relentless, irresistible musical sequence of apocalypse ("1999") and the raunchy sex that he proposes as the only possible response – "Little Red Corvette," "Let's Pretend We're Married," "Delirious" and, well, just about every other song on the album.

163 | Heart Like a Wheel
LINDA RONSTADT
CAPITOL 1974

"There's no way that I can be objective and say one album is better than another," Ronstadt told ROLLING STONE in 1978. "I never listen to them anyway." But millions of other people did, especially to this record, where she displays her vocal flexibility and rock grit on "You're No Good" and a country twang on a cover of Hank Williams Sr.'s "I Can't Help It (If I'm Still in Love With You)." Collaborating with producer Peter Asher, Ronstadt blends quality oldies (the Everly Brothers' "When Will I Be Loved?") and hip songwriters of her era (Lowell George, Anna McGarrigle), gracing each composition with her golden voice.

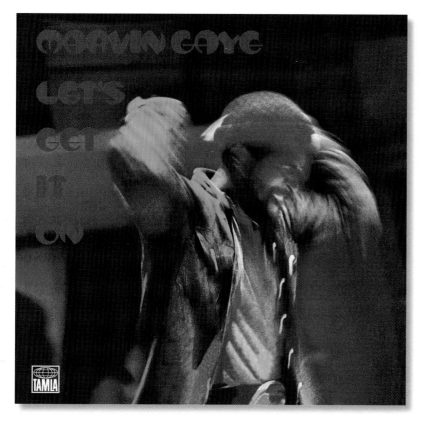

"I think sex is great. I think sex is sex and love is love. I think they can be and are separated. I think they are beautiful together, but they are two separate things."
(RS 158, APRIL 11TH, 1974)

164 | Let's Get It On

MARVIN GAYE
MOTOWN 1973

"I mumble things into the microphone," Gaye said. "I don't even know what I'm saying, and I don't even try to figure it out. If I try, it doesn't work. If I relax, those mumbles will finally turn into words. It's a slow, evolving process, something like the way a flower grows." On this album, those words turn into meditations on the gap between sex and love and how to reconcile them – an adult version of the Motown tunes Gaye had built his career on. Songs like "Just to Keep You Satisfied" and "You Sure Love to Ball" are some of the most gorgeous music of Gaye's career, resplendent with sweet strings and his clear-throated, non-mumbled crooning.

165 Imperial Bedroom

ELVIS COSTELLO AND THE ATTRACTIONS
COLUMBIA 1982

"I was trying to think or feel my way out of a defeated and exhausted frame of mind to something more glorious," Costello said of his seventh album. With his lyrics about marital stress growing more complex (this was his first album to include a lyric sheet), he decided that their sound should reflect that same ambition. So he enlisted producer Geoff Emerick – the engineer on *Sgt. Pepper's Lonely Hearts Club Band* – and experimented with what was his idea of an adult sonic palette: accordions, Mellotron, horns and whatever else struck his fancy. Not all of the songs reveal their charms quickly, but "Man Out of Time" is immediately soaring and sorrowful.

166 Master of Puppets

METALLICA
ELEKTRA 1986

Metallica's third album has a lyrical theme: manipulation. "It deals pretty much with drugs," singer-guitarist James Hetfield said. "Instead of you controlling what you're taking and doing, it's drugs controlling you." It also has a sonic theme: really loud guitars, played fast, with no regard for the hair metal that was then dominating the airwaves. When the band slows down on "Welcome Home (Sanitarium)," it just emphasizes the unrelenting nature of the rest of the songs. Recorded during three months in Copenhagen, *Master of Puppets* was bassist Cliff Burton's last album with Metallica; he died in September 1986, when the band's bus crashed.

"Revenge and guilt are the only emotions I know about and that I know I can feel. Love? I dunno what it means really, and it doesn't exist in my songs."

(RS 251, NOVEMBER 3RD, 1977)

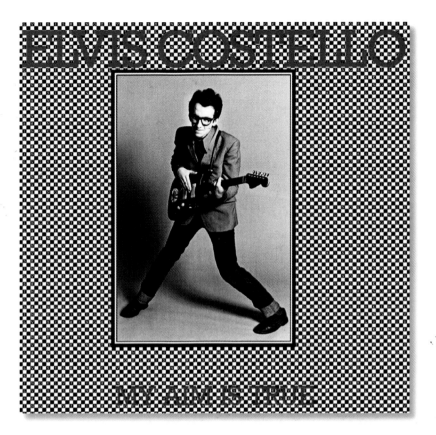

ELVIS COSTELLO

MY AIM IS TRUE

167 | My Aim Is True

ELVIS COSTELLO
COLUMBIA 1977

Costello on the fuel for his debut: "I spent a lot of time with just a big jar of instant coffee and the first Clash album [see No. 78], listening to it over and over." The music doesn't have the savage attack of the Clash – it's more pub rock than punk rock – but the songs are full of punk's verbal bite, particularly "Waiting for the End of the World" ("Dear Lord, I sincerely hope you're coming/'Cause you really started something"). The album's opening lines – "Now that your picture's in the paper being rhythmically admired" – and the poisoned-valentine ballad "Alison" established Costello as one of the sharpest, and nastiest, lyricists of his generation.

168 | Exodus
BOB MARLEY AND THE WAILERS
ISLAND 1977

As the title suggests, this album wasn't recorded in Jamaica; after Marley took a bullet in a 1976 assassination attempt, he relocated the Wailers to London. But tracks such as "Jammin'" are still suffused with the deep essence of reggae and life at home. "Three Little Birds," for example, had been written on the back step of Marley's home in Kingston, where he would sit and smoke herb. Each time Marley rolled a spliff, he would discard the seeds – and the birds of the song's title would pick them up. "The music have a purpose," Marley said, and his spiritual intent was never clearer than on the anthem "One Love," with its message of redemption and revolution.

169 | Live at Leeds
THE WHO
MCA 1970

Faced with the impossible task of following up the grand statement of *Tommy* [see No. 97], the Who just cranked up their amps. Rather than wade through eighty hours of American shows for a live album, Pete Townshend claimed he burned those tapes "in a huge bonfire" and selected a concert at Leeds University in England. *Live at Leeds* is a warts-and-all live album, including an accidental clunking sound on "My Generation." There's no finesse, just the pure power of a band able to play as loud as it wants to. When the Who blew up Eddie Cochran's "Summertime Blues" to Godzilla-like proportions, they invented Seventies arena rock.

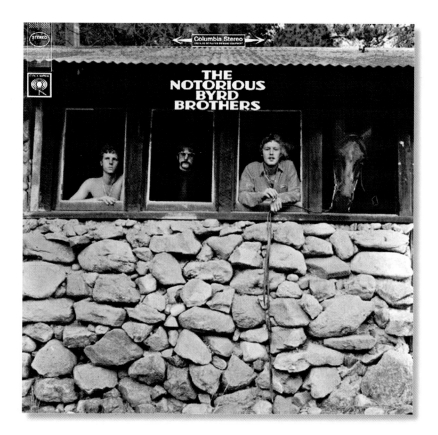

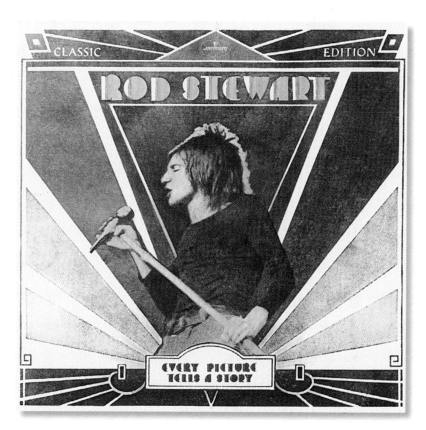

170 | The Notorious Byrd Brothers

THE BYRDS
COLUMBIA 1968

While recording their fifth album, Byrds guitarist David Crosby was fired and drummer Michael Clarke quit. According to legend, for the album-cover photo, the band erased Crosby's face – and replaced him with a horse. But despite the internal drama, the Byrds made *Notorious* a warm, gentle comedown for Sixties children facing up to the morning after the Summer of Love. The sound is melancholic but friendly, blending spacey studio effects and Moog synthesizers with guitars, strings and horns to build the elegiac mood of "Draft Morning" and "Goin' Back" as well as the optimistic surge of "Dolphin's Smile" and "Natural Harmony."

171 | Every Picture Tells a Story

ROD STEWART
MERCURY 1971

"We had no preconceived ideas of what we were going to do," Stewart said. "We would have a few drinks and strum away and play." With a first-class band of drinking buddies (including guitarist Ron Wood and drummer Mickey Waller), Stewart made a loose, warm, compassionate album, rocking hard with mostly acoustic instruments. "Mandolin Wind" was his moving ballad of a country couple toughing out a long winter on the farm; the title tune was a hilarious goof. But Stewart scored his first Number One hit with "Maggie May," his autobiographical tale of a young stud getting kicked in the head by an older lady.

Natural woman, Queen of Soul: Franklin in '68

Lady Soul

ARETHA FRANKLIN

In reminiscing about her 1968 album *Lady Soul*, Aretha Franklin proves that when it comes to respect, she can give as good as she can get. The singer first praises the "fabulous" work of producer Jerry Wexler, arranger Arif Mardin and engineer Tom Dowd, the triad who helped polish the gospel-tinged, sexually charged style that distinguished Franklin's groundbreaking R&B recordings during her tenure at Atlantic Records, in the late Sixties and Seventies. Next she acknowledges the songwriters showcased on the album – particularly Don Covay, who contributed "Chain of Fools," and Carole King, whose ballad "(You Make Me Feel Like) A Natural Woman" (co-written with Wexler and Gerry Goffin) appealed to Franklin on a number of levels. "[The lyrics] were typical of my personal experience," Franklin says. "It wasn't about a women's lib; it was just what I needed to say. And the song has a great melody. I wish I had the copyright!"

But, of course, as Mardin points out, most of the credit for *Lady Soul* belongs to Lady Soul herself. "For me, coming from Europe and from a jazz background, those album sessions were like going to school – to Aretha Franklin's University of Soul, you might say – and learning from one of the greatest singers ever," says the Turkish-born Mardin, who has also worked with Franklin as a producer during her post-Atlantic years. Mardin describes Franklin as having been "very nice, shy and unassuming" during the *Lady Soul* sessions but adds that the young diva never hesitated to assert her authority in the creative process. "Her piano playing was one of the most important aspects," Mardin says. "She always knew her tempo and her key, and she always had the arrangement down. She was the source; we would all work around her."

The results speak for themselves. More than thirty-five years after its release, *Lady Soul* still glistens, from Franklin's rousing cover of Curtis Mayfield's "People Get Ready" to "Ain't No Way," the deliriously sensual closing song (penned by Franklin's late sister, Carolyn). "It was something that happens very rarely," Mardin says. "That's why I'm in this business – so that I can have times like those."

172 | **Something/ Anything?**

TODD RUNDGREN
RHINO 1972

"I'm probably the whitest singer in the world," Rundgren told ROLLING STONE in 1972. "I have no 'soul' in the usual sense – but I can do this great feminine falsetto." On this tour-de-force double album, Rundgren employs that falsetto on two great singles: the hard-rocking "I Saw the Light" and the pop-soul ballad "Hello It's Me." For the rest of the album, he demonstrates his complete command of the studio, playing almost all the instruments himself, experimenting with a kaleidoscope of rock genres and even delivering a monologue on what poorly made records sound like, complete with examples of hiss and hum.

173 | **Desire**

BOB DYLAN
COLUMBIA 1976

Soon after completing *Blood on the Tracks* [see No. 16], Dylan started work on *Desire*, with lyrical input from collaborator Jacques Levy. In typical Dylan style, the recording was mostly bashed out in one all-night New York session, fueled in part by tequila. Guest singer Emmylou Harris didn't even get to rehearse her harmony vocals. The most intense moment came at the end, when Dylan struck up a new song he hadn't sung for the band before. As his wife, Sara, sat listening in the studio, Dylan sang "Sara," his heartbroken account of their crumbling marriage. It was the first time she heard the song – and that take ended up on the album.

174 | **Close to You**

THE CARPENTERS
A&M 1970

Karen Carpenter sang and drummed; her brother Richard arranged their lush music. Both contributed to their thoroughly wholesome image. "It's like we're Pat Boone, only a little cleaner," Richard lamented to ROLLING STONE in 1974. "As if all we do all day is drink milk, eat apple pie and take showers. I don't even like milk." *Close to You*, their second album, has two of their best ballads: "Close to You" and "We've Only Just Begun." In the early Seventies, the Carpenters epitomized the mainstream, but now their influence is audible in cooler, slightly less-clean indie bands: the Cardigans, Stereolab and "chamber pop" acts such as Belle and Sebastian.

175 | **Rocks**

AEROSMITH
COLUMBIA 1976

After *Toys in the Attic* proved that Aerosmith were more than a Stones caricature, the band flexed its muscles on the boastfully (and aptly) named *Rocks*, a buffalo stampede of rave-ups and boogies. During one typically madcap session, bassist Tom Hamilton and guitarist Joe Perry switched instruments on "Sick As a Dog"; when they came to the song's instrumental outro, Perry flipped the bass to singer Steven Tyler, grabbed his guitar and joined Hamilton and rhythm guitarist Brad Whitford for the final salvo. "We could have done it a lot easier by overdubbing," Perry admitted. "It wouldn't have had the same feel, though."

"You can get so frustrated in life that you just want to jump out the window. Funk tells you, 'Go ahead, man, but nobody gonna pay you any attention if you do.' It's a way of getting out of that bind you get in, mentally, physically."

GEORGE CLINTON
(RS 587 SEPTEMBER 20TH, 1990)

176 | One Nation Under a Groove

FUNKADELIC
WARNER BROS. 1978

When *One Nation* came out, Parliament Funkadelic ringleader George Clinton compared his visionary music with mainstream black pop: "James Brown, Jimi, Sly and ourselves took the whole other thing so far anyway that most of 'em ain't nowhere near catching up yet." But the public made *One Nation* Funkadelic's first million-seller, meaning a million people got down not just to the title track and to guitar-heavy make-out soul like "Into You," but to scatological philosophizing like "The Doo Doo Chasers," in which the Funk Mob cooks up "A musical bowel movement/Designed to rid you of moral diarrhea." As the man once said, free your ass and your mind will follow.

CURTIS MAYFIELD & *The Impressions*

THE ANTHOLOGY
1961 - 1977

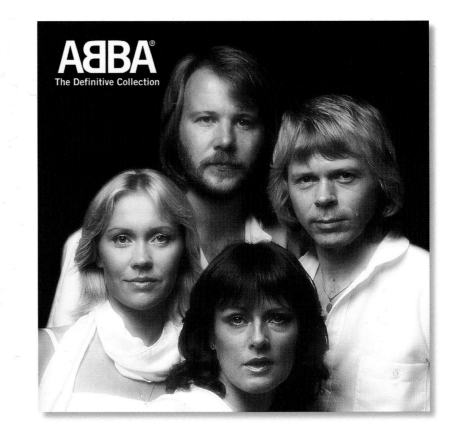

177 | The Anthology 1961-1977

CURTIS MAYFIELD AND THE IMPRESSIONS
MCA 1992

Mayfield was Professor Soul, teaching sociocultural awareness while dispensing hard lessons and tough love. Starting with the gospel-rooted vocal group the Impressions, he crafted romantic ballads ("Gypsy Woman"), inspirational anthems ("People Get Ready"), orchestrated funk workouts ("Move On Up") and edgy street narratives ("Superfly"), all of which are collected here. When Mayfield died in 1999 — nine years after being paralyzed in a stage accident — his manager, Marv Heiman, offered this epitaph: "He wanted people to think about themselves and the world around them, making this a better place for everyone to live." Amen.

178 | The Definitive Collection

ABBA
UNIVERSAL 2001

Pete Townshend once said, "I remember hearing 'S.O.S.' on the radio in the States and realizing that it was Abba. But it was too late, because I was already transported by it." These Swedish pop stars became the world's biggest group in the 1970s, with a streak of Nordic despair under the sparkly melodies. Agnetha Faltskog and Frida Lyngstad were the bewitching frontwomen in the sequinned pantsuits; their husbands Björn Ulvaeus and Benny Andersson wrote global hits like the joyful "Dancing Queen," the double-divorce drama "Knowing Me, Knowing You" and their haunting farewell, "Thank You for the Music."

179 | The Rolling Stones, Now!

THE ROLLING STONES
ABKCO 1965

As the Stones were taking London by storm with their insouciant refraction of R&B, the *Daily Mail* noted their "doorstep mouths, pallid cheeks and unkempt hair" – all of which would later become the most copied image in rock. A charming exuberance pervades *Now!*, the Stones' third U.S. release, with its hot-rod takes on Chuck Berry, Bo Diddley, Willie Dixon and Muddy Waters, plus – at the urging of manager-producer-guru Andrew Loog Oldham – four attempts at re-creating the stateside flava on their own compositions, the best of which, "Heart of Stone," introduces the crucial Stones element of menace into the mix.

180 | Natty Dread

BOB MARLEY AND THE WAILERS
ISLAND 1974

Natty Dread was the first Wailers album to give Marley top billing, and Marley's first without original Wailers Peter Tosh and Bunny Livingston. This was rebel music – from the opening "Lively Up Yourself" (a call to dance to the reggae beat or take to the streets, depending on how you looked at it) to "Them Belly Full (But We Hungry)," which warned that "a hungry mob is an angry mob." "No Woman, No Cry" was a compassionate gospel-flavored song about not giving up hope. Marley co-credited the song to Vincent Ford – a friend who'd given him a place to live years before and who ran a backyard soup kitchen in Kingston – to keep his operation afloat.

181 | Fleetwood Mac

FLEETWOOD MAC
WARNER BROS. 1975

Mick Fleetwood, John McVie and his missus, Christine, had been through myriad lineups before finding California couple Lindsey Buckingham and Stevie Nicks. Surmounting "cultural differences" (Buckingham's description), the group clicked, generating big radio songs such as "Say You Love Me" and "Rhiannon," and Buckingham contributed solid guitar work, arrangements and vocals that bridged the wildly divergent styles of McVie and Nicks. "We would get to know one another as friends only to a certain point," Buckingham remarked. But that didn't prevent them from going on to record 1977's *Rumours* [see No. 26], one of the biggest records ever.

182 | Red Headed Stranger

WILLIE NELSON
COLUMBIA 1975

Newly signed to Columbia, Nelson was feeling ambitious. "It was the first time I had 'artistic control,'" he recalled. "So I thought I would just start writing." Nelson had penned the song "Red Headed Stranger" years before; on a drive back to Austin after a Colorado ski trip, he fleshed out the yarn – his wife, Connie, writing down the lyrics as they came out of his mouth. He kept the arrangements extremely spare, in sharp contrast to the gussied-up music coming out of Nashville at the time. The songs locked together to tell a riveting and heartfelt multitrack tale of murder and infidelity, and the concept album became one of Nelson's biggest hits.

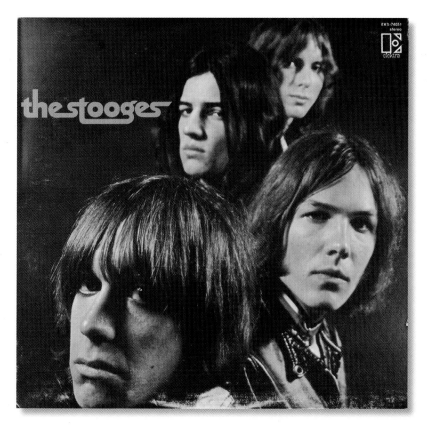

183 | The Stooges

THE STOOGES
ELEKTRA 1969

Fueled by "a little marijuana and a lotta alienation," Michigan's Stooges gave the lie to hippie idealism, playing with a savagery that unsettled even the most blasé clubgoers. The band was signed to Elektra, despite label head Jac Holzman's misgivings that "the Stooges could barely play their instruments. How were we going to get this on record?" Ex-Velvet Underground member John Cale produced a primitive debut wherein, amid Ron Asheton's wah-wah blurts, Iggy Stooge (né James Osterberg) snarled seminal punk classics such as "I Wanna Be Your Dog," "No Fun" and "1969." The record stiffed, but it undeniably gave birth to punk rock.

"The music drives me into a peak freak. I can't feel any pain or realize what goes on around me. I'm just feeling the music and when I dive into a sea of people, it is the feeling of the music, the mood. Nobody ever knows how it is going to end up."
IGGY POP
(RS 55, APRIL 2ND, 1970)

184 | Fresh

SLY AND THE FAMILY STONE
EPIC 1973

As the Seventies unfurled, Sly Stone became progressively flakier, frequently disappointing fans at his concerts by keeping them waiting . . . all night. "Sometimes you don't feel your soul at 7:30," he explained. Happily, the increasingly dissolute soul pioneer had one more ace up his sleeve: the intoxicating "If You Want Me to Stay," in which he holed up in the basement of his vocal range while a fidgety bass line kept running up and down the stairs. This burst of residual genius was surrounded by various idiosyncratic gestures, the oddest of which was a ragged take on Doris Day's "Que Sera, Sera." *Fresh* would be Stone's last Top Ten album.

185 | So

PETER GABRIEL
GEFFEN 1986

Gabriel got funky on the 1982 single "Shock the Monkey," and it took him four years to follow up the hit. The similarly visceral "Sledgehammer" slammed *So* into the mainstream, and its hold on radio and MTV deepened with the upbeat "Big Time," the gothic love ballad "In Your Eyes" (beautifully employed by filmmaker Cameron Crowe in *Say Anything*) and the inspirational "Don't Give Up," a duet with Brit art thrush Kate Bush, who was shown locked in a five-minute embrace with Gabriel in the video. Said his wife, Jill, of a marriage that had barely survived a series of dual affairs, "I managed to punish him. He managed to punish me better."

For $6,000, they made a masterpiece: Johnny, Tommy, Joey, Dee Dee (from left) in London.

Ramones

RAMONES

Boston, Styx, Toto – do you remember we did a show with Toto?" Joey Ramone asked in a 1997 interview with the band, rolling his eyes. The hostile musical environment into which the Ramones released their debut still gave him chills. "It was 1976, the height of disco and corporate rock, and we were like nobody else." It was because of that difference that *Ramones* became a Molotov cocktail that set the nascent British punk scene ablaze. "'Judy Is a Punk' mentioned punk before anyone," said Tommy Erdelyi, a.k.a. Tommy Ramone, the band's original drummer. "And Joey sang with a cockney accent because he loved English bands like Herman's Hermits. The funny thing is, when English groups like the Clash started, they all sang with cockney accents. Joey from Queens [N.Y.] initiated cockney singing in punk rock!"

Ramones' call to arms began with its grainy cover photo. Posed in front of a Lower East Side tenement, the band members offered an affront to the bell-bottomed pretty-boy rockers of the day. But the cover was scarcely preparation for the sonic violence inside – when the band recorded a real chain saw for the intro to "Chain Saw," it could barely be differentiated from Johnny Ramone's hammering guitar.

Ramones was recorded at Plaza Sound, a now-defunct studio on the eighth floor of Radio City Music Hall that featured a Wurlitzer pipe organ, a sprawling Rockettes rehearsal room and art-deco decor "straight out of a Shirley Temple movie," said Erdelyi. Still, he remembered less-than-ideal conditions: "We recorded everything with $50 guitars in less than a week, for $6,000! It was absurd!" While that added to the group's rough aesthetic, he felt that it caused the album's sonic complexity to be overlooked. "We experimented with what we called pingpong stereo," Erdelyi said. "It's like early Beatles or Cream records, where guitar is in one channel, bass is in the other, the drums are in the middle, and it sounds bizarre. That's one of the things that makes *Ramones* sound…"

"Schizophrenic?" asked Joey.

A junkyard assemblage of Beach Boys' bubblegum, Stooges-style guitar mayhem and numbing, Andy Warhol-influenced repetition, the Ramones' scavenger approach remains most evident in the sing-along chorus to "Blitzkrieg Bop." "There was this line from Rufus Thomas' 'Walking the Dog' that went: 'Hi-ho's nipped her toes,'" Erdelyi remembered. "But instead of 'hi-ho,' I said, 'Hey-ho.'" Calling this mongrel mix "urban roots music," Erdelyi knew the Ramones were ahead of their time — just not how far ahead. "When we went into the studio, we knew what we were doing was important," he said. "What we didn't know was that we were gonna change [music] – that we'd still be imitated twenty years later."

"Those were really good days. Great people. Everybody in that group was a genius at what they did. That was a great group, man. There'll never be another Buffalo Springfield. Never."

NEIL YOUNG
(RS 193, AUGUST 14TH, 1975)

186 Buffalo Springfield Again

BUFFALO SPRINGFIELD
ATCO 1967

Buffalo Springfield boasted three major songwriters: Stephen Stills, Neil Young and Richie Furay. That's one reason they were already splitting apart when they made their second record (another was Young's distaste for "groupies, drugs, shit"). *Again* harnesses masterful L.A. folk rock (Stills' "Bluebird"), pioneering country rock (Furay's "Child's Claim to Fame") and raw R&B rock (Young's "Mr. Soul"). It ends with Young's suitelike "Broken Arrow," a brief, prescient hint of how brilliant and odd his solo career would later be. He called the song "the end of something – and the beginning." Less than a year later, the band called it quits.

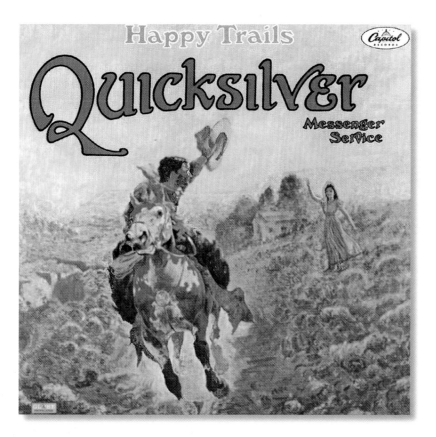

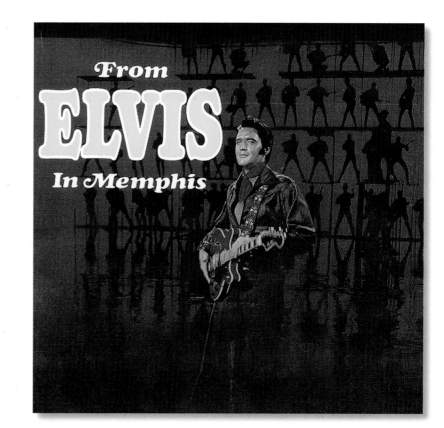

187 | Happy Trails

QUICKSILVER MESSENGER SERVICE
CAPITOL 1969

If you weren't there, then this just might be the next best thing: the definitive live recording of the mid-Sixties San Francisco psychedelic-ballroom experience. Mostly taped at the two Fillmores, in San Francisco and New York, Quicksilver Messenger Service's second album captures twin guitarists John Cipollina and Gary Duncan in high, bright flight, making rare magic from a couple of old Bo Diddley numbers ("Mona," "Who Do You Love?"), while the gorgeous, composed intricacies of "Maiden of the Cancer Moon" and the acid-flamenco studio epic "Calvary" prove that psychedelia was about much more than just tripping out.

188 | From Elvis in Memphis

ELVIS PRESLEY
RCA VICTOR 1969

"I had to leave town for a little while," Presley sings in the first track. Along with his 1968 TV special, this record announced he was back. Cut at Chips Moman's American Studios, it is little short of astounding. With help from a crack crew of Memphis musicians, Presley masterfully tackles quality material from country ("I'm Movin' On"), gospel ("Long Black Limousine"), soul ("Only the Strong Survive") and pop ("Any Day Now") as well as message songs ("In the Ghetto"). The same sessions also yielded another album, *Back in Memphis*, as well as one of Presley's greatest singles, the towering pop-soul masterpiece "Suspicious Minds."

189 | Fun House

THE STOOGES
ELEKTRA 1970

With garage-savvy ex-Kingsmen keyboardist Don Gallucci producing their second album, the Stooges made their most fully realized effort, despite their collective drug problems. "We had a certain purity of intention," Iggy Pop asserted. "I don't think we did ever get it from the drugs. I think they killed things." They couldn't kill what he has called the relentless "troglodyte groove" the band had on *Fun House*. "I stick it deep inside," Iggy growls on "Loose," one of the album's typically confrontational tracks. Later, on "1970," he insisted, ad infinitum, "I feel all right," and there's no question you wouldn't want any of whatever he was on.

190 | The Gilded Palace of Sin

THE FLYING BURRITO BROTHERS
A&M 1969

"We're a rock & roll band that sounds like a country band," Gram Parsons said of the Burritos, whose first album was an obscure Sixties masterpiece that drew the blueprint for both Seventies country rock and today's alt-country. Parsons and Chris Hillman formed the Burritos after they both quit the Byrds; in many ways, *Gilded Palace* picks up where the Byrds' *Sweetheart of the Rodeo* left off. Together, the mercurial Parsons and the levelheaded Hillman concocted a crazily coherent statement of irony-fueled hillbilly anthems, inventive covers and achingly beautiful two-part harmonies, all underscored by Sneaky Pete Kleinow's radical pedal-steel guitar.

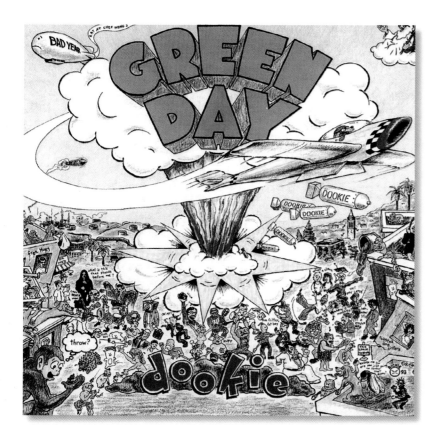

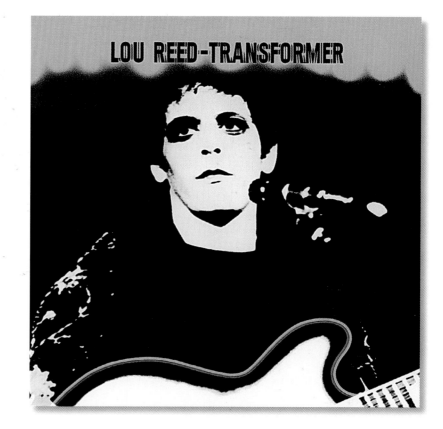

191 **Dookie**

GREEN DAY
REPRISE 1994

The album that jump-started the Nineties punk-pop revival. The skittish *Dookie* was recorded in little more than three weeks, and singer-guitarist Billy Joe Armstrong blazed through all the vocals in two days. "Right from getting the drum sound, everything seemed to click," their A&R man (and *Dookie* producer) Rob Cavallo marveled. "Click" is indeed the operative word here, also describing Billy Joe's airtight, three-minute shots like "Welcome to Paradise" and "Basket Case." But nowhere did everything click better than on the infectious smash "Longview" – which Armstrong described as "cheap self-therapy from watching too much TV."

192 **Transformer**

LOU REED
RCA 1972

David Bowie counted the former Velvet Underground leader as a major inspiration – and paid back the debt by producing *Transformer*. The album had glam flash courtesy of *Ziggy Stardust* guitarist Mick Ronson as well as Reed's biggest hit, "Walk on the Wild Side" – which brought drag queens and hustlers into the Top Twenty – and the exquisite ballad "Perfect Day." It was Reed's first producer, VU impresario Andy Warhol, who inspired the lead cut when he suggested "Vicious" as a song title. "You know, like, 'Vicious/You hit me with a flower,'" Warhol elaborated. Reed took him at his word, penning the song and cribbing the lines verbatim.

193 Blues Breakers

JOHN MAYALL WITH ERIC CLAPTON
DERAM/UNIVERSAL 1966

The Blues Breakers became one of London's hottest acts as soon as ex-Yardbird Clapton arrived, but that wasn't what he'd bargained for. "He just wanted to play his guitar," Mayall remembered. As things turned out, Clapton's solos on *Blues Breakers* were to inspire his cult; this is when "Clapton Is God" graffiti first started to appear in London, and this record shows why. Along with the band's expert renderings of Freddie King's "Hideaway" and Robert Johnson's "Ramblin' on My Mind," the LP contains a nutty take on Ray Charles' "What'd I Say," whose long drum solo gave Clapton a preview of what he'd soon experience in Cream.

194 Nuggets: Original Artyfacts From the First Psychedelic Era, 1965-1968

VARIOUS ARTISTS
RHINO 1972

This collection of Sixties garage rock, compiled by rock critic and soon-to-be Patti Smith guitarist Lenny Kaye, became a touchstone for Seventies punks and, years later, for the aftershock of post-punk. The twenty-seven-track, two-LP set was a radical idea in 1972: While rock was getting bigger, *Nuggets* established a new canon out of forgotten AM-radio hits – brutally simple singles like the Standells' "Dirty Water," the Shadows of Knight's "Oh Yeah!" and the Count Five's "Psychotic Reaction." Rhino expanded *Nuggets* into a sprawling four-CD box in 1998.

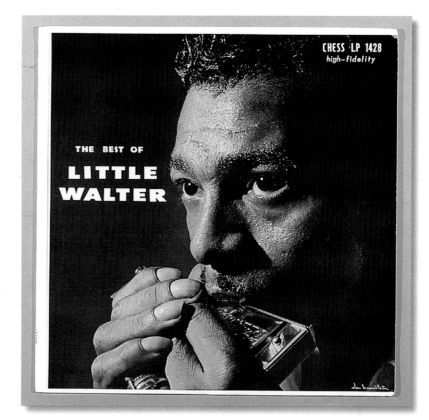

195 | Murmur

R.E.M.
A&M 1983

"We wanted to have this kind of timeless record," guitarist Peter Buck said of R.E.M.'s debut, and this "technically limited" band (according to producer Don Dixon) did just that. Buck was a rock scholar who had worked in a record store; singer Michael Stipe unspooled his lyrics as if they constituted some new secret language. *Murmur* is full of ringing guitar and mystery. The lyrics and the melodies seem buried, almost subliminal, and even the songs with something approximating hooks, such as "Radio Free Europe," resist clarity. *Murmur* was a founding document of alternative rock, released just as Gen X was heading off to college.

196 | The Best Of

LITTLE WALTER
CHESS 1964

While the other players in Muddy Waters' band were electrifying the blues, Little Walter was doing something unprecedented. Holding his harmonica and a microphone in his cupped hands, Walter attacked the instrument with the authority of the bop sax players who'd influenced him, bringing a dynamic new sound to Chicago blues. In 1952, after Walter's own "Juke" topped the R&B charts, he started his own group. Walter was a disciplined musician, but he had less control of his personal life. "He was hellacious when he drank," said Lazy Lester Johnson. Walter died at thirty-seven after suffering severe head injuries in a street fight.

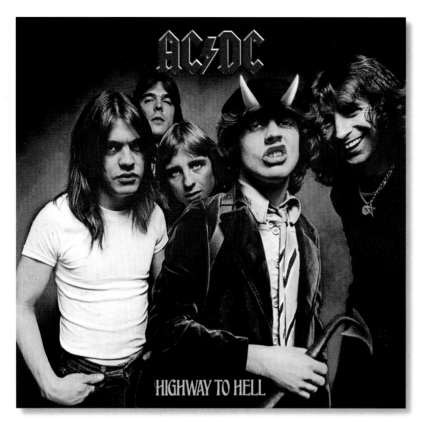

197 Highway to Hell

AC/DC
EPIC 1979

Upon being promoted from the band's driver to its lead singer, Bon Scott immediately came up with his singular formula for recording vocals: He downed half a bottle of bourbon, chased it with some weed and a fat rail of blow, and proclaimed, "I'm ready." Then he got the take. Scott was a force of nature, and by AC/DC's fourth studio album, he and guitarist Angus Young had become an explosive one-two punch. "You'd need several volumes of Britannica," Young noted, "just to chronicle what Bon got up to in one day." Inevitably, Scott's wicked ways caught up with him, and he was dead six months after *Highway*'s release.

198 The Downward Spiral

NINE INCH NAILS
NOTHING/INTERSCOPE 1994

"When I rented the place, I didn't realize it was that house," claimed NIN's Trent Reznor about recording *Spiral* in the one-time home of Manson-family victim Sharon Tate. Despite "a million electrical disturbances," Reznor made the most successful album of his career – a cohesive, willful and overpowering meditation on the central theme running through all of NIN's videos, live shows, music and lyrics: control. While *Spiral* has its share of Reznor's trademark industrial corrosiveness, it's balanced by the tentatively hopeful (and intensely personal) "Hurt" and soundscapes inspired by David Bowie's *Low*.

199 | Parsley, Sage, Rosemary and Thyme

SIMON AND GARFUNKEL
COLUMBIA 1966

Simon and Garfunkel's third album – the first Columbia album to feature 8-track recording – yielded uptempo hits such as "The 59th Street Bridge Song." But the real gems are such poetic reveries as the strings-laden "Dangling Conversation" and the ballad "For Emily, Wherever I May Find Her," which features Art Garfunkel singing solo. "For Emily" summons, at least partly, the spirit of Emily Dickinson, while "Dangling Conversation" has been compared to T.S. Eliot's "The Love Song of J. Alfred Prufrock," though Paul Simon called it an attempt to make the theme of "The Sound of Silence" more personal.

200 | Bad

MICHAEL JACKSON
EPIC 1987

Excessive? Michael Jackson? After *Thriller* turned him into an international pop phenomenon, he spent $2 million and two years of work on the follow-up. The title song came with a seventeen-minute video by Martin Scorcese that cost another $2 million. *Bad* gave Jackson more hits to add to his collection: "I Just Can't Stop Loving You," "Bad," "The Way You Make Me Feel" and "Man in the Mirror." He also began to vent some of his darker emotions in public, raging against treacherous women in the violent fantasies of "Smooth Criminal" and the paranoia of "Dirty Diana." Before long, Jackson had retreated to the safety of the Neverland ranch.

201 | Wheels of Fire

CREAM
POLYDOR 1968

Half studio album, half live album, Wheels of Fire not only has the definitive Cream tune – "White Room" – but it is also incontrovertible proof of Eric Clapton's skill. "Crossroads," a live reworking of Robert Johnson's blues classic, features one of the most blazing guitar solos ever recorded.

202 | Dirty Mind

PRINCE
WARNER BROS. 1980

A mix of slinky funk, synth-driven rock, jittery pop and sexual innuendo, *Dirty Mind* hinted where Prince was headed. It includes the world's merriest done-me-wrong song, "When You Were Mine," and the incest ditty "Sister." "I wasn't being deliberately provocative," Prince said. "I was being deliberately me."

203 | Abraxas

SANTANA
DIGITAL SOUND 1970

"Black Magic Woman," the Top Five hit from *Abraxas*, is definitive Santana: Afro-Latin grooves and piercing lyrical psychedelic blues guitar. It was a cover of a Fleetwood Mac song written by one of Carlos Santana's guitar heroes, Peter Green. The album's other hit was also a cover: Tito Puente's "Oye Como Va."

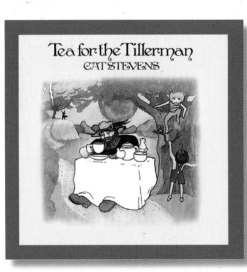

204 | Tea for the Tillerman

CAT STEVENS
A&M 1970

With its chamber-pop arrangements, *Tea for the Tillerman* is one of the British folkie's most ambitious albums. Both the hit single "Wild World" and the bleak ballad "Hard-Headed Woman" find him condemning his ex, Patti D'Arbanville – who later shacked up with Mick Jagger.

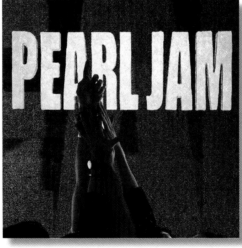

205 | Ten

PEARL JAM
EPIC 1991

When their debut came out, Pearl Jam were competing with Nirvana in a grunge popularity contest they were bound to lose. Yet *Ten* is a near-perfect record: Eddie Vedder's shaky, agonized growl and Mike McCready's wailing guitar solos on "Alive" and "Jeremy" push both songs to the brink and back again.

206 | Everybody Knows This Is Nowhere

NEIL YOUNG WITH CRAZY HORSE
WARNER BROS. 1969

Neil Young and Crazy Horse hadn't been together for more than eight weeks when they cut this album. It has the feel of a jam session conducted by master jammers, especially "Down by the River," "Cinnamon Girl" and "Cowgirl in the Sand."

Hit men: Lamont Dozier, Eddie and Bobby Holland (from left) writing another smash at Motown's Detroit studios in the mid-Sixties

Holland, Dozier, Holland

The "Motown sound" was largely the product of Eddie Holland, Lamont Dozier and Brian Holland. Working out of a cinder-block studio in the Hitsville offices, the songwriting and production trio wed R&B to pop in Number One singles such as "Reach Out, I'll Be There," by the Four Tops, and "Baby Love," by the Supremes. They were inducted into the Rock & Roll Hall of Fame in 1990.

How much arguing went on in your writing room at Motown?
Eddie Holland: I wanted to do "Where Did Our Love Go" with Mary [Wilson] singing lead, instead of Diana [Ross], because I thought Mary's voice was softer. But I was double-teamed by my brother and Lamont.
Were any of your songs a surprise hit?
EH: We weren't knocked out about "Baby I Need Your Loving." It sat around for six months before we gave it to the Four Tops.

Do you ever listen to your own songs?
EH: Never. Sometimes it took me two weeks to finish one lyric. After I was done, I didn't want to hear about it.
Brian Holland: I was driving in Vegas and the Supremes' "I Hear a Symphony" came on. I said, "Man, my brother wrote some lyrics!"
EH: Berry Gordy told me, "Eddie, you're a genius." I laughed and said, "After all these years, you acknowledge me."

207 | Wish You Were Here

PINK FLOYD
CAPITOL 1975

The Floyd's follow-up to *The Dark Side of the Moon* was another essay on everyday lunacy, dominated by the liquid-rock suite "Shine On You Crazy Diamond," a poignant allusion to errant ex-member Syd Barrett. "Have a Cigar" is a searing blast at the music biz, with the classic line, "Which one's Pink?"

208 | Crooked Rain, Crooked Rain

PAVEMENT
MATADOR 1994

Pavement's second album made love and rock & roll its great subjects, with bouncy pop songs, epic stretches of lyrical noise and "Range Life," a sweet country ballad that slagged the Smashing Pumpkins, then shifted to poignant longing for the right way to settle down.

209 | Tattoo You

THE ROLLING STONES
VIRGIN 1981

Tattoo You was lean, tough and bluesy – the Stones relying on their strengths, as if they'd matured into the kind of surefire bluesmen they'd idolized as kids. It spent nine weeks at Number One on the strength of "Start Me Up," in which Mick Jagger snuck the line "Girl, you'd make a dead man come" onto the radio.

210 | Proud Mary: The Best of Ike and Tina Turner

IKE AND TINA TURNER
EMI 1991

"Tina sounded like screaming dirt," the duo's first label boss once said. He meant it as a compliment. On early singles like "Fool in Love," she has wild power and raw vulnerability. Then come the rock & roll covers, the Seventies funk and "River Deep, Mountain High." Amazing.

TINA TURNER

"I loved it when it first came out. We had auditioned a girl and she had sung 'Proud Mary.' This is like eight months later, and Ike said, 'You know, I forgot all about that tune.' And I said, 'Let's do it, but let's change it.' So in the car Ike plays the guitar and we just sort of jam. And we just sort of broke into the black version of it."

(RS 93, OCTOBER 14TH, 1971)

211 | **New York Dolls**
NEW YORK DOLLS
MERCURY 1973

"Could you make it with Frankenstein?" they asked, not kidding. Glammed-out punkers the New York Dolls snatched riffs from Chuck Berry and Fats Domino and fattened them with loads of attitude and reverb. Produced by Todd Rundgren, songs like "Personality Crisis" and "Bad Girl" drip with sleaze and style.

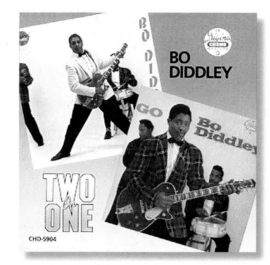

212 | **Bo Diddley/ Go Bo Diddley**
BO DIDDLEY
MCA 1959

Diddley's influence on rock & roll is inestimable, from the off-kilter rhythmic thump of "Pretty Thing" to his revved-up take on singing the blues. This album – a repackaging of his first two records – has many of his best singles, including "I'm a Man" and "Who Do You Love?"

213 | **Two Steps From the Blues**
BOBBY BLAND
BEAT GOES ON 1961

Bland said he found his falsetto after he had his tonsils out, and his stirring, guttural howl is epitomized by "Little Boy Blue" and "Cry, Cry, Cry," which erase any distinction between blues and soul. "I Pity the Fool" and "Lead Me On" may just be some of the purest, most heartbroken singing you'll ever hear.

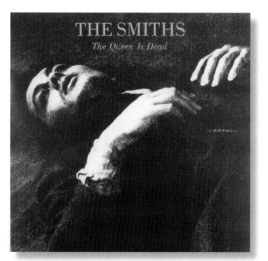

214 | **The Queen Is Dead**
THE SMITHS
SIRE 1986

The original kings of British mope rock could have earned that title on the basis of this album alone. The Smiths' third set is full of quiet rage ("The Queen Is Dead"), epic sadness ("There Is a Light That Never Goes Out") and strummy social commentary ("Frankly Mr. Shankly").

215 | **Licensed to Ill**
BEASTIE BOYS
DEF JAM 1986

Recorded when the three New York rappers were barely out of high school, *Licensed to Ill* remains a revolutionary combination of hip-hop beats, metal riffs and some of the most exuberant, unapologetic smart-aleck rhymes ever made. No wonder it went on to become the best-selling rap album of the Eighties.

216 | **Look-Ka Py Py**
THE METERS
SUNDAZED 1970

The Meters were the house band for New Orleans' genius producer Allen Toussaint and played on Seventies landmarks such as LaBelle's *Nightbirds*. These instrumentals – sampled by rappers including Nas and Salt-N-Pepa – are funk of the gods, with monster bass and the off-the-beat drumming of Ziggy Modeliste.

P.E. in '88: Chuck D (second from left), Terminator X (top) and Flavor Flav (front)

It Takes a Nation of Millions to Hold Us Back

PUBLIC ENEMY

I hated that record," says Public Enemy's lead man Chuck D. Believe it or not, he's referring to "Bring the Noise," the frenetic first track of the group's agit-rap masterpiece, *It Takes a Nation of Millions to Hold Us Back.* Public Enemy had recorded the song in October 1987 for the soundtrack of the forgettable *Less Than Zero.* When Chuck (a.k.a. Carlton Ridenhour) first heard the final version, he says, "I practically threw it out the window."

He changed his mind later that year when Public Enemy were on tour in England. "I kept hearing people ask, 'What's this record you've got out? People are going crazy over it,'" he

remembers. "I was like 'OK, pull that acetate out, and let's play it [in concert].' People went berserk."

"Bring the Noise," along with "Rebel Without a Pause" and "Don't Believe the Hype" – all conceived in 1987 at the group's Hempstead, Long Island, studio, Spectrum City – would become the foundation of *It Takes a Nation of Millions.* Chuck may have been disgruntled over "Bring the Noise," but he always liked "Rebel Without a Pause," the track that introduced Public Enemy's trademark sirenlike horn squeals. Hank Shocklee of PE's production team, the Bomb Squad, says that "Rebel" started out as a response to Eric B. and Rakim's "I

Know You Got Soul." "We were going for something that had the same feel but with more aggression," Shocklee says. "Because we were angry."

For "Rebel," PE coupled piercing squeals (a snippet from the J.B.'s "The Grunt" played backward) with James Brown's "Funky Drummer" ("Because that song was my milk," says Shocklee). Then it fell on Chuck to write the lyrics. "I remember locking myself in the house for twenty-four hours," Chuck says. He emerged with verses that emulated Rakim's off-the-rhythm flow but stayed true to his own booming-baritone persona ("Soul, rock & roll, comin' like a rhino"); Chuck also dropped the name of black activist Joanne Chesimard, hinting at the political direction that his rhymes would soon take.

"Don't Believe the Hype," recorded just before "Bring the Noise," was Chuck's first foray into full-fledged polemics, in this case against the media. The lyrics were inspired by a slight against Chuck by New York-area radio DJ Mr. Magic. PE had serious doubts about that song, too. "We thought 'Hype' was just garbage," says Shocklee. Again, they saw the response the song got when DMC (of the group Run-DMC) blasted the track out of his Bronco in Harlem on a Saturday night. "The whole block was grooving to it," says Shocklee.

In January 1988, it all fit together. "You had the combination of the noise from 'Rebel,'" says Chuck, "the tempo of 'Bring the Noise' and the subject matter of 'Don't Believe the Hype.' It set off *Takes a Nation* pretty nice."

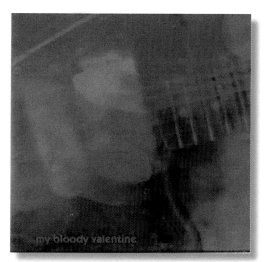

217 | Loveless

MY BLOODY VALENTINE
WARNER BROS. 1991

A shoegazer masterpiece, the second My Bloody Valentine album reportedly cost more than $500,000 and bankrupted the British band's label. It was worth every penny: *Loveless* expanded the possibilities for noise as a form of melody, combining its dizzying guitar drone and Bilinda Butcher's ethereal vocals.

218 | New Orleans Piano

PROFESSOR LONGHAIR
ATLANTIC 1972

There may never have been a funnier, sunnier piano player. His rolling, rumba-tinged style, yodeling vocals and whistling make tracks such as "Tipitina" swinging blasts of joy. *New Orleans Piano* collects Atlantic singles from 1949 to 1953, including the ultimate party anthem "Mardi Gras in New Orleans."

219 | War

U2
ISLAND 1983

U2 were on the cusp of becoming one of the Eighties' most important groups when *War* came out. It's the band's most overtly political album, with songs about Poland's Solidarity movement ("New Year's Day") and Irish unrest ("Sunday Bloody Sunday") charged with explosive, passionate guitar rock.

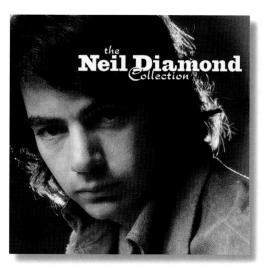

220 | The Neil Diamond Collection

NEIL DIAMOND
MCA 1999

This pop-rock star cut some of his best material from 1958 to '73 – the era this anthology documents. His melodramatic delivery is a guilty pleasure that never gets less pleasurable – or less guilty – than when he's belting "Sweet Caroline," "Cherry, Cherry" or "I Am . . . I Said."

221 | Nebraska

BRUCE SPRINGSTEEN
COLUMBIA 1982

Recorded on a four-track in Springsteen's bedroom, *Nebraska*'s songs were stark, spooky acoustic demos that he decided to release "bare." Packed with hard-luck tales of underdogs, this album ends with "Reason to Believe," one of those songs where Springsteen's search for faith inspires faith itself.

222 | Doolittle

PIXIES
4AD/ELEKTRA 1989

Kurt Cobain himself acknowledged the Pixies' influence on the soft/loud dynamic that powered "Smells Like Teen Spirit." *Doolittle* is a mix of the band's earlier hardcore storms, Black Francis' self-described "stream of unconsciousness" rants, and the strange melodicism and surf-metal guitar that defined the Pixies.

223 | **Paid in Full**
ERIC B. AND RAKI
ISLAND 1987

Ice-grilled, laid-back, diamond-sharp: Rakim is a front-runner in the race for Best Rapper Ever, and this album is a big reason why. *Paid in Full* was one of the first hip-hop records to fully embrace Seventies funk samples on stone hip-hop classics such as "I Know You Got Soul" and the title track.

224 | **Toys in the Attic**
AEROSMITH
COLUMBIA 1975

This is where Aerosmith perfected their raunchy blues-rock sound, with guitarist Joe Perry laying down some of the Seventies' most indelible riffs on "Walk This Way" and "Sweet Emotion," and Steven Tyler stepping up with an album full of unforgettable songs about his favorite topic: sex.

225 | **Nick of Time**
BONNIE RAITT
CAPITOL 1989

After being dumped by her previous label, blues rocker Raitt exacted revenge with this multiplatinum Grammy-award winner. Producer Don Was helped her sharpen the songs without sacrificing any of her slide-guitar fire. And as Raitt herself pointed out, her tenth try was "my first sober album."

BONNIE RAITT

"Every song on there is about somebody who had to have lived this long. 'I Ain't Gonna Let You Break My Heart Again' – I had that song for eleven years, and until this album I couldn't really mean it."

(RS 577, MAY 3RD, 1990)

226 | **A Night at the Opera**
QUEEN
HOLLYWOOD 1975

"Queen will be the Cecil B. DeMille of rock," proclaimed singer Freddie Mercury, and this is where the band let its over-the-top tendencies loose, with heavy metal ("Sweet Lady"), pop ("You're My Best Friend") and the most operatic of all rock songs, "Bohemian Rhapsody."

227 | The Kink Kronikles
THE KINKS
REPRISE 1972

Covering the years 1966 to 1970, this double-disc set anthologizes the second act in the Kinks' venerable career. Observational narratives such as "Waterloo Sunset" reveal Ray Davies to be a master miniaturist. "That's what I write about," Davies remarked, "the immense smallness of life."

228 | Mr. Tambourine Man
THE BYRDS
COLUMBIA/LEGACY 1965

"Wow, man, you can even dance to that!" said Bob Dylan when he heard the Byrds' heavily harmonized, electric twelve-string treatments of his material. The Byrds' tender-but-tough debut defined folk rock with Pete Seeger and Dylan covers, Los Angeles studio savvy and punchy, ringing guitars.

229 | Bookends
SIMON AND GARFUNKEL
COLUMBIA/LEGACY 1968

Paul Simon has said this is "the quintessential Simon and Garfunkel album." It is certainly far-ranging, a mostly dark, beautifully written voyage that includes both the epic "America" and the *Graduate* theme "Mrs. Robinson," still a pop-radio staple. The duo produced the record themselves, with brilliant restraint.

230 | The Ultimate Collection
PATSY CLINE
UTV 2000

Her career was cut short when she died in a plane crash at thirty, but Cline made her mark as one of country's great singers. Country hits "Walkin' After Midnight" and "I Fall to Pieces" also made it to the pop charts. Her version of "Crazy" was a godsend to struggling writer Willie Nelson.

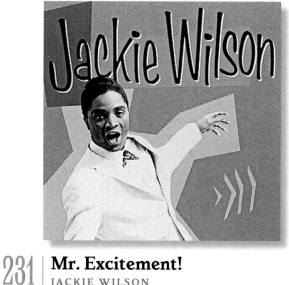

231 | Mr. Excitement!
JACKIE WILSON
RHINO 1992

Wilson was an knockout live performer who made R&B that rocked and also sang ballads with a voice, said arranger Dick Jacobs, "like honey on moonbeams." The highlight of this three-disc set is the endless build of "Your Love Keeps Lifting Me (Higher and Higher)."

232 | The Who Sings My Generation
THE WHO
MCA 1965

The Who introduce themselves in maximum-R&B mode: power-chorded reductions of James Brown ballads. But when Pete Townshend was badgered by a manager into beefing up his laid-back demo of "My Generation," the resulting explosion knocked a hole in the future.

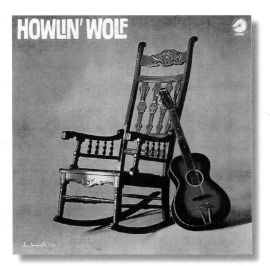

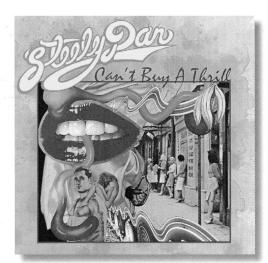

 233 | **Howlin' Wolf**
HOWLIN' WOLF
CHESS/MCA 1962

"The Rocking Chair Album" features an outrageous set of sex songs written by Willie Dixon, including "Shake for Me," "The Red Rooster" and "Back Door Man." In 1971, on *The London Howlin' Wolf Sessions,* Wolf finally taught an enraptured Eric Clapton how to play "The Red Rooster."

234 | **Like a Prayer**
MADONNA
SIRE/WARNER BROS. 1989

"I like the challenge of merging art and commerce," Madonna told ROLLING STONE. Artistic recognition was won with her most personal set of songs, including "Till Death Do Us Part" and "Oh Father"; commerce with "Express Yourself" and the title track, whose video had the Vatican talking about blasphemy.

235 | **Can't Buy a Thrill**
STEELY DAN
MCA 1972

Working as hired songwriters by day, Donald Fagen and Walter Becker rehearsed this debut in executives' offices by night. "We play rock & roll, but we swing," said Becker. For proof, check the cool lounge-jazz rhythms of "Do It Again" and the hot guitar of "Reelin' in the Years."

MADONNA

"In the past, my albums tended to be a reflection of current influences. This album is more about past musical influences. The songs 'Keep It Together" and 'Express Yourself,' for instance, are sort of my tributes to Sly and the Family Stone. 'Oh Father' is my tribute to Simon and Garfunkel, who I loved. Also, the overall emotional context of the album is drawn from what I was going through when I was growing up – and I'm still growing up."

(RS 548, MARCH 23RD, 1989)

 236 | **Let It Be**
THE REPLACEMENTS
TWIN/TONE 1984

Copping a Beatles title was cheeky; attaching it to a post-punk masterpiece was a sign of maturity. Said Paul Westerberg, "This was the first time I had songs that we arranged, rather than just banging out riffs." Mixing punk, pop and country with wry lyrics, he wrote "Unsatisfied" for his lagging bandmates.

237 | **Run-DMC**
RUN-DMC
PROFILE 1984

"It's good to be raw," said Run, and the metallic guitar powering "Rock Box" proved it when the song became the first rap video on MTV. Run-DMC's debut ditches party rhymes to codify B-boy style and make history, from the way they dress to their hard beats to the everyday subject matter of "It's Like That."

238 | **Black Sabbath**
BLACK SABBATH
WARNER BROS. 1970

Recorded in a single twelve-hour blurt by a hippie-leaning former blues band, this lumbering debut conjures up a new, sludgy sound: the birth pains of heavy metal. The slide guitar on "Wizard" and the grungy boogie of "Wicked World" would influence not only future metal spawn but even the sound of Nirvana.

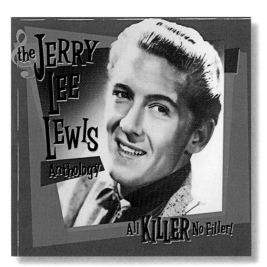

239 | **All Killer, No Filler!**
JERRY LEE LEWIS
RHINO 1993

Lewis is best known for his frenzied, piano-pumping Sun sides cut in the late Fifties, yet his career as a country hitmaker lasted decades. Listen to "What Made Milwaukee Famous (Has Made a Loser Out of Me)" and you might agree with the Killer that "Elvis was the greatest, but I'm the best."

 240 | **Freak Out!**
THE MOTHERS OF INVENTION
RYKODISC 1966

A master guitarist and provocateur, Frank Zappa made more than sixty albums, but the first was perhaps the most groundbreaking. The double-disc *Freak Out!* declares the arrival of a visionary weirdo who dabbles in doo-wop, pop-song parody, protest tunes, art rock and avant-garde classical.

241 | **Live Dead**
GRATEFUL DEAD
WARNER BROS. 1969

After two expensive studio albums put the Dead $100,000 in debt, this live set was more than just cheap, it was pivotal. For the Dead, the magic happened onstage, as demonstrated by the glorious twenty-three-minute jam-outs on "Dark Star" and a cover of Bobby Bland's "(Turn On Your) Lovelight."

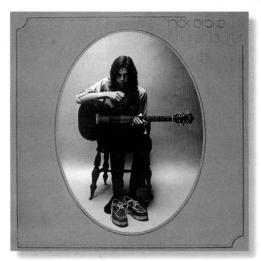

242 **Bryter Layter**

NICK DRAKE
ISLAND 1970

Compared to the British folkie's other records, Nick Drake's second album could almost be called upbeat. Almost. With John Cale, Richard Thompson and other members of Fairport Convention assisting him, Drake jazzes up the arrangements on songs such as "Poor Boy" but leaves his voice stark and fragile.

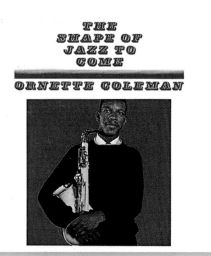

243 **The Shape of Jazz to Come**

ORNETTE COLEMAN
ATLANTIC 1959

Coleman's sound was so out-there, one audience at an early gig threw his tenor sax over a cliff. He switched to alto and pioneered free jazz: no chords, no harmony, any player can take the lead. Here, his music can be just as lyrical as it is demanding, particularly on the haunting "Lonely Woman."

244 **Automatic for the People**

R.E.M.
WARNER BROS. 1992

"It doesn't sound a whole lot like us," warned guitarist Peter Buck, but that was the point of R.E.M.'s ninth album. Largely acoustic, and with string parts arranged by Led Zeppelin's John Paul Jones, this musical left turn finds a haunted beauty in songs like "Everybody Hurts" and "Drive."

245 **Reasonable Doubt**

JAY-Z
ROC-A-FELLA/PRIORITY 1996

"The studio was like a psychiatrist's couch for me," Jay-Z told ROLLING STONE, and his debut is full of a hustler's dreams and laments. It established Jay as the premier freestyle rapper of his generation and includes a filthy guest appearance from a sixteen-year-old Foxy Brown on "Ain't No Nigga."

246 **Low**

DAVID BOWIE
RCA 1977

Moving to Berlin to kick cocaine, Bowie hooked up with producer Brian Eno. *Low* was the first of the trilogy of albums they made, full of electronic instrumentals and quirky funk like "Sound and Vision." The same year, Bowie also produced Iggy Pop's *Lust for Life* and *The Idiot*, both recorded in Berlin.

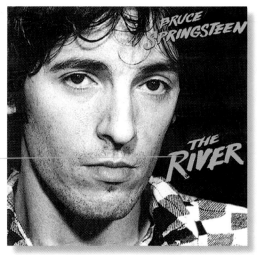

247 **The River**

BRUCE SPRINGSTEEN
COLUMBIA 1980

Springsteen said it took him five albums to begin writing about real relationships, about "people tryin' to find some sort of consolation, some sort of comfort in each other." *The River* balances those stories of heartbreak with E Street romps through bar-band R&B, rockabilly and their own brand of epic rock.

Dictionary of Soul
OTIS REDDING
RHINO 1966

"Try a Little Tenderness" was a Bing Crosby hit from the Thirties until Redding turned it into pure Memphis soul. On *Dictionary*, he does the same with "Tennessee Waltz" and the Beatles' "Day Tripper," as well as his own ballads "Fa-Fa-Fa-Fa-Fa (Sad Song)" and "My Lover's Prayer."

Metallica
METALLICA
ELEKTRA 1991

Bon Jovi producer Bob Rock helped create one of the best-selling metal albums of all time, led by "Enter Sandman" and the ballad "Nothing Else Matters." "It's scary to look out and see couples hugging during that song," frontman James Hetfield said. " 'Oh, fuck, I thought this was a Metallica show.'"

> "A one-riff song…The whole intro, the verse, the bridge, the chorus, all that stuff, is the same riff. 'Enter Sandman' was also the first song written for the album. That's why it's the leadoff track. To me, it was 'Here's the new vibe gone right to the extreme.'"
>
> LARS ULRICH
> RS 611, SEPTEMBER 22ND, 1991

James Hetfield's handwritten lyrics to Metallica's "Enter Sandman"

 250 **Trans-Europe Express**
KRAFTWERK
CAPITOL 1977

This German group's sound sought to eliminate the distinction between men and machines. Kraftwerk's robot-synthesizer grooves influenced electrodisco hitmakers, experimental geniuses such as Brian Eno and rappers including Afrika Bambaataa, who lifted the title track for "Planet Rock."

251 **Whitney Houston**
WHITNEY HOUSTON
ARISTA 1985

She had been a model and a nightclub singer when she cut this smooth R&B debut. Her vocal gifts and technique are astounding; even slick tracks such as "Greatest Love of All" stick. Best song: "How Will I Know," perky synth-funk evoking Houston's godmother, Aretha Franklin.

252 **The Village Green Preservation Society**
THE KINKS
REPRISE 1968

Having shed their early garage-rock grit in favor of more baroque arrangements, the Kinks made one of their loveliest albums with *Village Green*, Ray Davies' nostalgic ode to British pastoral life. The sound is delicate, like a picture of a small town vanishing before your eyes.

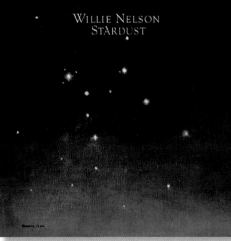

253 **The Velvet Rope**
JANET JACKSON
VIRGIN 1997

Jackson left behind her girl-next-door image forever with *The Velvet Rope*, an album of sexy, confessional, freewheeling hip-hop soul. She fuses Joni Mitchell and Q-Tip in "Got 'Til It's Gone," but the shocker is her girl-girl version of Rod Stewart's "Tonight's the Night."

254 **Stardust**
WILLIE NELSON
COLUMBIA/LEGACY 1978

Stardust is Nelson's love song to old-time American music: At the height of his country popularity, the crooner digs up his favorite Tin Pan Alley standards – "Georgia on My Mind," "Unchained Melody," "Don't Get Around Much Anymore" – making them swing as if he had just come up with them in his La-Z-Boy.

255 **American Beauty**
GRATEFUL DEAD
RHINO/WARNER BROS. 1970

The Dead were never better in the studio than on the down-home stoner country of *American Beauty*. Released just six months after the folkie classic *Workingman's Dead* [see No. 262], *Beauty* has some of the band's most beloved songs, including "Box of Rain" and "Friend of the Devil."

256 | Crosby, Stills and Nash
CROSBY, STILLS AND NASH
ATLANTIC 1969

"I've seen Crosby, Stills and Nash burnin' ass," Jimi Hendrix declared in 1969. "They're groovy, Western-sky music." Hendrix knew what he was talking about. The trio first combined its golden hippie harmonies on this debut, featuring "Marrakesh Express" and the seven-minute "Suite: Judy Blue Eyes."

257 | Buena Vista Social Club
BUENA VISTA SOCIAL CLUB
WORLD CIRCUIT/NONESUCH 1997

Here's an idea for a blockbuster: Take L.A. rock guitarist Ry Cooder, stick him in a Havana studio with a crew of legendary Cuban musicians, and just let the old guys play their asses off. Against all odds, *Buena Vista Social Club* defied Nineties-pop formulas and became a huge word-of-mouth hit.

258 | Tracy Chapman
TRACY CHAPMAN
ELEKTRA 1988

Somehow, this young folk singer came out of nowhere to catch everyone's ear during the hair-metal late Eighties. Chapman had already spent time strumming her acoustic guitar for spare change on the streets around Boston, but her gritty voice and storytelling made "Fast Car" hit home.

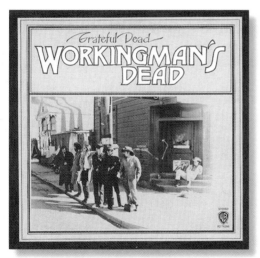

259 | Workingman's Dead
GRATEFUL DEAD
RHINO/WARNER BROS. 1970

"We weren't feeling so much like an experimental music group," Jerry Garcia said. "More like a good old band." On *Workingman's Dead,* the Dead strip down for eight spooky country and folk tunes that rival the best of Bob Dylan, especially on the morbid "Black Peter" and "Dire Wolf."

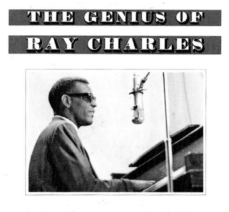

260 | The Genius of Ray Charles
RAY CHARLES
RHINO 1959

Charles spent the Fifties working hard to pioneer his own sound: fusing jazz, gospel and the blues into a new soul style that changed American music. But here he relaxes: *Genius* is easy-swinging pop, featuring big-band accompaniment. When he sings "Am I Blue?," the only answer is "Hell, yeah!"

261 | Child Is Father to the Man
BLOOD, SWEAT AND TEARS
COLUMBIA/LEGACY 1968

Organist Al Kooper founded BST after leaving the Blues Project. The idea was an eclectic rock-jazz collective, the horns up front with the guitars, and touches of folk and classical as well. On songs by Tim Buckley and Randy Newman, as well as the hard-bitten original "I Can't Quit Her," it worked.

Cobain kills a drum kit at a 1990 show at Raji's in L.A.

Nevermind

NIRVANA

The week before I flew to L.A. [to produce *Nevermind*], Kurt [Cobain] sent a cassette, which was done on a boombox," says producer Butch Vig. "It was really terrible sounding. You could barely make out anything. But I could hear the start to 'Teen Spirit,' and I knew it was amazing."

Vig, along with mixer Andy Wallace, made sure that *Nevermind*'s brilliant songs didn't get lost in the same cheap production as on the band's first album, *Bleach*. Vig spent a little more than a month recording and mixing the album with Cobain, bassist Krist Novoselic and drummer Dave Grohl at Sound City Studios in Van Nuys, California.

"They were living in this apartment complex, and it was chaos," Vig remembers. There'd be graffiti on the walls, and the couches were upside down. They'd stay up every night and go down to Venice Beach until six in the morning. I'd go into the studio at noon and they'd wander in around four."

Rowdy lifestyles aside, Vig says the recording went smoothly, except when it came time for the restrained "Something in the Way."

"No matter how subtly they'd try to play," Vig says, it was too aggressive. "Kurt walked into the control room and said it just had to sound like this – he was barely whispering, and playing the guitar so quietly you could barely hear it. It was mesmerizing. I pulled a couple of mikes in, and we built the whole song around it."

Mixing the record, the band and producer hit another snag. "Kurt kept trying to bury his voice," says Vig. "I kept arguing, 'You can't do that. Your vocal performance is as intense as the drums and the bass and the guitar.'"

Vig eventually won the argument, but his mixes didn't make it onto the album. The band decided to hire an outside engineer. Andy Wallace, who'd worked with Slayer, gave *Nevermind* its incredible sonic sheen – something Cobain never admitted to being comfortable with. Talking about "Teen Spirit," he told Nirvana biographer Michael Azerrad, "It's such a perfect mixture of cleanliness and nice, candy-ass production.... It may be extreme to some people who aren't used to it, but I think it's kind of lame, myself."

262 | Cosmo's Factory
CREEDENCE CLEARWATER REVIVAL
FANTASY 1970

The third classic album that Creedence cranked out in less than a year, after *Green River* and *Willie and the Poor Boys*. Highlights: the choogling "Ramble Tamble," the eleven-minute guitar party "I Heard It Through the Grapevine" and the front-porch reverie "Lookin' Out My Back Door."

263 | Quadrophenia
THE WHO
MCA 1973

The album that brought back Vespa scooters, parkas and uppers: Pete Townshend drew on the Who's roots in the London mod scene of the early Sixties and composed this expansive, messy rock opera about a lonely teenage boy looking for love in the city. It gets even better when you check out the movie.

264 | There Goes Rhymin' Simon
PAUL SIMON
WARNER BROS. 1973

After his great 1972 solo debut, Simon could stop proving he could go it alone without Art Garfunkel. So he made the sunniest music of his career, lifted by the gospel, R&B and doo-wop rhythms he grew up loving. The hit: "Kodachrome," about "all the crap I learned in high school."

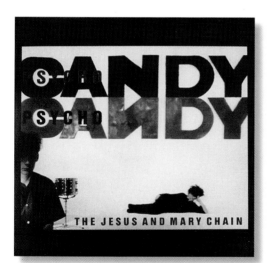

265 | Pyscho Candy
THE JESUS AND MARY CHAIN
WEA INTERNATIONAL 1985

Pretty Scottish boys surfing a wave of doom and gloom and enjoying every moment of it. The Jesus and Mary Chain's debut is a decadent alt-rock masterpiece of bubblegum pop – with "Just Like Honey," "My Little Underground" and "Never Understand" – drowned in feedback.

266 | Some Girls
THE ROLLING STONES
VIRGIN 1978

"Christ, Keith fuckin' gets busted every year," Mick Jagger fumed. Keith Richards was lost in drug hell, and the Stones were on the verge of destruction, but they bounced back with "Miss You," the sleazy "Shattered" and "When the Whip Comes Down." And Richards does his best song, "Before They Make Me Run."

267 | The Beach Boys Today!
THE BEACH BOYS
CAPITOL 1965

The Beach Boys were still into cars, girls and surfboards, but Brian Wilson was already a genius. He writes sweet California tunes here, from "When I Grow Up (to Be a Man)" to "Don't Hurt My Little Sister." And the haunting "She Knows Me Too Well" hits as deep as anything on *Pet Sounds*.

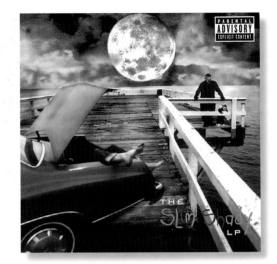

268 | **Going to a Go-Go**

SMOKEY ROBINSON
THE MIRACLES
MOTOWN 1965

Motown at its most debonair and sexy. Smokey Robinson works his sweeping soul falsetto over unbelievably sad ballads including "The Tracks of My Tears" and "Ooh Baby Baby" as the Miracles sob along. Even obscurities such as "Choosey Beggar" are top-notch.

269 | **Nightbirds**

LABELLE
EPIC 1974

"Lady Marmalade" has one of funkiest chants in Seventies disco: "Hey sister, go sister, soul sister, go sister!" Nobody did the disco girl-group thing quite like the ladies of Labelle: They were Funkadelic meets the Supremes, complete with platform heels, silver-lamé spacesuits and songs about New Orleans prostitutes.

270 | **The Slim Shady LP**

EMINEM
AFTERMATH/INTERSCOPE 1999

Here's where Eminem introduced himself as a crazy white geek, the "class-clown freshman/Dressed like Les Nessman." Hip-hop had never heard anything like Em's brain-damaged rhymes on this Dr. Dre-produced album, which earned Em respect, fortune, fame and a lawsuit from his mom.

EMINEM

271 | **Mothership Connection**

PARLIAMENT
MERCURY 1976

"Do not attempt to adjust your radio," the DJ announces as George Clinton leads his Detroit crew of extraterrestrial brothers through a visionary album of science-fiction funk, doing it to you in your ear hole with jams such as "Super-groovalisticprosifunkstication (The Thump Bump)."

"My album isn't for younger kids to hear. It has an advisory sticker, and you must be eighteen to get it. That doesn't mean younger kids won't get it, but I'm not responsible for every kid out there. I'm not a role model, and I don't claim to be."

(RS 811, APRIL 29TH, 1999)

272 | Rhythm Nation 1814

JANET JACKSON
A&M 1989

Jackson bought a military suit and ruled the radio for two years with this album. Along with producers Jimmy Jam and Terry Lewis, she fashions a grand pop statement with hip-hop funk ("Rhythm Nation"), slow jams ("Love Will Never Do [Without You]"), even hair metal ("Black Cat").

273 | Anthology of American Folk Music

HARRY SMITH, ED.
SMITHSONIAN FOLKWAYS 1952

This influential compilation inspired folk music, rekindled interest in the blues and shaped decades of pop. Joan Baez, Pete Seeger and Bob Dylan covered and/or rewrote many of the tracks, and Jerry Garcia cut his turntable speed in half in order to master the solos.

274 | Aladdin Sane

DAVID BOWIE
VIRGIN 1973

"I think *Aladdin* was much more in the area of 'Ziggy goes to America,'" Bowie remarked of the *Ziggy* sequel written largely during his first extensive U.S. tour. "Time" bridges the two albums, but "The Jean Genie" and a raunchy cover of "Let's Spend the Night Together" show a louder, harder, sexier Bowie.

275 | The Immaculate Collection

MADONNA
SIRE/WARNER BROS. 1990

Like the 1987 remix album, *You Can Dance*, this is a perfect Madonna CD: nothing but good songs. You get timeless pop such as "Holiday," provocations like "Papa Don't Preach," dance classics like "Into the Groove" and a new Lenny Kravitz-produced sex jam, "Justify My Love," which samples Public Enemy.

276 | My Life

MARY J. BLIGE
MCA 1994

Graced by soulful samples and revisions of classic R&B, this Puff Daddy-helmed second album is Blige's most autobiographical. Upbeat jams like "Be Happy" were created during her struggle with substance abuse and a tumultuous relationship. "There's a real bad suicide spirit on there," she admitted.

277 | Folk Singer

MUDDY WATERS
CHESS/MCA 1964

Worried that the folk-music fad was luring listeners away from the blues, Chess Records directed Waters to record with acoustic instruments. These sessions – by Waters, Willie Dixon and a young Buddy Guy – went astonishingly well, and this pioneering "unplugged" set is beloved by blues and folk fans alike.

278 **Can't Get Enough**

BARRY WHITE
MERCURY 1974

In 1974, White had three albums on the charts simultaneously, all of which contained orchestrated hits that fanned the flames of disco fever. But the newly married maestro was also a master balladeer, and "I Can't Believe You Love Me" keeps the boudoir drama coming for ten-plus minutes.

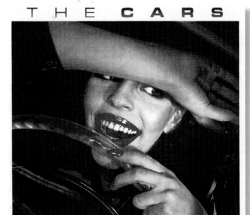

279 **The Cars**

THE CARS
ELEKTRA 1978

"We used to joke that the first album should be called *The Cars' Greatest Hits*," said guitarist Elliot Easton. Their debut was arty and punchy enough to be part of Boston's New Wave scene and yet so catchy that nearly every track ("My Best Friend's Girl," "Just What I Needed") landed on the radio.

280 **Five Leaves Left**

NICK DRAKE
ISLAND 1969

Peter Buck of R.E.M. once said that you could turn a Nick Drake song up all the way, but it would still sound quiet. Drake's 1969 debut – recorded while he was still at Cambridge University – introduced the world to his gorgeous, melancholy folk on songs such as "Time Has Told Me."

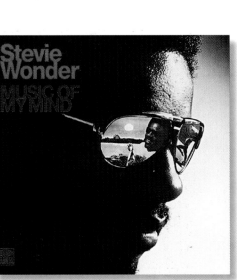

281 **Music of My Mind**

STEVIE WONDER
MOTOWN 1972

Recording after his onerous contract with Motown had expired, a newly empowered Wonder flexed his artistic control on *Music of My Mind*, making a relaxed love-smitten warm-up for the blockbusters to come and playing nearly every funky note on classics such as "Love Having You Around."

282 **I'm Still in Love With You**

AL GREEN
HI/THE RIGHT STUFF 1972

After topping the R&B and pop charts with *Let's Stay Together*, Green released his second LP of that year, one that was even more sensual than its predecessor. "Love and Happiness" is a slow-building masterpiece: His band provided the subtle groove, and Green added a mountain of soul.

283 **Los Angeles**

X
SLASH/RHINO 1980

The quintessential L.A. punk band made the first great West Coast punk album with its debut. *Los Angeles* is best known for its city-defining anthem and the torrid "Johnny Hit and Run Paulene"; produced by Ray Manzarek of the Doors, it also shows that punk and classic rock can be occasional friends.

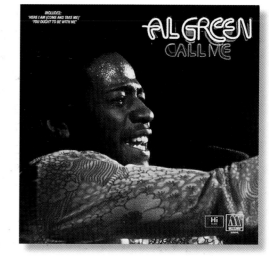

284 | Anthem of the Sun
GRATEFUL DEAD
RHINO/WARNER BROS. 1968

The Dead's second album was built from multiple live performances and studio takes, which were faded in and out of each track in an attempt to re-create the alchemy of the band's shows. Jerry Garcia said, "We really mixed [the album] for the hallucinations, you know?" One listen, and you did.

285 | Something Else by the Kinks
THE KINKS
REPRISE 1968

The Kinks' most tuneful, reflective album yet, *Something Else* was anchored by two of their greatest songs: "Waterloo Sunset" and "Death of a Clown." The album didn't make much of a mark on the U.S. charts, but it did set the table for the band's pastoral masterpiece, *Village Green Preservation Society*.

286 | Call Me
AL GREEN
HI/THE RIGHT STUFF 1973

By the time they recorded the graceful, almost perfect *Call Me*, Green and producer Willie Mitchell could do little wrong. To hammer that home, Green showed he could rival Ray Charles as an interpreter of country songs on the killer downtempo cover of Hank Williams' "I'm So Lonesome I Could Cry."

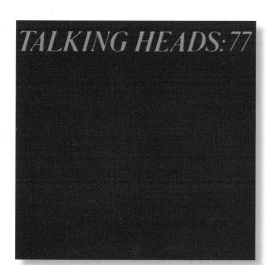

287 | Talking Heads: 77
TALKING HEADS
SIRE 1977

The Heads wore button-down shirts and embraced a tightly wound normality as rebellion. "For a long time, I felt, 'Well, fuck everybody,' " David Byrne told *Punk* magazine in 1976. "Well, now I want to be accepted." The result was the tense, ingeniously constricted sound of Talking Heads' debut.

288 | The Basement Tapes
BOB DYLAN AND THE BAND
COLUMBIA 1975

Dylan and the Band juiced up rock and folk into a loose-limbed stoner free-for-all during these sessions, most of which took place in 1967 in the basement of the Band's house in Woodstock, New York. Bootleggers turned tracks such as "This Wheel's on Fire" into classics, and *Tapes* was officially released eight years later.

289 | White Light/White Heat
THE VELVET UNDERGROUND
POLYDOR 1967

Drowning their songs in guitar fuzz and drone, The Velvet Underground captured the toe-clenching freakouts of their live show with their second album — the most extreme disc in VU's extreme catalog. The blow-your-wig-back highlight: "Sister Ray," seventeen minutes of amplifiers screaming.

290 | Kick Out the Jams

MC5
ELEKTRA 1969

It's the ultimate rock salute: "Kick out the jams, motherfuckers!" Recorded live in Detroit by Rob Tyner and his anarchist crew, *Kick Out the Jams* writhes and screams with the belief that rock & roll is a necessary act of civil disobedience. The proof: It was banned by a Michigan department store.

291 | Meat Is Murder

THE SMITHS
SIRE 1985

Inspired by Can riffs, bookended by lengthy, brutal songs about corporal punishment and the horrors of the cattle industry, *Murder* is the darkest entry in the U.K. group's catalog. On "How Soon Is Now?," Morrissey sums up with great pathos and hilarity what a drag it is to be shy. More pathos would come.

292 | We're Only in It for the Money

THE MOTHERS OF INVENTION
RYKODISC 1968

"What's the ugliest part of your body?" asked Frank Zappa. Answer: your brain. *Only in It for the Money* is a milestone of studio mischief and a merciless satire of anything that pissed Zappa off during flower power's heyday – drippy hippies, the Establishment, whatever.

293 | Weezer (Blue Album)

WEEZER
DGC 1994

When it came out, Weezer's debut was merely a cool, quirky power-pop album with a couple of hit singles: "Buddy Holly" and "Undone (The Sweater Song)." But Rivers Cuomo's band became a major influence on young sad-sack punkers who today claim Weezer as one of emo's pioneers.

294 | Master of Reality

BLACK SABBATH
WARNER BROS. 1971

The greatest sludge-metal band of them all in its prime. *Paranoid* may have bigger hits, but *Master of Reality*, released a mere six months later, is heavier. The highlight is "Sweet Leaf," a droning love song to marijuana. But the vibe is perfectly summed up by the final track, "Into the Void."

295 | Coat of Many Colors

DOLLY PARTON
BUDDHA 1971

Parton's starkest, most affecting album. The title track is about wearing rags but keeping your pride; the rest is more hard country. On "Traveling Man," Parton's mom runs off with the singer's boyfriend; on "If I Lose My Mind," her boyfriend has sex with another woman in front of her.

296 | **Fear of a Black Planet**
PUBLIC ENEMY
DEF JAM 1990

The lyrical flap surrounding "Welcome
to the Terrordome" couldn't overwhelm
Public Enemy's widescreen vision of
hip-hop on their third album, which included the righteous noise of "Fight the
Power," the uplifting sentiment of
"Brothers Gonna Work It Out" and the
agit-funk of "911 Is a Joke."

297 | **John Wesley Harding**
BOB DYLAN
COLUMBIA 1967

Recovering from his 1966 motorcycle
crash, Dylan took a left turn into country music and ascetic mysticism on this
disc, connecting to Nashville through a
host of characters from the Bible and
America's rugged history. And with "All
Along the Watchtower," he wrote the
most ominous rock song ever.

"Mostly it's cartoon-type material. I
make up this one cat who's funny. He
goes through these strange scenes.'
You put it in music, just like you put
blues in music.... Most of the time I
can't get it on the guitar, you know?
Most of the time I'm just laying
around daydreaming, hearing all this
music. If you go to the guitar and try
to play it, it spoils the whole thing."
JIMI HENDRIX
(RS 54, MARCH 19TH, 1970)

Jimi Hendrix's handwritten lyrics to "Voodoo Chile"

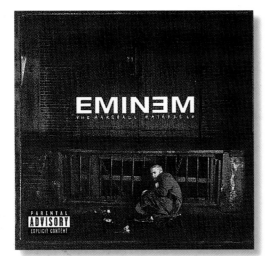

298 | The Marshall Mathers LP

EMINEM
AFTERMATH/INTERSCOPE 2000

Before his second LP, Eminem was a shock rapper with a sense of humor; after *Mathers*, he was the voice of a generation. "I'm not a role model, and I don't claim to be," he said, but on songs like "The Real Slim Shady," he creates a vast, pissed-off audience. And no one could deny the narrative heft of "Stan."

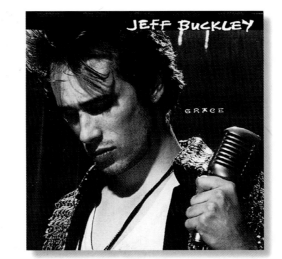

299 | Grace

JEFF BUCKLEY
COLUMBIA 1991

Buckley had a voice like an oversexed angel, and the songs here shimmer and twist and ripple. On the fierce rocker "Eternal Life," he upends Led Zeppelin's take on the blues, even as he honors it: Instead of a hellhound on his trail, Buckley, who drowned in 1997, sings about immortality bearing down on him.

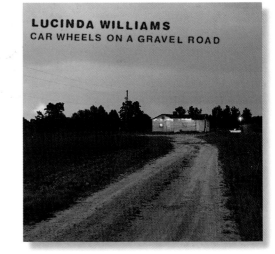

300 | Car Wheels on a Gravel Road

LUCINDA WILLIAMS
MERCURY 1998

It took three torturous years to finish, but it was worth it; there are no bad songs on this alt-country masterwork. The title track is one of Williams' best: Over guitars that owe more to the Stones than to the Opry, she tell a story about the rootlessness of American life.

301 | Odelay

BECK
DGC 1996

Burrowing into the studio with the Dust Brothers, Beck came back with a Technicolor version of his Woody Guthrie-meets-Grandmaster Flash vision, demonstrating to all his rock peers on "Devil's Haircut" and "Where It's At" that turntables had a brighter future than refried grunge.

302 | Songs for Swingin' Lovers

FRANK SINATRA
CAPITOL 1956

Here is an album that means to deny the rock & roll that was then changing America—and succeeds. The songs were standards, most ten or twenty years old, and Sinatra and arranger Nelson Riddle were bent on jazzy, hip sophistication. "I've Got You Under My Skin" still stands as a Sinatra high point.

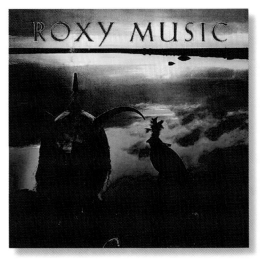

303 | Avalon

ROXY MUSIC
VIRGIN 1982

Peter Sinfield, producer of Roxy Music's angular and wild 1972 debut, said that on *Avalon* they "ran out of naiveté." Their sound was now woozy and lush, horny yet mature. And also unabashedly romantic. A synth-soul landmark, *Avalon* was their biggest hit, their swan song and the pinnacle of rock elegance.

304 | **The Sun Records Collection**

RHINO, 1994

Blues without polish, country without corn and rockabilly played with brainless abandon: This collection of Fifties Sun releases has acknowledged greats (Elvis Presley, Johnny Cash, Jerry Lee Lewis) and lesser-known gems (Bill Justis' spiky "Raunchy"). Lewis' take: "It took all of us to screw up the world."

305 | **Nothing's Shocking**

JANE'S ADDICTION
WARNER BROS. 1988

They thought Led Zeppelin were a funk band, and when they learned this was not true, they carried on anyway. Initially released wrapped in ribbed rubber, Jane's major-label debut rewrites pre-Nirvana rock history, reconciling punk and metal with shredding riffs on oceanic songs.

306 | **BloodSugarSexMagik**

RED HOT CHILI PEPPERS
WARNER BROS. 1991

The Peppers spent a decade trying to recapture this high point, best known as the album where they went touchy-feely (and multiplatinum) with the ballad "Under the Bridge." The story behind the story was guitarist John Frusciante's energizing, songful riffs and huge assist from producer Rick Rubin.

307 | **MTV Unplugged in New York**

NIRVANA
GEFFEN 1994

Nirvana shine brightly on this live set because the volume is just low enough to let Kurt Cobain's tortured tenderness glow. The powerful, reverent covers of Lead Belly, Bowie and Meat Puppets songs sum up Nirvana as a haunted, theatrical and, ultimately, truly raw band.

308 | **The Miseducation of Lauryn Hill**

LAURYN HILL
RUFF HOUSE/COLUMBIA 1998

Hill took Seventies soul and made it boom and signify to the hip-hop generation on her solo debut. The production was subtle and glorious on heartbreakers such as "Ex-Factor" (reportedly about Wyclef Jean) and the swinging sermon "Doo Wop (That Thing)."

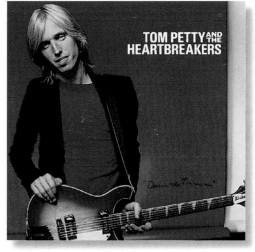

309 | **Damn the Torpedoes**

TOM PETTY AND THE HEARTBREAKERS
MCA 1979

With hair like Jagger's and a voice like Dylan's in tune, Tom Petty and his bar band de-frilled classic rock: In 1979, he filed for bankruptcy; then *Torpedoes* took off, mostly because "Here Comes My Girl" seemed to keep the promises those Jagger et al. forgot they'd made.

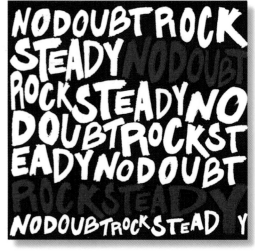

310 | The Velvet Underground
THE VELVET UNDERGROUND
POLYDOR 1969

The album that turned folk music inside out. The Velvet Underground began as the black-booted antidote to the flower-power sound of the Sixties. Their disillusion, exhaustion and ache on *VU* is explosive, and the churning rhythm guitar in "What Goes On" could shame most lead guitarists.

311 | Surfer Rosa
PIXIES
4 A D/ELEKTRA 1988

Smack in between hardcore punk and alternative, it was impossible to deconstruct the Pixies' ferocious howl. Their secret weapon was leaping from sweet to screamin' (which Kurt Cobain admitted to boosting): On "Gigantic," Kim Deal sings like Peppermint Patty as the band drives a spike into Eighties rock.

312 | Rock Steady
NO DOUBT
INTERSCOPE 2001

In which No Doubt do dancehall and techno but reveal themselves to be a great New Wave band: On "Don't Let Me Down" (produced by Ric Ocasek), they sound more like the Cars than the Cars. Bassist Tony Kanal compared *Steady* to *Return of the Jedi*: "It's, like, full of Ewoks. You know, just happy."

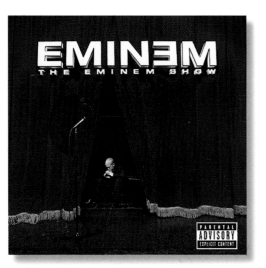

313 | The Eminem Show
EMINEM
INTERSCOPE 2002

Eminem's bittersweet victory lap: the stomping "Square Dance," the almost cuddly "Without Me," the cracks showing in "Hailie's Song" when he says he's insecure. Just add tension from legal woes: "I thought I was goin' to jail. But the scariest thought was, 'How am I going to tell Hailie?'"

314 | Back Stabbers
THE O'JAYS
EPIC/LEGACY 1972

After Vietnam, Watergate and the Watts riots, soul music slipped into darkness in the early Seventies. The title track of this Philly-soul album, made by a group named after a beloved Cleveland DJ, was the writing on the wall: symphonically funky and irretrievably paranoid, much like the times themselves.

315 | Burnin'
THE WAILERS
TUFF GONG/ISLAND 1973

Righteous and seriously in the pocket, this is the last Wailers album with Peter Tosh and Bunny Wailer. Bob Marley's soulful cry is almost rivaled by the sticky organ riffs and fat-bottom beats, and their original version of "I Shot the Sheriff" is far creepier and more desperate than Eric Clapton's hit cover.

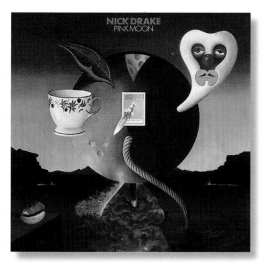

316 | **Pink Moon**
NICK DRAKE
ISLAND 1972

Drake recorded his last album in a couple of nights, mailed the tapes to Island Records and checked himself into a psychiatric ward. If the music were as dark as the lyrics, it might be unlistenable. But Drake's soothing vocals and unadorned acoustic picking make *Moon* unfold with supernatural tenderness.

317 | **Sail Away**
RANDY NEWMAN
WARNER BROS. 1972

Producer Lenny Waronker called him the King of the Suburban Blues Singers. This is Newman's quiet masterpiece, less rock than a fuck-you cabaret. Even now, "Political Science" ("Let's drop the big one/And see what happens") is relevant; either Newman is brilliant or we haven't come a long way, baby.

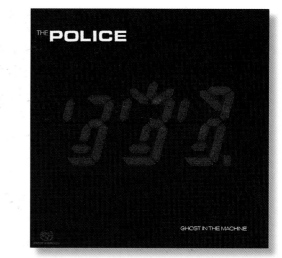

318 | **Ghost in the Machine**
THE POLICE
INTERSCOPE 1981

Recording on the island of Montserrat, the previously punkish trio hit the big time by adding strings and sociopolitical commentary to their sound. "Every Little Thing She Does Is Magic" is a pop smart bomb, and "Invisible Sun," about the violence in Northern Ireland, is genuinely moving.

319 | **Station to Station**
DAVID BOWIE
VIRGIN 1976

The title track is where Bowie proclaims himself the Thin White Duke. Thin he was: *Station to Station* was recorded in a blizzard of cocaine in Los Angeles. "TVC 15" is New Orleans R&B as robotic funk; "Golden Years" is James Brown from outer space, with Bowie's amazing falsetto.

320 | **The Very Best of Linda Ronstadt**
LINDA RONSTADT
RHINO 2002

So very So-Cal (her band became the Eagles), Ronstadt was more empathetic interpreter than songwriter. But could she ever knock out a pop single. Among the guilty pleasures is "Long Long Time," where she sounds like a girl next door with a voice that can peel chrome.

321 | **Slowhand**
ERIC CLAPTON
UNIVERSAL 1977

Slowhand was the nickname given to Clapton by the Yardbirds. On this quintessential Seventies album, he mixes candlelit love songs and guitar-hero riffs; "Cocaine" and "Wonderful Tonight" are the hits, but don't overlook "Next Time You See Her," a tender melody loaded with a death threat to a lover's suitor.

U2 on the "Joshua Tree" tour (from left): Larry Mullen Jr., the Edge, Bono, Clayton

The Joshua Tree

U2

Working with U2 is like being in an avalanche of expectations and possibilities," Daniel Lanois says of his experience co-producing the band's landmark 1987 *The Joshua Tree*, his second U2 effort after 1984's *The Unforgettable Fire*. "I went in to do some preproduction, some sketches. I knew at that time that they were onto something clear and specific."

Attempting to retain the intimate feel of those demos, sessions began in a ramshackle studio set up in a rural Irish farm. "Adam [Clayton, U2's bassist] had been looking to buy himself a house and found this beautiful place," says Lanois.

Bono reportedly struggled with marital difficulties during *The Joshua Tree*'s genesis, which may explain the sense of loss that haunts the album, from despairing abandon on "With or Without You" to "One Tree Hill," a memorial to an associate killed in a motorcycle accident. The chilling anti-heroine ode "Running to Stand Still" had a less grisly inspiration. "That title came from Bono's brother, who was in the computer business," Lanois recalls. "He said to Bono, 'I can't take this anymore – I feel like I'm running to stand this business just to pay the bills.'"

According to Lanois, many of what are now considered U2 classics almost weren't. After arduous sessions for "Where the Streets Have No Name" – whose difficult arrangement forced Lanois "to stand at a big blackboard like a teacher in a science class, conducting the band with a pointer" – co-producer Brian Eno nearly erased the song in frustration. "Too much emphasis was being placed on [the song]; he was tired of it," Lanois says, chuckling. "But it felt like an opening scene, so we made it the record's first track."

"I Still Haven't Found What I'm Looking For" began its life as a song called "The Weather Girls." "We agreed the song wasn't going to make the record, but it had this great beat, so we created a new song on top of it," he says. "It always had this R&B gospel rhythm to it. I remember humming a traditional melody in Bono's ear; he said, 'That's it! Don't sing anymore!' and went off and wrote the melody as we know it.

"I think *Joshua Tree* was probably the conclusive record of the sound we were going after," Lanois continues. "U2 really welcomed new angles and experimentation; they realized that another way of looking at their music allowed access to doors they didn't know about. It's ongoing for them."

322 | Disintegration
THE CURE
ELEKTRA 1989

According to the kids on *South Park,* this is the best album ever made. According to many depressive Eighties-minded kids, it's the *only* album ever made. On "Fascination Street," Robert Smith's voice shakes like milk as he makes adolescent angst sound so wonderfully, wonderfully pretty.

323 | Jagged Little Pill
ALANIS MORISSETTE
MAVERICK 1995

The album where a Canadian teen-pop dolly remade herself as a fire-breathing rock priestess. She rails against treacherous men ("You Oughta Know"), conformity ("Hand in My Pocket") and the preponderance of spoons when all you need is a knife ("Ironic"). A Nineties rock classic.

324 | Exile in Guyville
LIZ PHAIR
CAPITOL 1993

A studio expansion of Phair's homemade Girlysound cassettes, *Exile*'s frank sex talk caused a stir. But it's the lacerating honesty of tracks such as "Divorce Song" that sticks, and "Fuck and Run" is one of the saddest songs ever written about dreaming of romance and settling for less.

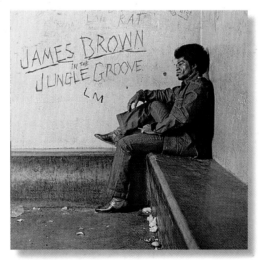

325 | Daydream Nation
SONIC YOUTH
GEFFEN 1988

Sonic Youth have had a long, brilliant career making trippy art punk, and this is their ultimate triumph. Thurston Moore and Lee Ranaldo's guitars are like antennae picking up otherworldly signals and channeling them into the scuzzy urban haze of "Teen Age Riot" and "Eric's Trip."

326 | In the Jungle Groove
JAMES BROWN
POLYDOR 1986

A compilation of Mr. Dynamite's singles from the Seventies, including the earliest recordings with his band the J.B.'s. The "Funky Drummer" break may be the most sampled drum loop ever, and on "Give It Up or Turn It a Loose," Brown drops the heaviest funk of his – or anyone's – life.

327 | Tonight's the Night
NEIL YOUNG
WARNER BROS. 1975

Young made this album as a tribute to two friends who died from drugs, Crazy Horse guitarist Danny Whitten and roadie Bruce Berry. Young sounds like he's on the edge of a breakdown in the mournful ballads "Tired Eyes" and "Speakin' Out," recorded with a loose, heavily emotional sound.

328 | Help!
THE BEATLES
CAPITOL 1965

The moptops' second movie was a Swinging London goof, but the soundtrack included the classics "You've Got to Hide Your Love Away" and "Ticket to Ride," as well as the lovely "I've Just Seen a Face." *Help!* didn't break new ground, but it paved the way for the Beatles' next stop: *Rubber Soul*.

329 | Shoot Out the Lights
RICHARD AND LINDA THOMPSON
HANNIBAL 1982

The British folk-rock duo's last album together is a harrowing portrait of a marriage gone bad, made as their own marriage collapsed. The catchiest song is called "Wall of Death"; the scariest is "Walking on a Wire." They agreed to tour, and audiences got to see Linda attack Richard onstage.

330 | Wild Gift
X
RHINO 1981

John Doe and Exene Cervenka harmonize about doomed love over L.A. garage-rock thrash, changing the emotional language of punk. They were the White Stripes of their day, a young couple messing with country and blues in gems such as "Adult Books," "Beyond and Back" and "We're Desperate."

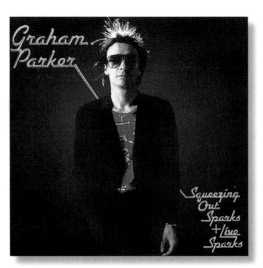

331 | Squeezing Out Sparks
GRAHAM PARKER
ARISTA 1979

An angry young crank in the mode of Elvis Costello and Joe Jackson, Parker, a former gas-station attendant, rode the wave of U.K. punk. His fifth album combines bar-band rock with New Wave hooks, but his bitter paranoia also shines through on "Protection" and "Nobody Hurts You."

332 | Superunknown
SOUNDGARDEN
A&M 1994

They were the Seattle punk scene's headbanging answer to *Led Zeppelin II*. But they became real songwriters on *Superunknown*, shaping their angst into grunge anthems like "Black Hole Sun." "We realized the importance of melody," said Chris Cornell. "Maybe we've been listening to Bryan Ferry."

333 | Aqualung
JETHRO TULL
CAPITOL 1971

Tull were hairy prog-rock philosophers who decried organized religion ("Hymn 43") and modern hypocrisy ("Aqualung") while managing to incorporate flute solos. With several FM-radio hits, this was the record that made Tull into a major arena band. The cover painting gave Seventies kids nightmares.

334 | **Cheap Thrills**
BIG BROTHER AND THE HOLDING COMPANY
SONY 1968

Janis Joplin said, "We're just a sloppy group of street freaks." But these San Francisco acid rockers were the most simpatico band she ever had, especially when its raw racket backs her up on "Piece of My Heart," perhaps her greatest recording.

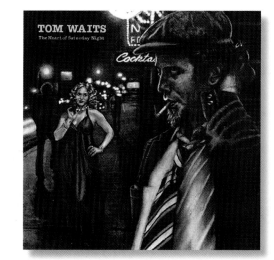

335 | **The Heart of Saturday Night**
TOM WAITS
ELEKTRA/ASYLUM 1974

By the time Waits made his second album, he'd fully developed his talent for growling, jazzy beatnik gutter tales, and largely dispensed with the love songs. He does it best on "Diamonds on My Windshield" and "The Ghosts of Saturday Night."

336 | **Damaged**
BLACK FLAG
SST 1981

MCA refused to release this, denouncing it as "immoral" and "anti-parent." High praise, but Black Flag lived up to it, defining L.A. hardcore punk with violent guitar and the pissed-off scream of Henry Rollins, especially on "TV Party" and "Rise Above." Punks still listen to *Damaged*, and parents still hate it.

ARTIFACTS

"I went to Robbie and asked , 'How did that come out of you?' He said that ['The Night They Drove Old Dixie Down' was] from being with Levon so long and being in that place and that time.… He wanted to write that song right at Levon, to let him know how much those things meant to him."
BAND ROAD MANAGER JONATHAN TAPLIN
(RS 266, JUNE 1ST, 1978)

Robbie Robertson's handwritten lyrics to the Band's "The Night They Drove Old Dixie Down"

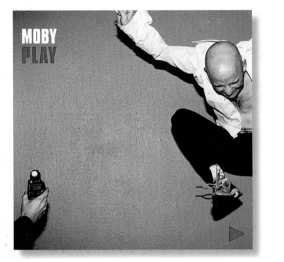

337 | Play
MOBY
V2/BMG 1999

Play was the techno album that proved a Mac could have a soul. Moby took ancient blues and gospel voices and layered them with dance grooves, creating songs such as "Porcelain" and "Natural Blues," which have a strange, haunting beauty – and enhanced countless TV commercials.

338 | Violator
DEPECHE MODE
WARNER BROS. 1990

For many Depeche Mode fans, *Violator* is the crowning glory of the boys' black-leather period. In "Sweetest Perfection," "Halo" and "World in My Eyes," they turn teen angst and sexual obsession into grand synth-pop melodrama, and their attempt at guitar rock resulted in a hit with "Personal Jesus."

339 | Bat Out of Hell
MEAT LOAF
SONY 1977

Meat Loaf's megaselling, megabombastic breakthrough was written by pianist Jim Steinman, who'd intended the material for a new version of *Peter Pan*. This is one of rock's most theatrical, grandiose records, yet Loaf bring real emotion to "Two Out of Three Ain't Bad" and "Paradise by the Dashboard Light."

340 | Berlin
LOU REED
RCA 1973

Reed followed up his breakthrough album, *Transformer*, with *Berlin*, which he called "my version of *Hamlet*." A bleak song cycle about an abusive, drug-fueled relationship, it's hugely ambitious but also one of the gloomiest records ever made – slow, druggy and heavily orchestrated by producer Bob Ezrin.

MEATLOAF

"All I can say is: You can't take this shit seriously."
(RS 278, NOVEMBER 16TH, 1978)

341 | Stop Making Sense

TALKING HEADS
WARNER BROS. 1984

This soundtrack to Jonathan Demme's 1984 concert film functions as a greatest-hits and a band history. It begins with a spare version of "Psycho Killer" and builds to an expansive "Take Me to the River," where the Heads are joined by members of the P-Funk mob. Eighties art funk at its finest.

342 | 3 Feet High and Rising

DE LA SOUL
TOMMY BOY 1989

At the end of the Eighties, De La Soul rolled out their new style of "D.A.I.S.Y. Age," which stood for "Da Inner Sound, Y'All." They led the Native Tongues posse – no gold chains, just samples, skits, jokes and beats, biting everyone from P-Funk to Hall and Oates and Johnny Cash.

343 | The Piper at the Gates of Dawn

PINK FLOYD
CAPITOL 1967

"I'm full of dust and guitars," Pink Floyd's Syd Barrett told ROLLING STONE. Here's what that sounded like. The band's debut is all playful, psychedelic imagery and acid guitars. "Astronomy Domine" shows the group's pop side; "Interstellar Overdrive" shows its spacier freakouts.

344 | At Newport 1960

MUDDY WATERS
MCA 1960

A stomping live document of the period when Waters started reaching a wider pop audience. *Newport* still works as a splendid intro to the Chicago blues: It's got his classics – "Hoochie Coochie Man," a torrid "Got My Mojo Working" – delivered by a tough, tight band, anchored by harp genius James Cotton.

345 | Roger the Engineer (a.k.a. Over Under Sideways Down)

THE YARDBIRDS
WARNER BROS. 1966

Jeff Beck played briefly in the Yardbirds, but his presence is heavily felt here, where he pushed the Brit blues rockers in a more adventurous, psychedelic direction. Case in point: his mind-bending riff on "Over Under Sideways Down."

346 | Rust Never Sleeps

NEIL YOUNG AND CRAZY HORSE
WARNER BROS. 1979

The live *Rust Never Sleeps* is essential Young, full of impossibly delicate acoustic songs and ragged Crazy Horse rampages. Highlights: "My My Hey Hey" (a tribute to Johnny Rotten), a surreal political spiel called "Welfare Mothers" and "Powderfinger," where Young's guitar hits the sky like never before.

Leiber and Stoller

Stoller, Presley and Leiber (from left) on the "Jailhouse Rock" set, 1957; the sheet music for "Hound Dog" (below). first cut by Big Mama Thornton.

Songs by Jerry Leiber and Mike Stoller have been recorded by Elvis Presley, the Beatles, James Brown – and just about everyone else. Their witty, sophisticated R&B was marked by singles like Presley's "Jailhouse Rock," Ben E. King's "Spanish Harlem" and the Drifters' "On Broadway." They were inducted into the Rock & Roll Hall of Fame in 1987.

Where did your ideas come from?

STOLLER: Sometimes it was things that caught our attention. Like with "Yakety Yak." We were in Jerry's apartment and he was in the kitchen making tea. I started playing this funny rhythm and he yelled, "Take out the papers and the trash." I yelled back one line about spending cash, and we knew we had a song.

What was the inspiration for "Hound Dog"?

LEIBER (LYRICIST): It was an old song Mike found by Furry Lewis called "You're a Dirty Mutha Furrier, Don't You Know?" I asked him where he got it, and he said, "I just stuck my hand in a pile of records and it came out."

How do you feel about all the cursing in songwriting nowadays?

LEIBER: I think it's a commercial put-on to attract young kids. But there are people like Snoop Dogg who use a four-letter word out of real temperament and feeling.

Who's your favorite lyricist?

LEIBER: Irving Berlin. I could never find a better word for anything in his lyrics.

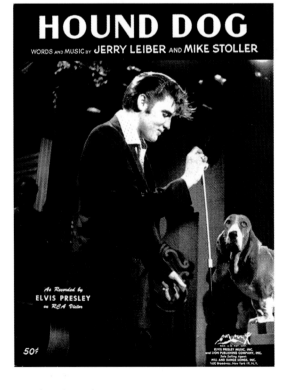

347 | Brothers in Arms
DIRE STRAITS
WARNER BROS. 1985

Mark Knopfler started writing "Money for Nothing" when he overheard a New York appliance salesman's anti-rock-star, anti-MTV rant. The song, of course, became a huge MTV hit, and this album shows off Knopfler's incisive songwriting and lush guitar riffs on "Walk of Life" and "So Far Away."

348 | 52nd Street
BILLY JOEL
COLUMBIA 1978

The intensive roadwork dictated by the success of *The Stranger* produced a leaner, rock-oriented follow-up, typified by "Big Shot." Like Elton John, Joel assimilated whatever styles (jazz, Latin rhythms) suited his purpose. "I don't want to limit my diet," he said, "sampling only one vegetable in the garden."

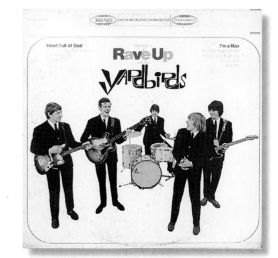

349 | Having a Rave Up With the Yardbirds
THE YARDBIRDS
EPIC 1965

Freed from Eric Clapton's blues purism and spurred by Jeff Beck's reckless exhibitionism, the Yardbirds launched a noisy rock & roll avant-garde. Partially recorded at Chess in Chicago and Sun in Memphis, this is the bridge between beat groups and psychedelia.

350 | 12 Songs
RANDY NEWMAN
REPRISE 1970

Newman's second disc remains one of his finest, with Ry Cooder and a few of the Byrds contributing to the loose, confident sound. The songs are prime caustic, funny Newman – especially the piano rockers "Mama Told Me (Not to Come)" and "Have You Seen My Baby?" and the tormented "Suzanne."

BILLY JOEL

"I don't know what the hell I'm doing when I'm writing. I'm just going. I work myself up into this state. For weeks, I'm empty. I got nothing. I'm dry, I walk around, I'm the worst person in the world, I got stubble, I smoke, I drink, I get bombed. I curse at everything, I throw things, I think it's all over. And then I click. I don't analyze it, I don't intellectualize it, I just do it."

(RS 280, DECEMBER 14TH, 1978)

351 | **Between the Buttons**
THE ROLLING STONES
ABKCO 1967

Andrew Loog Oldham called it the "most English of Stones albums." Music-hall piano rubs up against "Let's Spend the Night Together" and psychedelic soul of "Ruby Tuesday." And the lovely "She Smiled Sweetly" is offset by yet another great Chuck Berry rip, "Miss Amanda Jones."

352 | **Sketches of Spain**
MILES DAVIS
COLUMBIA 1960

This collaboration between Davis and arranger Gil Evans took fifteen orchestral sessions to record and six months to assemble. It wasn't an attempt to play Spanish music but to suggest it; its muted beauty contains enormous passion. But is it jazz? Davis responded, "It's music, and I like it."

353 | **Honky Château**
ELTON JOHN
MCA 1972

After a couple of weightier singer-songwriter outings, it was delightful to hear Elton John revel in the simple pop pleasures of "Honky Cat." Written in four days, and using his signature touring band for the first time, *Honky Château* is a snapshot of an artist loosening up and coming into his full powers.

354 | **Singles Going Steady**
BUZZCOCKS
IRS 1979

Singles collects eight British 45s into a perfect punk album. This Manchester group took the sound of the Ramones and made it jittery and even faster. Songs such as "Everybody's Happy Nowadays" define a world of permanently frustrated punk desire.

355 | **Stankonia**
OUTKAST
LAFACE 2000

"We call it slumadelic," said Big Boi of OutKast's far-reaching blend of hip-hop, funk, rock and otherworldly sounds. "Miss Jackson" was something new for rap: an apology to the mother of an ex-girlfriend. And the sadly still timely "B.O.B. (Bombs Over Baghdad)" twitches to techno beats and screeching guitar.

356 | **Siamese Dream**
THE SMASHING PUMPKINS
VIRGIN 1993

On their second disc, the Pumpkins pushed further from Nineties alt-rock to a grander, orchestrated sound with multiple guitar parts, strings and a Mellotron. Alt-rock ended up following the band on their trip: *Siamese Dream* is packed with hits ("Cherub Rock," "Today").

NEW
ORDER
——
SUBSTANCE
1987

357 | **Substance**
NEW ORDER
QWEST 1987

This assemblage of twelve-inch singles and remixes charts New Order's transformation from gloom rockers to electrodisco pioneers. The highlights – club hits including "Blue Monday" and "Bizarre Love Triangle" – are full of bass melodies that young bands such as Interpol are still trying to figure out.

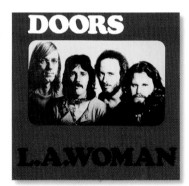

358 | **L.A. Woman**
THE DOORS
ELEKTRA 1971

Jim Morrison said that the Doors wanted to "get back to what we did originally: just be very primitive in our approach, very relaxed." Recorded in their rehearsal room with Morrison's mike set up in the bathroom, this was a bluesier, confident Doors, epitomized by "Riders on the Storm." Morrison died soon after.

359 Ray of Light
MADONNA
MAVERICK 1998

For her first post-motherhood disc, Madonna and producer William Orbit showed the world that electronica doesn't have to be cold. Songs like the title track and "Nothing Really Matters" are beat-driven but restrained – filled with warmth and wonder. *Ray* also features her best singing ever.

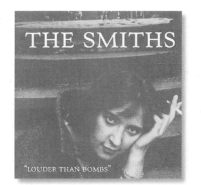

360 American Recordings
JOHNNY CASH
AMERICAN/SONY 1994

After a decade of neglect by the country establishment, Cash returned with a stark acoustic album produced by Rick Rubin. "There was nothing to hide behind, and that was scary," said Cash. With everything from gospel to a Danzig cover, it was a reminder that a giant still walked among us.

361 Louder Than Bombs
THE SMITHS
SIRE 1987

Designed to whet U.S. interest while the Smiths completed a new LP, this dazzling assortment of singles and album tracks became an unintended epitaph when the group dissolved. The band's best songs are here, from "How Soon Is Now" to "William, It Was Really Nothing."

362 Mott the Hoople
MOTT
COLUMBIA 1973

David Bowie's "All the Young Dudes" had revived Mott's career, but Ian Hunter "wanted people to know that David didn't create this band." Producing themselves, they weathered skepticism and studio fistfights to record this examination of rock as "a loser's game"; *Mott* became their greatest success.

363 Is This It
THE STROKES
RCA 2001

The objective of *Is This It,* said Strokes singer Julian Casablancas, "was to be really cool and non-mainstream, and be really popular." Recorded literally under the streets of New York, this blast of guitar-combo racket passionately reconciled those seemingly contradictory aspirations, and accomplished both.

364 Rage Against the Machine
RAGE AGAINST THE MACHINE
EPIC 1992

"I believe in this band's ability to bridge the gap between entertainment and activism," declared Zack de la Rocha, whose radical politics found sympathetic muscle in Tom Morello's howling one-guitar army, making a furor unheard since the MC5 and Clash.

365 Regatta de Blanc
THE POLICE
A&M 1979

The Police may have been lumped in with U.K. punk, but Sting said the mission was always to "sell great music to masses of people." They did that with *Regatta,* an album best known for "Message in a Bottle" but distinguished by the mutant reggae of "The Bed's Too Big Without You" and "Walking on the Moon."

366 Volunteers
JEFFERSON AIRPLANE
RCA 1969

Guitarist Jorma Kaukonen called Paul Kantner's revolutionary cheerleading "naive," but that didn't prevent the band from delivering this album with anthemic fervor. Also here: the gorgeous "Wooden Ships" and "Eskimo Blue Day," where Grace Slick sings, "The human name doesn't mean shit to a tree."

367 | Siren
ROXY MUSIC
ATCO 1975

"New customers are always welcome!" Bryan Ferry joked as "Love Is the Drug" became his band's first U.S. hit. This delicious LP of lounge-lizard ennui, inspired in part by Ferry's girlfriend, Jerry Hall, draws upon Roxy's arty roots even as it anticipates the even more rarified atmospheres of *Avalon* [see No. 303].

368 | Late for the Sky
JACKSON BROWNE
ASYLUM 1974

On his dark third album, Browne explored, in the words of one ROLLING STONE reviewer, the "romantic possibility in the shadow of apocalypse." There's an undercurrent of dread on *Late for the Sky*, from "Before the Deluge" to "For a Dancer" – not to mention a lot of obvious songwriting genius.

369 | Post
BJÖRK
ELEKTRA 1995

"I have to re-create the universe every morning when I wake up," Björk said, explaining her second solo album's utter lack of musical inhibition. *Post* bounces from big-band jazz ("It's Oh So Quiet") to trip-hop. Fun fact: For her vocals, Björk extended her mike cord to a beach so she could sing to the sea.

370 | The Eagles
THE EAGLES
ASYLUM 1972

This debut created a new template for laid-back L.A. country-rock style. Behind the band's mellow message – "Take It Easy," "Peaceful Easy Feeling" – was a relentless drive. "Everybody had to look good, sing good, play good and write good," Glenn Frey told Cameron Crowe in ROLLING STONE.

371 | The Ultimate Collection 1948-1990
JOHN LEE HOOKER
RHINO 1991

"Boogie Chillen" was Hooker's first hit and one of the last songs he played on this earth. In between that was a lifetime of pure mojo. *Collection* houses that song, "Boom Boom," and a voice Bonnie Raitt said could "tap into all the pain he'd ever felt."

372 | (What's the Story) Morning Glory?
OASIS
EPIC 1995

With their second album, the fighting Gallagher brothers embraced the Stones and Beatles comparisons, then went ahead and established themselves as a rock & roll force in their own right with barnburners ("Roll With It") and epic tunes like the glorious "Wonderwall."

373 | CrazySexyCool
TLC
ARISTA 1994

Things were not well with TLC during the making of *CrazySexyCool*: Lisa "Left Eye" Lopes was lighting fires, and the group was in a financial slide that would end in bankruptcy proceedings. But they emerged with the most effervescent and soulful R&B pop anyone had seen since the Supremes.

374 | Funky Kingston
TOOTS AND THE MAYTALS
MANGO 1973

Loose, funky, exuberant, *Kingston* is the quintessential document of Jamaica's greatest act after Bob Marley. Showcasing some of the Maytals' best songs ("Pressure Drop") and borrowing from soul, pop and gospel, *Kingston* introduced the world to the great Toots Hibbert.

375 Greetings From Asbury Park, N.J.

BRUCE SPRINGSTEEN
COLUMBIA 1973

When he started out, he was the pimp's main prophet. Springsteen's opening shot dazzled with rapid-fire, poetic street jive. "Blinded by the Light," "Spirit in the Night" and "Growin' Up" are R&B-folk songs populated by a cast of gypsies, tramps and thieves.

376 Sunflower

THE BEACH BOYS
CARIBOU 1970

One year after they were dropped by Capitol, and just as Brian Wilson began his psychological descent, the Beach Boys scraped together the remarkable *Sunflower.* The warm harmonies and dreamy textures of "Cool, Cool Water" and "Forever" show Carl and Dennis Wilson stepping up to fill Brian's space.

377 Modern Lovers

MODERN LOVERS
RHINO 1976

Jonathan Richman moved from Boston to New York as a teenager in hopes of sleeping on Lou Reed's couch. That influence shows on the two-chord anthem "Roadrunner." Recorded in 1972 but not released until 1976, *Lovers* turned the tough sounds of the Velvets into an ode to suburban romanticism.

378 More Songs About Buildings and Food

TALKING HEADS
SIRE 1978

Spawned in the punk scene of 1970s Manhattan, the Talking Heads struck out in a surprising direction with their second album, weaving in funk and gospel (including a cover of Al Green's "Take Me to the River") and announcing themselves as the newest of the New Wave bands.

379 A Quick One (Happy Jack)

THE WHO
MCA 1966

The Who were caught in the middle of an experimental phase, and the results were fascinatingly quirky. The cover of the theme from *Batman* shows the quartet having fun; Pete Townshend's mini-opera "A Quick One While He's Away" foreshadows his songwriting ambition.

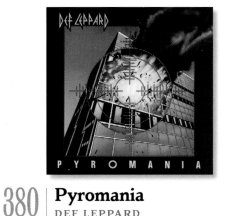

380 Pyromania

DEF LEPPARD
MERCURY 1983

A perfect balance of melodic hooks and metal: Before he met Shania Twain, producer Mutt Lange crammed an arena-ready sound and stacks of choruses onto *Pyromania.* "The choruses on things like 'Rock of Ages' were enormous," said singer Joe Elliott. The band was written off by critics, but the kids understood.

381 Pretzel Logic

STEELY DAN
MCA 1974

Donald Fagen and Walter Becker make their love of jazz explicit, covering Duke Ellington and copping the intro of "Rikki Don't Lose That Number" from hard-bop pianist Horace Silver. The guitars on their third LP are dialed back for a sound that's slick and airtight without being cold. The lyrics? As twisted as ever.

382 Enter the Wu-Tang: 36 Chambers

WU-TANG CLAN
LOUD/RCA 1993

East Coast hip-hop made a return in 1993, thanks to a nine-man troupe of Staten Island, New York, MCs with a fascination for Hong Kong martial-arts mythology and producer RZA's love of menacing atmospherics. Hip-hop had been harder, but it had rarely been this dirty.

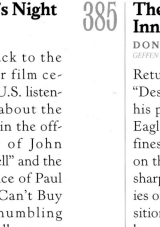

383 | Country Life

ROXY MUSIC
VIRGIN 1974

The ultra-cool murmur of Bryan Ferry's voice could not be better suited to the warm musical setting offered by guitarist Phil Manzanera. *Life* brims with romantic pop and sleek arrangements that hint at a lifestyle of luxury, style and erotic allure; "Thrill of It All" is a high-water mark for art rock and glam.

384 | A Hard Day's Night

THE BEATLES
CAPITOL 1964

This soundtrack to the Richard Lester film cemented all that U.S. listeners had heard about the Beatles' genius in the off-kilter beauty of John Lennon's "If I Fell" and the rockabilly bounce of Paul McCartney's "Can't Buy Me Love." A humbling footnote: The album was recorded in one day.

385 | The End of the Innocence

DON HENLEY
GEFFEN 1989

Returning to the theme of "Desperado" and much of his past work, the former Eagle hitched some of his finest melodies (especially on the gentle title track) to sharply focused lyrical studies of men in troubled transition – from youth to adulthood, from innocence to responsibility.

386 | Elephant

THE WHITE STRIPES
V2 2003

Jack and Meg White's minimalist garage rock proves it has more depth and power than even their more optimistic critics expected. On tracks like the slow-burning "Seven Nation Army" and "The Hardest Button to Button," Jack White's songwriting talent finally matches his blues fan-boy, art-school shtick.

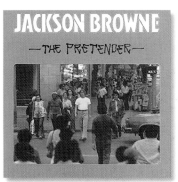

387 | The Pretender

JACKSON BROWNE
ASYLUM 1976

The confident, easy pulse of Southern California folk rock mutated into something far more weighty with Browne's fourth album. His first wife committed suicide while he was writing these songs, and they took a bitter turn. "Say a prayer for the pretender," he sings, "who stared out so young and strong, only to surrender."

388 | Willy and the Poor Boys

CREEDENCE CLEARWATER REVIVAL
FANTASY 1968

Sharp social criticism ("Fortunate Son") and party music ("Down on the Corner") take a ride on the Creedence bandwagon: Jon Fogerty's ability to wed swamp rock with catchy, complex arrangements gave *Willy* a durability few rock albums can match.

389 | Good Old Boys

RANDY NEWMAN
REPRISE 1974

Newman draws on his roots in the blues and New Orleans boogie to uncork this blistering portrait of the American South. He shows that he was pop's most cutting satirist on "Rednecks" – a song that doesn't spare Northern or Southern racism; Newman said he still gets nervous playing it in some cities.

390 | For Your Pleasure

ROXY MUSIC
VIRGIN 1973

Keyboardist Brian Eno's last album with Roxy Music is the pop equivalent of Ultrasuede: highly stylish, abstract-leaning art rock. The collision of Eno's and singer Bryan Ferry's clashing visions gives *Pleasure* a wild, tense charm – especially on the driving "Editions of You" and "Do the Strand."

Presley begins his reign, 1956.

Elvis Presley

ELVIS PRESLEY

When Elvis Presley walked into RCA Studios in Nashville for his first recording sessions after being signed to the major label, in 1955, he was, recalls his producer, Chet Atkins, "maybe apprehensive" about the prospect of working in an environment more regimented than Memphis' Sun Records. There, he had rehearsed and recorded free of time constraints, with little direction from Sun founder Sam Phillips in the control room. Having heard about Phillips' approach, Atkins stayed out of the way during the sessions, hoping to capture the startling intensity and seeming spontaneity of Elvis' five Sun singles.

What unfolded surprised Atkins nonetheless. "He's the first fella I ever remember working with who would go into the studio and take his time, take all night to do one song," he said. "Back in those days, we'd do four songs in three hours – and they sounded like it, of course."

Elvis hit his stride quickly in the studio, gaining confidence in his instincts as the hits piled up. "I remember once going to make a suggestion," Atkins recounts. "[Elvis] turned it down. I said to myself, 'Well, he's his own man now; he wants to conduct the sessions himself.' So I never offered any more advice."

Atkins has one other indelible memory from those years, dating from the initial RCA sessions (which produced the albums *Elvis Presley* and *Elvis*). Once, Atkins remembers, "Elvis split his pants." He chuckles softly. "I think they were black pants with a pink stripe down the side. He sent back to the hotel for a new pair and threw the old ones out in the hall. The next day or so the receptionist said, 'Chet, what do you want me to do with these old dirty pants?' I said, 'You better keep 'em. They'll be worth a lot of money someday.' 'Nah,' she turned up her nose. About six months later, she was trying to get on *I've Got a Secret*, or one of those shows, because she got Elvis' pants."

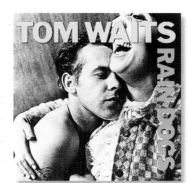

391 **Blue Lines**
MASSIVE ATTACK
VIRGIN 1991

One of the most influential records of the Nineties, *Lines* was perhaps the first post-hip-hop masterpiece: a combination of rap, dub and soul that gave birth to what used to be called trip-hop, and now we just call chill-out. "What's important to us is the pace," said the band's 3D, "the weight of the bass and the mood."

392 **Eliminator**
ZZ TOP
WARNER 1983

Pure Americana: this song cycle about burning rubber, high heels and adrenaline took fuzzed-out Texas blues guitar and lashed it around rollicking boogie. ZZ Top's megaplatinum album also had a high-gloss Eighties sheen and singles like "Sharp Dressed Man" that would help it sell some 10 million copies.

393 **Rain Dogs**
TOM WAITS
POLYGRAM 1985

"I like weird, ludicrous things," Waits once said. That understatement plays out most clearly on *Rain Dogs,* his finest portrait of the tragic kingdom of the streets. Waits abandons his grungy minimalism on the gorgeous "Downtown Train" and gets backing by Keith Richards on "Big Black Mariah."

394 **Anthology**
THE TEMPTATIONS
MOTOWN 1995

Indisputably the greatest black vocal group of the modern era, this quintet created masterpiece after masterpiece of chugging, gospel-tinged soul. *Anthology* captures a slice of the Temps' prime, including "My Girl," "I Can't Get Next to You" and "I Wish It Would Rain." What's not to like?

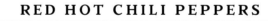

RED HOT CHILI PEPPERS

395 **Californication**
RED HOT CHILI PEPPERS
COLUMBIA 1999

Turning their focus completely to songs instead of jams, the Red Hot Chili Peppers steered frontman Anthony Kiedis' voice into a radio-friendlier wail on *Californication.* That, and the reappearance of guitarist/secret weapon John Frusciante helped form beautifully composed songs such as "Scar Tissue."

"It was always very funny to me, the way the Chili Peppers were perceived as this macho jock thing. We took off our shirts a lot, and Anthony wrote a lot of songs abut sex. But I feel the music is frequently feminine. I've always been, like, the girly-boy."

FLEA
(RS 839, APRIL 27TH, 2000)

396 | Illmatic

NAS
COLUMBIA 1994

Other rappers were harder and better-armed, but nobody captured the creeping menace of life on the streets like this twenty-year-old from New York's Queensbridge projects. With lines like "I never sleep, 'cause sleep is the cousin of death," Nas showed more poetic style than any MC since Rakim.

397 | (Pronounced Leh-Nerd Skin-Nerd)

LYNYRD SKYNYRD
MCA 1973

From the git-go, these Southern rockers played hard, lived hard and shot from the hip (with three guitars!). Discovered and produced by Al Kooper, Skynyrd offered taut rockers including "Poison Whiskey" and the ultimate anthem, "Freebird."

398 | Dr. John's Gumbo

DR. JOHN
ATCO 1972

After a series of eerie, voodoo-stoked records, pianist Mac Rebennack – a.k.a. Dr. John – returned to his New Orleans roots with spirited covers of classics such as "Iko Iko" and "Junko Partner." With his rolling piano figures and gritty vocals, Dr. John rekindled interest in the New Orleans sound.

399 | Radio City

BIG STAR
ARDENT 1974

Like the Velvet Underground, Big Star's influence far outstripped their sales. On this lean, guitar-driven LP they come up with a new, upside-down pop sound, filtering their love of the Beatles through their Memphis-soul roots. Towering achievement: the blissful, sad "September Gurls."

"'Graceland' and 'The Boy in the Bubble' each took three or four months to write. There would be long stretches where I was throwing out stuff. I wrote a whole 'Boy in the Bubble' and threw it out.

"If it's a subject that's close to me personally, it takes longer – there's a lot of avoidance. I don't want to write something hurtful to myself."

PAUL SIMON
(RS 485, OCTOBER 23RD, 1986)

Paul Simon's handwritten lyrics to "Graceland"

400 | Sandinista!

THE CLASH
EPIC 1980

The Clash's ballooning ambition peaked with *Sandinista!*, a three-album set named after the Nicaraguan revolutionary movement. Joe Strummer and Mick Jones reached beyond punk and reggae into dub, R&B, calypso, gospel and even a kids' chorus on "Career Opportunities" – whatever crossed their minds.

401 | Rid of Me

PJ HARVEY
ISLAND 1993

Like Patti Smith, she wanted to be Bob Dylan. Unlike Patti Smith, she played guitar very, very loud. Polly Jean Harvey's second album, recorded with Steve Albini, is charged with aggressive eroticism and rock fury. It careens from blues to goth to grunge, often in the space of a single song.

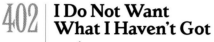

402 | I Do Not Want What I Haven't Got

SINÉAD O'CONNOR
CHRYSALIS 1990

O'Connor's second LP is most remembered for her dramatic reading of Prince's "Nothing Compares 2 U." But *I Do Not Want* delivers true originality and range, from the maternal warmth of "Three Babies" to the fiddle and beatbox of "I Am Stretched on Your Grave."

403 | Strange Days

THE DOORS
ELEKTRA 1967

The Doors stretch into darker, more baroque sounds on their second album. The catchy single, "Love Me Two Times," is overshadowed by the mood of foreboding and alienation in most songs, especially "People Are Strange" and "When the Music's Over," which demands, "We want the world and we want it now!"

404 | Time Out of Mind

BOB DYLAN
COLUMBIA 1997

The first of Dylan's two late-career triumphs. Producer Daniel Lanois' dark, atmospheric settings envelop Dylan in a sonic fog appropriate to the isolation and distance he sings of in a ravaged, weary voice. The songs – especially "Love Sick" and "Not Dark Yet" – are ghostly but forceful.

405 | 461 Ocean Boulevard

ERIC CLAPTON
RSO 1974

Boulevard marked Clapton's return from heroin addiction, and its mellow, springy groove left guitar histrionics behind. He paid tribute to Robert Johnson and Elmore James, but it was his cover of Bob Marley's "I Shot the Sheriff" that gave him his first Number One hit.

406 | Pink Flag

WIRE
HARVEST 1977

This first-generation U.K. punk band made sparse tunes that erupted in combustible snippets on its twenty-one-track debut album. America never got it, but *Pink Flag* – as revolutionary discs tend to do – influenced some important bands, including the Sonic Youth, Elastica and R.E.M.

407 | Double Nickels on the Dime

MINUTEMEN
SST 1984

"Our band could be your life," sing the Minutemen on "History Lesson – Part 2," and never did a lyric better articulate punk's Everyman aesthetic. Guitarist D. Boon and bassist Mike Watt push each other to fast, funny and agitated heights. Sadly, Boon would die a year later in a van accident.

408 Mezzanine

MASSIVE ATTACK
VIRGIN 1998

Tricky had split, and three years had passed since Massive Attack's last proper album, but *Mezzanine* returned the Bristol, England, collective to prominence. Cocteau Twins' Elizabeth Fraser was the designated chanteuse, and her icy voice stands out against the earthy backdrops of songs like "Teardrops."

409 Beauty and the Beat

GO·GO'S
A&M 1981

The most popular girl group of the New Wave surfed to the top of the charts with this hooky debut. Everyone knows "We Got the Beat" and "Our Lips Our Sealed," exuberant songs that livened up the Top Forty, but the entire album welds punkish spirit to party-minded pop.

"The Go-Go's are different. Admitting you like us is like admitting you like Twinkies. Twinkies taste good, but my God, Twinkies? Who are you kidding."

JANE WIEDLIN
(RS 375, AUGUST 5TH, 1982)

410 Van Halen

VAN HALEN
WARNER BROS. 1978

This debut gave the world a new guitar hero (Eddie Van Halen) and charismatic frontman (David Lee Roth). Tunes such as "Runnin' With the Devil" and "Ain't Talkin' 'Bout Love" put the swagger back in hard rock, and Van Halen's jaw-dropping technique, particularly on "Eruption," raised the bar for rock guitar.

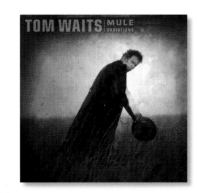

411 Mule Variations

TOM WAITS
EPITAPH 1999

After five silent years, *Variations* was the victorious return of Waits' rawboned, bluesy art rock. Using found instruments for rhythm and Smokey Hormel's angular guitar for color, Waits careers from carnival barker to croaky balladeer. The highlights: the sad but sweet "Hold On" and "House Where Nobody Lives."

412 Boy

U2
ISLAND 1980

Too ingenuous for punk, too unironic for New Wave, U2 arrived on *Boy* as big-time dreamers with the ambition to back it up. The Dublin foursome boasted Bono's arena-ready voice and Dave "the Edge" Evans' echoey, effects-laden guitar, as well as anthemic songs such as the club favorite "I Will Follow."

413 Band on the Run

WINGS
APPLE 1972

Paul McCartney and Wings trekked to EMI's studio in Lagos, Nigeria, for seven stressful weeks to make *Band*, regarded by many as McCartney's finest post-Beatles hour. Opening with the one-two punch of "Band on the Run" and "Jet" (named after Paul's dog), it proved that McCartney still knew how to rock.

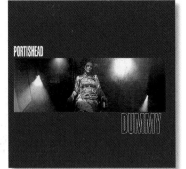

414 | Dummy

PORTISHEAD
POLYGRAM 1994

Portishead used some of the same building blocks as fellow Bristol, England, triphoppers Massive Attack – woozy break beats, jazzy samples, live guitar, girl singer/guy programmer dynamic – but Beth Gibbon's brooding, pop-cabaret vocals showed to the world that you could feel real pain over a trip-hop groove.

415 | The "Chirping" Crickets

BUDDY HOLLY AND THE CRICKETS
MCA 1957

Holly was only twenty-one when the Crickets cut these tracks, some on an Oklahoma Air Force base. With these standards – "That'll Be the Day," "Oh Boy," "Maybe Baby," "Not Fade Away" – Holly melded country, rockabilly and R&B into rock & roll for the ages.

416 | The Best of the Girl Groups Volumes 1 and 2

VARIOUS ARTISTS
RHINO 1990

In the lean years between Elvis and the Beatles, the girl groups kept the spirit of rock & roll alive. This package has the classics: The Shirelles are the sleek ones, the Ronettes are the sexy ones, and the Shangri-Las are the scary biker chicks hanging on the corner.

417 | Changesone

DAVID BOWIE
RCA 1976

Bowie's first greatest-hits collection sums up the finest disguises of his golden years. He plays the sex-crazed glitter rocker of "Rebel Rebel," the sensitive poet of "Changes," the lonely astro boy of "Space Oddity" and the utterly deranged soul crooner of "Young Americans." And the man was just getting started.

418 | The Battle of Los Angeles

RAGE AGAINST THE MACHINE
EPIC 1999

Some punk, lots of funk, plenty of metal and a mother lode of political fury – it all added up to Rage's loudest album, their last before the band fell apart in 2000. Tom Morello's boombastic guitar effects sounded even more pissed off than Zack de la Rocha's raps.

419 | Presenting the Fabulous Ronettes

THE RONETTES
ABKCO 1964

More a Spanish Harlem street gang than a girl group, the Ronettes were pop goddesses dressed as Catholic schoolgirls gone to hell and back. Phil Spector builds his Wall of Sound as his teen protégée (and future wife) Ronnie Spector belts "Be My Baby" and "Walking in the Rain."

420 | Kid A

RADIOHEAD
CAPITOL 2000

Just when they seemed destined to become the next U2, Radiohead made this fractured, twitchy record. Despite esoteric nods to electronica ("Idioteque") and free jazz ("The National Anthem"), they morphed those sounds into a surprisingly accessible elegy to tenderness – and had a hit anyway.

421 | Grievous Angel

GRAM PARSONS
REPRISE 1973

Parsons helped invent country rock with the Byrds and the Flying Burrito Brothers, but he perfected it here. Emmylou Harris was his ideal singing partner, and their voices blend in the high lonesome wail of "Brass Buttons" and "$1,000 Wedding." Weeks after finishing the album, Parsons was dead at twenty-six.

"You know, I think every revolutionary act is an act of love. Every song that I've written, it is because of my desire to use music as a way to empower and re-humanize people who are livin' in a dehumanizing setting. The song is in order to better the human condition. Every song that I've ever written is a love song."

ZACK DE LA ROCHA
RS 826, NOVEMBER 25TH, 1999

422 | At Budokan

CHEAP TRICK
EPIC/LEGACY 1979

After three studio albums, Cheap Trick were bigger in Japan than in their native America. But this record of a live Tokyo gig became their first U.S. hit. The Japanese schoolgirls are practically the lead instrument here, screaming their lungs out to "Surrender" and "I Want You to Want Me."

423 | Anthology

DIANA ROSS AND THE SUPREMES
MOTOWN 2001

In the genius assembly-line soul of Motown, the Supremes were their own hit factory, all glamour and heartbreak. There may be no more spine-tingling moment in pop than in "You Keep Me Hangin' On," when Ross sings, "Why don't you be a man about it/And set me free?"

424 | Sleepless

PETER WOLF
ARTEMIS 2002

Wolf accomplishes a rare feat on this modern blues album: He sings about adult romance without sounding jaded. The former J. Geils Band singer testifies about true love in his soulful growl, with help from friends such as Mick Jagger ("Nothing But the Wheel") and Keith Richards ("Too Close Together").

425 | Another Green World

BRIAN ENO
E.G. 1975

After years as a rock eccentric, Eno was exploring new ideas about ambient music. But he said goodbye to song form with this album of pure synthetic beauty, mixing lush electronics ("Becalmed") with acoustic instruments ("Everything Merges With the Night") to cast a truly hypnotic spell.

426 Outlandos d'Amour

THE POLICE
A&M 1978

They would get bigger, but they never sounded fresher. The Police were punks who could play their instruments, absorbing reggae into the spare, bouncy sound of their debut album. "Roxanne," "Next to You" and "So Lonely" proved that Sting was already a top-notch pop songwriter.

427 To Bring You My Love

PJ HARVEY
ISLAND 1995

Harvey sings the blues like Nick Cave sings gospel: with more distortion, sex and murder than you remember. *Love* was a towering goth version of grunge. Harvey's whisper is even scarier than her scream in morbid rockers such as "Down by the Water" and "Working for the Man."

428 Here Come the Warm Jets

BRIAN ENO
E.G. 1974

The former Roxy Music keyboardist's first solo album pioneered a new kind of glammy art rock: jagged, free-form and dreamy. "Baby's on Fire" and "Needle in the Camel's Eye" are vicious rockers with detached vocals, and Robert Fripp's warped guitars swarm and stutter.

429 All Things Must Pass

GEORGE HARRISON
CAPITOL 1970

Harrison had almost enough songs stored up from his Beatles days for a triple LP – the gas starts to run out on Side Six jams such as "Thanks for the Pepperoni." But with Eric Clapton and Ringo Starr on board, spiritual guitar quests like "My Sweet Lord" and "What Is Life" became classics.

GEORGE HARRISON

"Don't forget, John and Paul had been more satisfied from their ego point of view, having written all those tunes with the Beatles. Especially after 1966, I was starting to write loads of tunes, and one or two songs per album wasn't sufficient with me. By the time *All Things Must Pass* came, it was like being constipated for years, then finally you were allowed to go. I had seventeen tracks, and I really didn't want to chuck any away at the time – although I'm sure lots of them in retrospect could have been chucked away. I wanted to get shut of them so I could catch up to myself."

(RS 511, OCTOBER 22ND, 1987)

430 #1 Record

BIG STAR
FANTASY 1972

Alex Chilton and Chris Bell were the Memphis whiz kids at the heart of Big Star. They mixed British pop finesse with all-American hard rock, from the surging "Feel" to the acoustic "Thirteen." Big Star didn't sell many records at the time, but over the years they inspired artists such as R.E.M. and Jeff Buckley.

431 | In Utero
NIRVANA
GEFFEN 1993

After the success of *Nevermind*, Nirvana hired the misanthropic Steve Albini to record their new album, and Geffen wanted them to clean up a few of the results. Some of this tension shows in white-noise ruckus like "Serve the Servants," but the only thing that can explain the scalding "Rape Me" is inner pain.

432 | Sea Change
BECK
DGC 2002

Breakups are painful, but breakup records are rarely this lovely. *Sea Change* is the pristine sound of everything falling apart, a glossy take on a bummed-out Sixties folk sound. The music seems to be floating up from the bottom of the ocean; the words were straight from Beck's broken heart.

433 | Tragic Kingdom
NO DOUBT
TRAUMA/INTERSCOPE 1995

No Doubt thought they were the last of the ska revivalists, but they were actually the first of the neo-New Wavers. Gwen Stefani thought she was a pierced Madonna, but she belts "Spiderwebs" like Ethel Merman. The haters thought "Just a Girl" was a novelty, but it was only the first single.

434 | Boys Don't Cry
THE CURE
ELEKTRA/ASYLUM 1979

Before they became a goth-pop group, the Cure were a minimalist, inventive post-punk power trio. *Boys* is all hummable hooks, choppy guitars and mopey vocals. "10:15 Saturday Night" and "Jumping Someone Else's Train" are ingenious: You wait for a guitar solo and get a club-footed bass line instead.

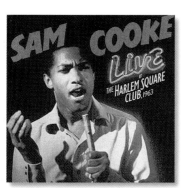

435 | Live at the Harlem Square Club, 1963
SAM COOKE
RCA 1985

Cooke was elegance and soul personified, but he works this Florida club until it's hotter than hell, all while sounding like he never breaks a sweat. He croons and strokes "For Sentimental Reasons" like a superlover, and when the crowd sings along with him, it's magic.

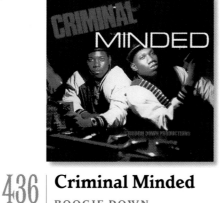

436 | Criminal Minded
BOOGIE DOWN PRODUCTIONS
B-BOY/LANDSPEED 1987

According to KRS-One, the whole world had a criminal mind, and his pioneering gangsta scenarios like "9 mm Goes Bang" were as much critique as celebration. DJ Scott LaRock was killed shortly after the album's release while trying to make the peace in a South Bronx street argument.

437 | Rum, Sodomy and the Lash
THE POGUES
WEA INTERNATIONAL 1985

With a voice like an ashtray, Shane MacGowan led this fabulous disaster of an Irish folk-punk band. Produced by Elvis Costello (who married bassist Cait O'Riordan), *Rum* careens between the maudlin "A Pair of Brown Eyes" and such explosive numbers as "The Sick Bed of Cuchulainn."

438 | Suicide
SUICIDE
MUTE U.S. 1977

These New York synth-punks evoke everything from the Velvet Underground to rockabilly. Martin Rev's low-budget electronics are violent and hypnotic; Alan Vega screams as a rhythmic device. Late-night listening to "Frankie Teardrop," a ten-minute-plus tale of a multiple murder, is not recommended.

439 | Q: Are We Not Men? A: We Are Devo!

DEVO
WARNER BROS. 1978

They came from Akron, Ohio, wore matching jumpsuits and had a sinister theory of devolution. Their debut album runs on rubber-punk guitars and mechanized New Wave beats, with a robotic, soul-chilling version of the Stones' "(I Can't Get No) Satisfaction."

440 | In Color

CHEAP TRICK
EPIC/LEGACY 1977

They were down-home Midwestern boys from Rockford, Illinois, but Cheap Trick had a rock & roll approach as twisted as guitarist Rick Nielsen's bow ties. With blond pin-up boy Robin Zander on vocals, the Trick rocked Beatles-style melodies such as "Oh Caroline," "Downed" and "Come On, Come On."

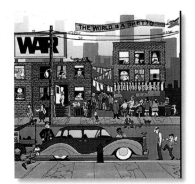

441 | The World Is a Ghetto

WAR
RHINO 1972

A band of badasses doing a Latin-funk song about a Latino TV show from the Fifties – that was "The Cisco Kid," and the band was War, L.A.'s answer to Parliament-Funkadelic. But War were serious: The title song is a sober reflection on inner-city life that hangs in the air like smoke from a riot.

442 | Fly Like an Eagle

STEVE MILLER BAND
CAPITOL 1976

After a 1972 car accident sidelined him for nearly a year, Miller came back with an irrepressible pop-rock sound that dominated Seventies radio: slick guitar boogie as catchy as Abba and as danceable as disco. Singles including "Rock 'n Me" and "Take the Money and Run" kept *Fly Like an Eagle* on the charts for nearly two years.

443 | Back in the USA

MC5
RHINO 1970

In the Sixties, the Motor City Five were the house band for the White Panther Party, devoted to "dope, guns and fucking in the streets." But here they channel their ferocious sound and politics into the concise, Chuck Berry-style riffs of "The American Ruse," "Looking at You" and "Shakin' Street."

444 | Music

MADONNA
MAVERICK 2000

Madonna aimed for "naked emotion" with this album, declaring, "This time, I've removed all the layers." But she also looked hot in her cowboy hat. French producer Mirwais brought the glitch-techno grooves, as Madonna sang with soul and fire in "I Deserve It" and "What It Feels Like for a Girl."

MADONNA

"I do my work privately, and take care of my daughter and try to be a decent girlfriend. These are kinds of quiet, introverted things. So I think that the whole waiting-to-be-sprung feeling is sort of bubbling under the surface and reflects in a lot of the music."

(RS 850, AUGUST 28TH, 2000)

445 ## Ritual de lo Habitual

JANE'S ADDICTION
WARNER BROS. 1990

Perry Farrell began the Lollapalooza tour and helped shape Nineties rock. But his proudest moment? "Been Caught Stealing," his insanely catchy ode to shoplifting. His band's third album became the sound of the Lollapalooza Nation: Led Zeppelin bravado with goth eyeliner.

446 ## Getz/Gilberto

STAN GETZ
POLYGRAM 1964

The menthol-cool Brazilian style of bossa nova met American jazz here, as saxman Getz teamed up with two Brazilian legends, guitarist-singer João Gilberto and pianist-songwriter Antonio Carlos Jobim. Gilberto's wife, Astrud, became a star herself with a sensual guest vocal on "The Girl From Ipanema."

447 ## Synchronicity

THE POLICE
INTERSCOPE 1983

"I do my best work when I'm in pain and turmoil," Sting told ROLLING STONE. And indeed, the dissolution of his first marriage produced some of his best work yet, including "King of Pain" and the stalker's anthem "Every Breath You Take." There was pain and turmoil in the band, too – it would be the Police's last album.

448 ## Third/Sister Lovers

BIG STAR
RYKODISC 1978

Big Star recorded their third and final album in 1974, but it didn't get released until 1978, in part because singer Alex Chilton sounds like he's having a nervous breakdown. It's a record of gorgeous, disjointed heartbreak ballads such as "Take Care," "Nighttime" and "Blue Moon."

449 ## For Everyman

JACKSON BROWNE
ELEKTRA/ASYLUM 1973

Browne emerged as the J.D. Salinger of the California singer-songwriter scene with his second album, capturing the transition from the idealistic Sixties to the disillusioned Seventies. He sings a moving update of "These Days," a song he originally wrote as a teenager for Velvet Underground singer Nico.

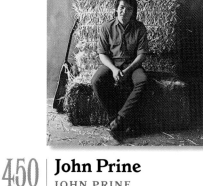

450 ## John Prine

JOHN PRINE
ATLANTIC 1971

Prine was a former mailman turned folk singer, and his debut is a vision of America that is unique in its generosity, tolerance and wit. Prine sang about smoking dope, but his empathy for old folks ("Hello in There") and a junkie Vietnam vet ("Sam Stone") makes most hippie songwriters sound smug.

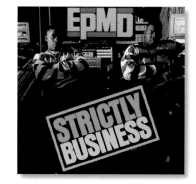

451 ## Strictly Business

EPMD
PRIORITY 1988

At the height of hip-hop's golden age, the summer of 1988, Erick Sermon and Parrish Smith, a.k.a. EPMD (Erick and Parrish Making Dollars), rolled out of Long Island with a new style of slow-grooving hip-hop funk. Cut in the era before artists cleared their samples, the title smash even takes a piece of "I Shot the Sheriff."

452 ## Love It to Death

ALICE COOPER
WARNER BROS. 1971

Onstage, Cooper was the shock-rock king who decapitated baby dolls, but his early studio albums are smart, razor-sharp attacks of Detroit rock. On *Love It to Death*, producer Bob Ezrin joins him for the twisted kicks of "Hallowed Be My Name" and the teen-spirit anthem "I'm Eighteen."

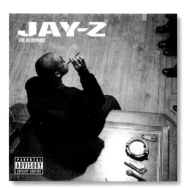

453 How Will the Wolf Survive?

LOS LOBOS
SLASH/WARNER BROS 1984

"We were kids with long hair and plaid shirts playing Mexican folk instruments," said Los Lobos' Louie Perez. But the band, lifelong friends from East L.A., became a surprise success, mixing traditional Mexican sounds with blues and rockabilly for tough, whomping roots rock.

454 Here, My Dear

MARVIN GAYE
MOTOWN 1978

It's one of the weirdest Motown records ever. Gaye's divorce settlement required him to make two new albums and pay the royalties to his ex-wife – the sister of Motown boss Berry Gordy. So Gaye made this bitterly funny double LP of breakup songs, including "You Can Leave, But It's Going to Cost You."

455 Tumbleweed Connection

ELTON JOHN
POLYGRAM 1971

John has always had a jones for the mythology of the American West. Along with lyricist Bernie Taupin, he indulges his cowboy fantasies in songs like "Burn Down the Mission." "Amoreena" plays unforgettably in the opening scene of the Al Pacino film *Dog Day Afternoon.*

456 The Blueprint

JAY-Z
ROC-A-FELLA/DEF JAM 2001

If Frank Sinatra had been born a Brooklyn rapper, *The Blueprint* is the album he would have made. It's all flash and bravado, with Jay-Z dissing rivals, talking smack about his troubles with the cops and flossing hard with ladies all around the world, as he samples everyone from the Doors to the Jackson 5.

457 Golden Hits

THE DRIFTERS
ATLANTIC 1968

By the early 1960s, the Drifters had evolved into the most suave soul group on the block. Even after Ben E. King went solo (scoring with "Stand by Me"), producers Jerry Leiber and Mike Stoller and the Drifters kept coming up with timeless odes to urban romance such as "Up on the Roof" and "Under the Boardwalk."

458 Live Through This

HOLE
GEFFEN 1994

On Hole's breakthrough album, Courtney Love wants to be "the girl with the most cake," and spends the whole album paying for it, in the melodic punk-rock anguish of "Miss World," "Softer, Softest" and "Doll Parts." Sadly, her husband Kurt Cobain's body was found just days before the album was released.

459 Love and Theft

BOB DYLAN
COLUMBIA 2001

Blood, desperation and wicked gallows humor are in the air as Dylan and his road band provide a raucous tour of twentieth-century musical America via jump blues, slow blues, rockabilly, Tin Pan Alley ballads and country swing. "Summer Days" sounds like the exact moment when R&B morphed into rock & roll.

460 Elton John

ELTON JOHN
POLYGRAM 1970

John doesn't exactly look like a rock star on the cover of his U.S. debut album. But he does have the tunes, with Paul Buckmaster's orchestrations and Bernie Taupin's lyrics, on piano ballads such as "Your Song" and the enigmatic rocker "Take Me to the Pilot." Elton John has been a rock star ever since.

461 | **Metal Box**
PUBLIC IMAGE LTD.
EMI U.K. 1979

After the Sex Pistols exploded, Johnny Rotten reclaimed his real name – John Lydon – and started his bold new band. PiL played eerie, futuristic art punk with dub bass and slashing guitar. The U.K. release *Metal Box* (retitled *Second Edition* in the U.S.) originally came as three vinyl discs in a metal film canister.

"The whole album deals with power. If life teaches us anything, it's that there's nothing that men and women won't do to get power. The album deals with power, wealth, knowledge and salvation – the way I look at it. If it's a great album – which I hope it is – it's a great album because it deals with great themes. It speaks in a noble language. It speaks of the issue or the ideals of an age in some nation, and hopefully, it would also speak across the ages. It'd be as good tomorrow as it is today. And would have been as good yesterday."

(RS 882, NOVEMBER 22ND, 2001)

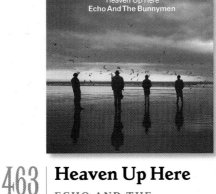

462 | **Document**
R.E.M.
CAPITOL 1987

R.E.M. were trying something new with each new album in the Eighties, but this straight-ahead rock move was the one that made them mainstream stars. "The One I Love" and "Finest Worksong" were hits, but the best-loved fan favorite is the manic "It's the End of the World As We Know It (and I Feel Fine)."

463 | **Heaven Up Here**
ECHO AND THE BUNNYMEN
SIRE 1981

The Bunnymen refresh psychedelia for the New Wave era with an arena of foggy guitars and doomy drums, while Ian McCulloch updates the aura of Jim Morrison. Melody meets melodrama on the title track and on "A Promise," where McCulloch sing-sobs a story of love gone wrong.

464 | **Hysteria**
DEF LEPPARD
POLYGRAM 1987

Def Leppard had a run of bad luck in the Eighties, especially when drummer Rick Allen lost his arm in a car crash on New Year's Eve 1984. But the lads admirably stuck by their old mate, who learned to play drums using his feet. The band was vindicated when *Hysteria* and "Pour Some Sugar on Me" became a smash.

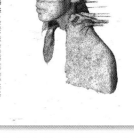

465 | **A Rush of Blood to the Head**
COLDPLAY
CAPITOL 2002

Chris Martin's ambition for his songwriting is simple: "Emotion that can make you feel sad while you're moving your legs." Coldplay churn out bighearted British guitar rock on their second album, with the romantic strains of "The Scientist," "Clocks" and "God Put a Smile Upon Your Face."

466 Live in Europe
OTIS REDDING
ATCO 1967

The Memphis soul man was a brilliant, methodical craftsman in the studio. But he also really knew how to bring it onstage. On this live album, Redding lives up to his reputation as a crowd flattener, exuding the warmth, humor and high spirits that always made him much, much more than a mere virtuoso.

467 Tunnel of Love
BRUCE SPRINGSTEEN
COLUMBIA 1987

After the big-scale *Born in the U.S.A.*, this came as a shock – Springsteen stripped down for an album of stark, intimate, mostly acoustic confessionals. The newly wed superstar gets personal on adult love songs such as "One Step Up" and "Walk Like a Man." The marriage may not have lasted – but the music does.

468 The Paul Butterfield Blues Band
THE PAUL BUTTERFIELD BLUES BAND
ELEKTRA/ASYLUM 1965

"Born in Chicago" is where the white youth of America got the notion they could play the blues. But this band had two killer guitarists – Michael Bloomfield, a rich kid from Chicago, and Elvin Bishop – and their blues knew no color boundaries.

469 The Score
THE FUGEES
RUFF HOUSE/COLUMBIA 1996

On their second album, the Fugees, led by Wyclef Jean, blend R&B and rap influences into an eclectic, politically aware sound on joints such as "Fu-Gee-La." But the track that grabbed everybody was the hip-hop-flavored cover of Roberta Flack's "Killing Me Softly," showcasing the amazing pipes of Lauryn Hill.

470 Radio
LL COOL J
DEF JAM 1985

LL Cool J was only sixteen when he released his first single, "I Need a Beat." A year later, he had the first hit on the fledgling Def Jam label. The sound he and producer Rick Rubin found on "I Can't Live Without My Radio," "That's a Lie" and "Rock the Bells" was harder and leaner than hip-hop had ever been before.

471 I Want to See the Bright Lights Tonight
RICHARD AND LINDA THOMPSON
HANNIBAL 1974

Richard played guitar like a Sufi-mystic Neil Young; wife Linda had the voice of a Celtic Emmylou Harris. *Bright Lights* is their masterwork of folk-rock dread. Radiohead even picked up some guitar tricks from "The Calvary Cross."

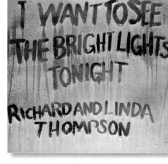

472 Faith
GEORGE MICHAEL
COLUMBIA 1987

When Michael left Wham!, he signified his new maturity by not shaving; thankfully, his music was still tasty pop candy. "I Want Your Sex" is one of the decade's best Prince imitations, and the best ballad is the spooky, soulful "Father Figure," which underscores the incestuous implications of the word *baby* in most lyrics.

473 The Smiths
THE SMITHS
SIRE 1984

"I recognize that mystical air/It means I'd like to seize your underwear," Morrissey moans, and rock music was never the same. The Smiths' debut is a showcase for Morrissey's morose wit and Johnny Marr's guitar chime, trudging through England's cheerless marshes in "Still Ill" and "This Charming Man."

474 **Armed Forces**

ELVIS COSTELLO AND THE ATTRACTIONS
RHINO 1979

Costello's third album is wound tight, full of paranoia and anger. The concept is personal politics; the original title was *Emotional Fascism,* and one of the songs is called "Two Little Hitlers." The keyboard-driven sound of "Accidents Will Happen" helped define New Wave.

475 **Life After Death**

THE NOTORIOUS B.I.G.
BAD BOY/ARISTA 1997

As the Roots' Ahmir Thompson put it, "Rakim is the Father, Biggie's the Son, and Jay-Z's the Holy Ghost." Released less than a month after Biggie's murder, *Life After Death* is two CDs of humor and bravado, no filler at all, as Biggie tops himself in "Mo Money Mo Problems" and "#!*@ You Tonight."

476 **Branded Man**

MERLE HAGGARD
CAPITOL 1967

Haggard's tough country sound was born in Bakersfield, California, a.k.a. Nashville West. His songs are full of drifters, fugitives and rogues, and this four-disc set – culled from his seminal recordings for Capitol as well as MCA and Epic – is the ultimate collection from one of country's finest singers.

477 **All Time Greatest Hits**

LORETTA LYNN
MCA 2002

Anyone who thinks country music is cute should listen to "Fist City," where Lynn threatens to beat down a woman if she doesn't lay off her man. The White Stripes worship this coal miner's daughter, and so should anyone with a taste for country gals who kick ass.

478 **Maggot Brain**

FUNKADELIC
WESTBOUND 1971

"Play like your mama just died," George Clinton told guitarist Eddie Hazel. The result was "Maggot Brain," ten minutes of Hendrix-style guitar anguish. This is the heaviest rock album the P-Funk crew ever created, but it also made room for the acoustic-guitar funk of "Can You Get to That."

GEORGE MICHAEL

"If you listen to a Supremes record or a Beatles record, how can you not realize that the elation of a good pop record is an art form? Somewhere along the way, pop lost all its respect. And I think I kind of stubbornly stick up for that."

(RS 518, JANUARY 28TH, 1988)

479 Mellon Collie and the Infinite Sadness

THE SMASHING PUMPKINS
VIRGIN 1995

Billy Corgan indulged his love of Seventies prog-rock on this double disc of alt-rock epics built around James Iha's ethereal guitar and Corgan's anguished keen; "Tonight, Tonight" and "1979" are the Pumpkins at their finest.

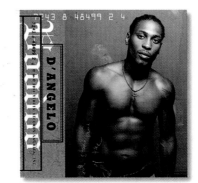

480 Voodoo

D'ANGELO
VIRGIN 2000

D'angelo recorded his second album at Electric Lady, the Manhattan studio built by Jimi Hendrix. There he studied bootleg videos of Sixties and Seventies soul singers and cooked up an album heavy on bass and drenched in a post-coital haze. The single "Untitled (How Does It Feel?)" sounds like a great lost Prince song.

481 Guitar Town

STEVE EARLE
MCA 1986

"I got a two-pack habit and a motel tan," Earle sings on the title track. By the time he released his debut at thirty-one, he had done two stints in Nashville as a songwriter and he wanted something else. *Guitar Town* is the rocker's version of country, packed with songs about hard living in the Reagan Eighties.

482 Entertainment!

GANG OF FOUR
WARNER BROS. 1979

Formed in 1977, gang of Four combined Marxist politics with punk rock. They played staccato guitar-driven funk, and the stiff, jerky aggression of songs such as "Damaged Goods" and "I Found That Essence Rare" invented a new style that's still influencing young bands such as the Rapture.

483 All the Young Dudes

MOTT THE HOOPLE
COLUMBIA 1972

Mott the Hoople were a hard-rock band with a Dylan fixation until David Bowie got ahold of them and turned them into glam rockers. He penned the androgyne title track and had Mott cover Lou Reed's "Sweet Jane." Mott would sound more soulful but never more sexy or glittery.

484 Vitalogy

PEARL JAM
EPIC 1994

Their previous album, *Vs.*, made Pearl Jam the most successful band in the world. They celebrated by suing Ticketmaster and making *Vitalogy*, where their mastery of rock's past and future became complete. Soulful ballads like "Nothingman" are matched by hardcore-influenced rockers such as "Spin the Black Circle."

485 That's the Way of the World

EARTH, WIND AND FIRE
COLUMBIA 1975

Before he got into African thumb piano and otherworldly philosophizing, founder Maurice White was a session drummer at Chess studios (that's him on Fontella Bass' "Rescue Me"). EWF's seventh album is make-out music of the gods; its title track is one of funk's most gorgeous ballads.

486 She's So Unusual

CYNDI LAUPER
EPIC/LEGACY 1983

Lauper's first band had broken up, she had filed for bankruptcy, and she was singing in a Japanese restaurant. Then this debut album of razor-sharp dance pop became the first by a female performer to score four Top Five hits, including "Girls Just Want to Have Fun" and "Time After Time."

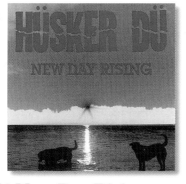

487 **New Day Rising**

HÜSKER DÜ
SST 1985

These three Minneapolis dudes played savagely emotional hardcore punk that became a key influence on Nirvana, among others. Guitarist Bob Mould and band created a roar like garbage trucks trying to sing Beach Boys songs, especially on the anthems "Celebrated Summer" and "Perfect Example."

488 **Destroyer**

KISS
MERCURY 1976

By the time their fifth album was released, Kiss were the most popular band in America, with sold-out stadium tours and eventually their own pinball machines, makeup line and a TV movie. Built around the proto power ballad "Beth," this is a ridiculously over-the-top party-rock album that just gets better with age.

489 **Yo! Bum Rush the Show**

PUBLIC ENEMY
DEF JAM 1987

On the debut by Long Island's hip-hop revolutionaries, rapper Chuck D and his production crew the Bomb Squad introduced a booming new sound and an urgent social and political message to rap, especially on "You're Gonna Get Yours" and "Miuzi Weighs a Ton."

490 **Tres Hombres**

ZZ TOP
WARNER BROS. 1973

A decade before the Texas blues trio became MTV stars, ZZ Top got their first taste of national fame with this disc, which features one of their biggest hits, the John Lee Hooker-style boogie "La Grange," as well as the boozy rocker "Jesus Just Left Chicago" and the concert anthem "Beer Drinkers and Hell Raisers."

CYNDI LAUPER

"People used to throw rocks at me for my clothes. Now they wanna know where I buy them, right? Doesn't that seem weird to you?"

RS 422,
MAY 24TH, 1984

491 **Born Under a Bad Sign**

ALBERT KING
STAX 1967

King's first album for the Stax label combines his hard, unflashy guitar playing with the sleek sound of the label's house band, Booker T. and the MG's. Hits such as "Crosscut Saw" and "Laundromat Blues" influenced Clapton and Stones, and earned King a new rock & roll audience.

492 **Touch**

EURYTHMICS
RCA 1984

Annie Lennox looked like a gender-bending robot zombie, but she sang with soul; producer Dave Stewart hid behind his beard and masterminded the sound. Together they made divine synth-pop, especially "Who's That Girl," a tale of kinked-up sexual obsession, and their biggest hit, "Here Comes the Rain Again."

493 ## Yankee Hotel Foxtrot

WILCO
NONESUCH 2002

When Reprise Records refused to release *Yankee Hotel Foxtrot*, Wilco posted it for free on the Internet. Two hundred thousand downloads later, Nonesuch Records (owned by the same company as Reprise) released the album – it became critical and commercial gold.

494 ## Boz Scaggs

BOZ SCAGGS
ATLANTIC 1969

The stone-solid grooves on this underrated gem come courtesy of the Muscle Shoals rhythm section; the soulful guitar comes courtesy of Scaggs and guest Duane Allman. Together, they made "Somebody Loan Me a Dime" an FM radio classic – ten minutes of knockout blues pleading and wailing.

495 ## New Boots and Panties!!

IAN DURY AND THE
BLOCKHEADS
RHINO 1977

Dury cut his teeth on the British pub rock circuit before his debut made him a cult star. He never managed to duplicate the brilliance of this punk-funk classic, but the album's impact is felt to this day – even introducing the phrase "sex, drugs and rock & roll" to the lexicon.

496 ## Give It Up

BONNIE RAITT
RHINO 1972

California darling Bonnie Raitt headed to Woodstock to cut her second LP – only to face near-monsoon weather. "It rained every day, my house had sand and salamanders," Raitt said. She took refuge in the studio and churned out gorgeous folksy blues, including a cover of Jackson Browne's "Under the Falling Sky."

497 ## The Stone Roses

THE STONE ROSES
SILVERTONE 1989

For a few glorious moments, the Stone Roses looked like they were going to lead another British Invasion. Instead, they fell apart – but first they made this incredible album, highlighted by the ecstatic eight-minute-long "I Am the Resurrection." It singlehandedly launched Nineties Brit pop.

498 ## Head Hunters

HERBIE HANCOCK
COLUMBIA 1973

"I was tired of everything being heavy – I wanted something lighter," Hancock said. With that in mind, the keyboardist shed his former backing band (as well as all guitars) and recorded this Miles-meets-Sly Stone masterpiece, a peak of the jazz-fusion movement, highlighted by "Chameleon" and "Watermelon Man."

499 ## Live at Cook County Jail

B.B. KING
MCA 1972

B.B. King was in the middle of a career renaissance when he stepped into Chicago's Cook County Jail in 1971. Laying down definitive renditions of his blues standards as well as his crossover hit "The Thrill Is Gone," B.B. wins over the hostile prisoners and proves why he is the king.

500 ## Aquemini

OUTKAST
LA FACE 1998

At a time when formulaic albums by Master P and Puff Daddy topped the charts, OutKast's André Benjamin and Big Boi unleashed an explosive hip-hop sound that used live musicianship, social commentary and a heavy dose of deep funk. Hits like "Rosa Parks" put the duo's hometown "Hotlanta" on the rap map.

The king and queen of the blues: B.B. King with his lifelong guitar Lucille. September 1994

The ballots were scored by the accounting firm of Ernst & Young and overseen by the ROLLING STONE editors. We assigned 100 points for each first-place vote, 50 points for each second-place vote, 33-1/3 points for each third-place vote and so on, down to 2 points for each fiftieth-place vote. We then ranked albums appearing on at least five ballots.

Bill Adler *Biographer, Run-DMC*

Lou Adler *Producer*

Vince Aletti *Senior editor, "Village Voice"*

Art Alexakis *Everclear*

Billy Altman *Writer*

Jeff Ament *Pearl Jam*

Roger Ames *Former chairman and CEO, Warner Music Group*

Billie Joe Armstrong *Green Day*

Dick Asher *Former CEO, Polygram*

James Austin *A&R, Rhino Records*

Michael Azerrad *Writer*

Irving Azoff *Azoff Music Management*

Martin Bandier *Chairman and CEO, EMI Music Publishing*

Peter Barakan *Radio host*

Johnny Barbis *Senior executive, DreamWorks Records*

Ken Barnes *Music editor, "USA Today"*

Frank Barsalona *Consultant, William Morris Agency*

David Bauder *Entertainment writer, AP*

Beck

Jules Belkin *President, Belkin Productions*

Andy Bell *Erasure*

Bill Belmont *VP, international operations, Fantasy*

Bill Bentley *Senior VP, Warner Bros. Records*

Steve Berkowitz *Senior VP, A&R, Legacy Recordings*

James Bernard *Co-founder, "The Source" and "XXL"*

Cathy Bernardy *Associate editor, "Goldmine" magazine*

Jim Bessman *Senior writer, "Billboard"*

Les Bider *Chairman and CEO, Warner/Chappell Music*

Scott Billington *VP, A&R, Rounder Records*

Rodney Bingenheimer *Radio personality*

David Bither *Senior VP, Nonesuch Records*

Hal Blaine *Drummer*

Jerry Blavat *Radio and TV personality*

Nathan Brackett *Senior editor, ROLLING STONE*

Harriett Brand *Senior VP, music, MTV Networks Europe and International*

Jon Bream *Critic, Minneapolis "Star Tribune"*

Harold Bronson *Co-founder, Rhino Records*

Duncan Browne *COO, Newbury Comics*

Jackson Browne

Bebe Buell

Solomon Burke

Cliff Burnstein *Co-owner, Q Prime*

James Burton *Guitarist*

Geezer Butler *Black Sabbath*

Jerry Butler

Joe Butler *The Lovin' Spoonful*

Tom Calderone *General manager, VH1*

Mike Carabello *Santana*

Jon Caramanica *Writer*

Rosemary Carroll *Partner, Carroll, Guido and Groffman*

Marshall Chess *Producer*

Deborah Chessler *Songwriter*

Lauren Christy *Producer, the Matrix*

Mitchell Cohen *Senior VP, A&R, Columbia Records*

Chris Connelly *Correspondent, ESPN*

Tom Constanten *Pianist, composer*

Tré Cool *Green Day*

Gerard Cosloy *Co-president, Matador Records*

Tommy Couch Sr. *President, Malaco Music Group*

Wayne Coyne *The Flaming Lips*

Bill Crandall *Editor, ROLLING STONE Online*

Cameron Crowe *Writer-director*

Clive Davis *Chairman and CEO, RCA Music Group*

Anthony DeCurtis *Contributing editor, ROLLING STONE*

Ron Delsener *Concert promoter*

John Densmore *The Doors*

Don DeVito *Producer*

Rob Dickins *Chairman, Instant Karma*

Bruce Dickinson *Marketing and A&R consultant*

Dion DiMucci

Dr. John

Antoine "Fats" Domino

Jancee Dunn *Contributing editor, ROLLING STONE*

The Edge *U2*

Ben Edmonds *Writer*

Gavin Edwards *Columnist, ROLLING STONE*

Graham Edwards *Producer, the Matrix*

Jenny Eliscu *Contributing editor, ROLLING STONE*

Missy Elliott

Thomas Erdelyi *The Ramones*

Melissa Etheridge

Suzan Evans *Executive director, Rock & Roll Hall of Fame*

Phil Everly *Everly Brothers*

Bob Ezrin *Producer*

Art Fein *Author, TV talk-show host*

Danny Fields *Writer, former Stooges and Ramones manager*

Jason Fine *Senior editor, ROLLING STONE*

Jim Fishel *Producer*

Bill Flanagan *Senior VP, MTV Networks*

Flea *Red Hot Chili Peppers*

Chet Flippo *Editorial director, Country Music Television*

Jason Flom *Chairman and CEO, Atlantic Records Group*

Ben Fong-Torres *Writer, broadcaster*

Richard Foos *CEO, Shout! Factory*

Pete Frame *Rock genealogist*

Chris Frantz *Talking Heads, Tom Tom Club*

David Fricke *Senior editor, ROLLING STONE*

John Frusciante *Red Hot Chili Peppers*

Richie Furay *Buffalo Springfield, Poco*

Elysa Gardner *Music reporter, "USA Today"*

Art Garfunkel

Rob Garza *Producer, Thievery Corporation*

David Geffen *Co-founder, DreamWorks*

Gregg Geller *Producer*

Gary Gersh *Founder, Strummer Recordings*

Andy Gershon *President, V2 Music Group*

Charlie Gillett *Author; radio broadcaster, BBC*

Mikal Gilmore *Music writer, ROLLING STONE*

Daniel Glass *President, Artemis Records*

Gerry Goffin *Lyricist, producer*

Jeff Gold *Owner, Recordmecca.com*

Michael Goldberg *Editor in chief, Neumu.net*

Gary Graff *Music journalist, author*

Ellie Greenwich *Songwriter*

Peter Guralnick *Author*

Brett Gurewitz *Founder, Epitaph Records*

Albert Hammond Jr. *The Strokes*

Davey Havok *AFI*

Jim Henke *VP of exhibitions and curatorial affairs, Rock & Roll Hall of Fame*

Raoul Hernandez *Music editor, "Austin Chronicle"*

James Hetfield *Metallica*

Robert Hilburn *Pop-music critic, "Los Angeles Times"*

Michael Hill *Writer, A&R consultant*

Chris Hillman *The Byrds*

David Hinckley *Critic at large, New York "Daily News"*

Susanna Hoffs *The Bangles*

Bruce Hornsby

Robert Hull *Executive producer, Time-Life Music*

James Hunter *Music critic, ROLLING STONE*

Scott Ian *Anthrax*

Don Ienner *President and CEO, Sony Music U.S.*

Bruce Iglauer *President, Alligator Records*

Bob Jamieson *Entertainment consultant*

Chris Jasper *Artist, president, Gold City Records*

Jeff Jones *Senior VP, Columbia Jazz/Legacy Recordings*

Craig Kallman *Co-president, Atlantic Records*

John David Kalodner *Senior VP, A&R, Sanctuary Records*

Tony Kanal *No Doubt*

Peter Katsis *VP of music, the Firm*

Jorma Kaukonen *Jefferson Airplane, Hot Tuna*

Lenny Kaye *Guitarist*

Carole King

Marc Kirkeby *Music archivist, writer*

Howie Klein *Former president, 415 Records and Reprise Records*

Greg Kot *Music critic, "Chicago Tribune"*

Howard Kramer *Director of curatorial affairs, Rock & Roll Hall of Fame*

Bob Krasnow *Producer*

Andrew Lauder *Co-founder, Evangeline Recorded Works*

David Leaf *TV writer, producer*

Brenda Lee

David Lefkowitz *Composer*

Michael Leon *Producer*

Arthur Levy *Writer-historian*

Joe Levy *Deputy managing editor, ROLLING STONE*

Alan Light *Writer*

Amy Linden *Journalist*

Kurt Loder *MTV News*

Greg Loescher *Editor, "Goldmine" magazine*

Roy Lott *President and COO, Virgin Records*

Leigh Lust *A&R, Elektra Records*

Stan Lynch *Tom Petty and the Heartbreakers*

Stephen Malkmus

Shirley Manson *Garbage*

Ray Manzarek *The Doors*

Joe McEwan *A&R consultant*

Paul McGuinness *Manager, U2*

Christine McVie *Fleetwood Mac*

Brad Mehldau *Jazz pianist*

Peter Mensch *Co-owner, Q Prime*

Milo Miles *Critic, NPR commentator*

Kirk Miller *Former associate editor, ROLLING STONE*

David Mills *TV producer, "Kingpin"*

Martin Mills *Founder, Beggars Banquet Records*

Willie Mitchell *Musician-producer*

Moby

Joseph Modeliste *The Meters*

Tom Moon *Music critic, "Philadelphia Inquirer"*

Tom Morello *Audioslave*

Bruce Morrow *Radio personality*

Steve Morse *Senior pop-music critic, "Boston Globe"*

Alan Moulder *Producer-engineer*

Jason Mraz

Dave Navarro *Jane's Addiction*

Tom Nawrocki *Former assistant managing editor, ROLLING STONE*

Ed Needham *Editor in chief, "Maxim"*

Ashley Newton *Executive VP, A&R, RCA Records*

Claude Nobs *Founder-director, the Montreaux Jazz Festival*

Yoko Ono

Mo Ostin *Chairman, DreamWorks Records*

Andy Paley *Producer-musician*

John Parrish *Musician*

George Pelecanos *Writer*

Michael Penn

Claudia Perry *Journalist, "Newark Star-Ledger"*

Michelle Phillips *The Mamas and the Papas*

Tony Pipitone *President, Warner Special Projects*

Steve Pond *Assistant professor, Cornell University*

George Porter Jr. *The Meters*

Robert Pruter *R&B editor, "Goldmine" magazine*

Parke Puterbaugh *Music journalist, ROLLING STONE*

Steve Ralbovsky *Senior VP, A&R, RCA Records*

Johnny Ramone *Ramones*

Marky Ramone *Ramones*

Sylvia Rhone *Chairman and CEO, Elektra Records*

Cory Robbins *President, Robbins Entertainment*

Ira Robbins *Editorial director, MJI Programming, Premiere Radio Network*

Robbie Robertson *The Band*

Cynthia Robinson *Sly and the Family Stone*

Bob Rock *Producer*

Rick Rubin *Producer; co-founder, Def Jam*

Paul Samwell-Smith *Producer, the Yardbirds*

Bob Santelli *Artistic director, Experience Music Project*

Austin Scaggs *Associate editor, ROLLING STONE*

Timothy B. Schmit *The Eagles*

Fred Schneider *The B-52's*

Jordan Schur *President, Geffen Records*

Andy Schwartz *Researcher-archivist, Rock & Roll Hall of Fame*

Bud Scoppa *Writer*

Gene Sculatti *Director of special issues, "Billboard"*

John Sebastian *The Lovin' Spoonful*

Pete Seeger

Joel Selvin *Music critic, "San Francisco Chronicle"*

Matt Serletic *Producer*

Paul Shaffer *Musical director, "Late Show With David Letterman"*

Ron Shapiro *Co-president, Atlantic Records*

Rob Sheffield *Contributing editor, ROLLING STONE*

Mike Shinoda *Linkin Park*

Tom Silverman *Founder and CEO, Tommy Boy Records*

Barbara Skydel *Senior VP, William Morris Agency*

Larry Sloven *Co-owner, executive producer, Hightone Records*

Joe Smith *Chairman, Unison Productions*

Britney Spears

Scott Spencer *Novelist*

Scott Spock *Producer, the Matrix*

Freddie Stewart *Sly and the Family Stone*

Gary Stewart

Brian Stoltz *Funky Meters, the Neville Brothers, Bob Dylan*

Keith Strickland *The B-52's*

John Sykes *CEO, Infinity Broadcasting*

Jeff Tamarkin *Editor in chief, "Global Rhythm" magazine*

Corey Taylor *Slipknot*

Al Teller *Consultant, Al Teller and Associates*

Bruce Thomas *Elvis Costello and the Attractions*

Touré *Contributing editor, ROLLING STONE*

Allen Toussaint *Producer-songwriter*

Roy Trakin *Senior editor, "Hits" magazine*

Lars Ulrich *Metallica*

Nick Valensi *The Strokes*

Hilton Valentine *The Animals*

Steven Van Zandt

Tom Vickers *A&R consultant*

Butch Vig *Garbage*

Phil Walden *President, Velocette Records*

Barry Walters *Music journalist, ROLLING STONE*

Bill Ward *Black Sabbath*

Harry Weinger *VP, A&R, Universal Music Enterprises*

Eric Weisbard *Curator, Experience Music Project*

Barry Weiss *President, Zomba Group*

Hy Weiss *Founder, Old Town Records*

Steve Weitzman *President, SW Productions*

Jann S. Wenner *Editor and publisher, ROLLING STONE*

Tina Weymouth *Talking Heads, Tom Tom Club*

Joel Whitburn *President, Record Research*

David Wild *Contributing editor, ROLLING STONE*

Lucinda Williams

Hal Willner *Music director, "Saturday Night Live"*

Muff Winwood *President, Sony U.K. A&R*

Richard Wright *Pink Floyd*

Robert Wright

Howard Wuelfing *Howlin' Wuelf Media*

Adam Yauch *Beastie Boys*

CREDITS

PAGES 5, 8, 12, 15, 16, 19, 20, 23, 24, 27, 28: Anthony Verde. PAGE 11: John Pratt/Keystone/Getty Images. PAGE 13: Glenn A. Baker/Redferns/Retna Ltd. PAGE 14: Central Press/Getty Images. PAGE 18: SUS/Camera Press/Retna Ltd. PAGE 21: Jim Britt/MichaelOchsArchives.com. PAGE 22: Harry Goodwin/MichaelOchsArchives.com. PAGE 25: Courtesy of Rock & Roll Hall of Fame and Paul Simonon. PAGE 26: Alice Ochs/MichaelOchsArchives.com. PAGE 40: Frank Driggs Collection/Getty Images. PAGE 42: Bettmann/Corbis. PAGE 44: Kwame Brathwaite. PAGE 46: Lex van Rossen/Redferns/Retna Ltd. PAGE 49: Norman Seeff. PAGE 50: Laurens Van Houten/Star File. PAGE 52: Denis O'Regan/Corbis. PAGE 54: Masayoshi Sukita/Bureau L.A. Collection/Corbis. PAGE 57: MichaelOchsArchives.com. PAGE 58: K.T./Hulton-Deutsch Collection/Corbis. PAGE 60: Hulton-Deutsch Collection/Corbis. PAGE 63: Lynn Goldsmith/Corbis. PAGE 65: Adrian Boot/Urban Image. PAGE 66: Ted Williams/Corbis. PAGE 69: Bettmann/Corbis. PAGE 70: Redferns/Retna Ltd. PAGE 72: Eddie Kramer/Kramer Archives Inc. PAGE 75: Allan Tannenbaum/Polaris. PAGE 78: Stephen Paley/MichaelOchsArchives.com. PAGE 83: Eddie Kramer/Kramer Archives Inc. PAGE 87: Courtesy of Collection of Tetsuo Hamada © Lennonono Music. PAGE 92: MichaelOchsArchives.com. PAGE 95: Evening Standard/Getty Images. PAGE 99: Bettmann/Corbis. PAGE 105: MichaelOchsArchives.com. PAGE 109: Roy Jones/Getty Images. PAGE 119: Al Pereira/MichaelOchsArchives.com. PAGE 123: Kevin Mazur/WireImage.com. PAGE 129: Jeff Albertson/Corbis. PAGE 132: MichaelOchsArchives.com. PAGE 137: TTI/Retna Ltd. PAGE 139: Hulton-Deutsch Collection/Corbis. PAGE 142: DPA/Landov. PAGE 145: Lynn Goldsmith/Corbis. PAGE 149: Mick Rock/Star File. PAGE 151: Ian Dickson/Redferns/Retna Ltd. PAGE 152: Glenn A. Baker/Redferns/Retna Ltd. PAGE 161: MichaelOchsArchives.com. PAGE 162: Jack Robinson/Hulton Archive/Getty Images. PAGE 164: Suzi Gibbons/Redferns/Retna Ltd. PAGE 166: TTI/Retna Ltd. PAGE 168: Courtesy of Everett Collection. PAGE 171: Collection of James Hetfield/Courtesy of Rock & Roll Hall of Fame/Design Photography Inc. PAGE 174: Charles Peterson/Retna Ltd. PAGE 176: Sian Kennedy/Retna Ltd. PAGE 181: Courtesy of Experience Music Project Permanent Collection. PAGE 186: Neal Preston/Corbis. PAGE 189: Collection of Robbie Robertson/Courtesy of Rock & Roll Hall of Fame/Design Photography Inc. PAGE 190: Glenn A. Baker/Redferns/Retna Ltd. PAGE 192: MichaelOchsArchives.com (top); AP Photo. PAGE 193: Michael Putland/Retna Ltd. PAGE 199: Gilloon/Camera Press/Retna Ltd. PAGE 200: Anthony Saint James/Retna U.K. PAGE 201: Collection of Paul Simon. Courtesy of Rock & Roll Hall of Fame/Design Photography Inc. PAGE 203: Neal Preston/Corbis. PAGE 205: Niels Van Iperen/Retna Ltd. PAGE 206: Wolfgang Heilemann/Camera Press/Retna Ltd. PAGE 208: Regan Cameron/Corbis Outline. PAGE 211: David Gahr/Columbia Records. PAGE 213: Michael Putland/Retna Ltd. PAGE 215: Joe Bangay/London Features. PAGE 217: Jay Blakesberg/Retna Ltd. PAGE 220: Estevan Oriol/Celebrity Pictures.

ACKNOWLEDGEMENTS: Thanks to Jann S. Wenner and Bob Wallace for making this book possible, and to John Dragonetti and KellyAnn Kwiatek for making it happen. This book also reflects the tireless work of the ROLLING STONE staff who produced the original RS 500 in 2003, notably research chief Sarah Pratt, copy chief Thomas Walsh and the indefatigable Tom Nawrocki. Nathan Brackett, Robert Buckley, Cliff Cerar, Bill Crandall, Jason Fine, David Fricke, Lauren Goldstein, Henry Groskinsky, Amelia Halverson, Aubree Lennon, Jodi Peckman, Michael Pirrocco, Corey Seymour, Sean Woods and Melissa Wygant all contributed their expert touch and immense patience.